The Chronicle of Exeter

The Chronicle of Exeter

1205–1722

Todd Gray

THE MINT PRESS

First published in Great Britain by The Mint Press, 2005

ISBN 1-903356-42-3

Cataloguing in Publication Data
CIP record for this title is available from the British Library

The Mint Press
76 Longbrook Street
Exeter, Devon
England EX4 6AP

Typeset by Kestrel Data, Exeter

Cover design by Delphine Jones

Printed and bound in Great Britain by
Short Run Press Ltd, Exeter

CONTENTS

FOREWORD

The history of the city of Exeter has fascinated me since I was a small boy. I asked questions and read everything I could find on Exeter's past – this has proved useful since I became Lord Mayor as I am asked many questions about the city, the guildhall and our long history.

Now Todd Gray brings us *The Chronicle of Exeter* which celebrates 800 years of Exeter's mayoralty and fills many gaps in our information about our past. The appearance of these four chronicles shows us the great service that so many men and women have undertaken for the people of Exeter.

Councillor Peter Wadham, Lord Mayor

For Malcolm and Molly Todd

INTRODUCTION

When, in 1590, John Hooker organised his *Chronicle of Exeter* he began 'modern Exeter' with the earliest mayors. Hooker knew that in the early thirteenth century King John had granted the status of mayor to the city's lead citizen and later writers went so far as to even claim it was the oldest such institution in the country. In fact it is unclear when this was first granted to Exeter. The earliest documentary evidence is a letter of 19 June 1205 which refers to the city's mayor.[1] London's mayoralty was established in about 1192, Winchester's by 1200[2] and it is likely that Exeter was earlier than 1205: the letter establishes that the city already had a mayor by that date as well as that the office was in operation at some earlier, as yet unknown, time. Hooker's account begins in 1216 but the three writers that followed him started theirs with 1200 and the supposed mayoralty of Henry Rifford who, it was thought, was followed in 1208 by John Fitz-Robert. Their accounts of these early years are thin owing to a general dependence upon the writings of Hooker.

Hooker's work was a list of each year's mayor along with any notable events covering nearly four hundred years. The manuscript remained in the city's archive after his death and, like his others works, was extensively used by later writers. Another chamberlain, Richard Izacke, compiled a second chronology in 1666. He included information from Hooker's text and then continued his own account up to the year 1676. One later writer observed that Izacke 'pilfered unblushingly' from Hooker[3] but at this date plagiarising, as it is perceived today, was commonplace. Later his son, Samuel, wrote a third chronology. His work was largely a reprint of his father's book but he also continued the account up to 1722. This went to several editions. There is also one more account: Richard Crossing, a city councillor, wrote his own version in 1681. This is the slimmest of the four chronicles. Crossing also copied copiously from Hooker and Richard Izacke and added his own notes as well. This book comprises the original contributions of each of these writers: they are taken from the manuscript copies of each of the earliest three writers and the printed edition of the last.[4]

The Chroniclers

For centuries John Hooker has dominated the writing of the history of Exeter and it was not until the middle of the twentieth century, with the arrival of W. G. Hoskins, that any other writer has come to be nearly as influential. Hooker was a local boy and in the Chronicle he noted he was born in 1525. He became the city's first chamberlain in 1555, was a Member of Parliament in 1568, edited Raphael Holinshed's *Chronicles* in 1586 and died in 1601. Hooker wrote with authority of a good part of the sixteenth century: he was a personal observer of many events. For the earlier period he used the city's documents which, as he noted in his Chronicle, he gathered together and organised. Hooker also used printed sources, particularly for national events. In his description of the year 1474 he mentioned four authors: Robert Fabyan whose *The Concordance of Histories* was first published in 1516, Richard Grafton who wrote *Abridgment of the Chronicles of England* which was printed in 1562 and also *Chronicle at Large* which appeared six years later, John Hardyng whose chronicle was printed by Grafton in 1543 and Polydore. Elsewhere he referred to using the works of Erasmus, Raphael Holinshead and John Fox.

His text was occasionally poorly put together. In some places he repeated himself and there is mis-numbering of the years from 1513 to 1518 where he continued to attribute the events of 1514 to 1515 as 1513, wrongly numbered the years 1516 and 1517 and did not correct himself until he wrote up the year 1518. A scribe may have copied parts of the manuscript which might indicate there was an earlier version. Hooker has also been criticised for being unreliable[5] but it is not surprising that occasionally he was inaccurate given there were no printed works on Exeter. He was completely reliant upon documentary sources and, presumably, on oral traditions.

Hooker's account was written at the end of the sixteenth century and he was careful to be appropriately respectful to Queen Elizabeth as well as to her mother Anne Boleyn. He was necessarily cautious about religion and yet decidedly favourable about the Reformation and negative in all respects of the popes. Perhaps he was on firmer ground when he expressed criticisms of several early members of the Courtenay family of nearby Powderham.

It is interesting that Hooker failed to keep the Chronicle up-to-date; he could have continued it for another ten years but ended it in 1590. His writing the Chronicle reflects a general interest in them at that time. His contemporary in Barnstaple, Adam Wyatt, also recorded local events and were others written for Plymouth, Tiverton, Torquay and many other towns and cities across England.[6]

Richard Izacke's Chronicle is an intriguing work. Like Hooker he was the city's Chamberlain and also lived through years which had been particularly challenging in terms of national and local politics. The city had been largely on the side of Parliament during the Civil War and then from 1649 through to 1660 it was in sympathy with Cromwell's governments. Then came the Restoration of Charles II in May 1660.

Izacke's manuscript is dated 23 January 1666 and it was published, finally, ten years later. It is worth pondering why he wrote it six years after the return of the king. Not surprisingly in his Chronicle he wrote with disapproval of the execution of King Charles in 1649 and noted the great local support for the restoration of the crown in 1660. The purpose of the Chronicle, and its publication, may have been more influenced by politics whereas Hooker's motivation may have been as part of his wider interest in historical record-keeping and writing. Izacke carefully edited Hooker's text and he tried to show a city loyal to its monarchs. He himself was a Royalist and had been punished as such when the Roundheads took over the city.[7] Izacke's own father, another Samuel, was appointed Town Clerk in 1624.[8]

Izacke's manuscript, which is printed hereafter, is much fuller than the printed version. The printed account for 1642 recorded that

All the trees in Northerny-hay Southern-hay – elms of above one hundred years growth – were felled and destroyed. The city was twice this year besieged by the King's Forces; first by my Lord Hopton about

Christmas, who having only viewed the same, presently drew off his army and marched into Cornwall. Secondly, by Prince Maurice, who laid close siege thereunto and 3 September following got possession thereof, being surrendered to him on Articles.

The manuscript noted for that year:

Walls erected in a lane by St Katharine's almshouse are to be again pulled down. No sea coal ashes are to be cast into the streets on pain of 4d for the first offence, the 2nd 12d. Mr Mayor is appointed to keep the only key of the powder house. 10s paid the messenger for bringing a writ for the election of new Parliament men here. The porters to be allowed candle light at their several gates. A watch to be kept every night winter and summer. All the trees in Northernhay and Southernhay taken down towards the making of carriages for the city's defence and other public uses in reference to war. 500 weight of match to be provided and brought into the common storehouse. An engineer sent for and here entertained, to whom for his welcome a gratuity of £10 is given, and also a stipend of £30 per annum settled on him for his attendance and service here. Ordinances or great guns to be mounted on their carriages and powder allotted to try them. The gates of the said city in these times of danger to be constantly shut at six of the clock at night, and iron chains to be provided for them for their better fortification. Edmond Prideaux esquire elected recorder of the said city. A present of £100 bestowed on the earl of Stamford general of the rebels in these western parts. Another present of £300 bestowed on Sir John Berkeley governor of the said city for his Majesty.

Samuel Izacke continued the Chronicle from 1678 to 1723. He was the son of Richard and, like the other two chroniclers, was also a Chamberlain. It was a family tradition to run the city: his grandfather Samuel had been Town Clerk, his uncle Nicholas was a mayor, his father Richard was Town Clerk from 1681 until his death in 1698 and he was Chamberlain from 1693 until his death in 1729.[9] He noted in his preface that he was continuing the work of his father but there does not appear to be any overriding political motivation in writing or publishing it. He corrected some mistakes of his father's, notably in moving the death of Raleigh from 1604 to 1618.

The final Chronicle was written by Richard Crossing. He described his work as 'a catalogue or particular of the antiquities &c special remarks of the city and chamber of the city of Exeter' but this does not appear to have had much public exposure. It was written in 1681 and was also based on the earlier works. The author was a supporter of Parliament during the Civil War and had been assiduous in his attendance as a councillor during the time in which the Roundheads were in control of Exeter but then largely withdrew from public service when the Royalists won. He resumed his full duties once the Parliamentarians regained Exeter.[10] Curiously, the Chronicle noted that he refused to serve as mayor in 1649 when the king had been executed. Of the execution of the king he noted himself it was a 'most sad time, the king this year was cruelly put to death'.

The office of mayor in Exeter

The mayors of Exeter have always been hugely influential although their role has continually changed. Eight hundred years ago local government appears to have been largely in the control of the earliest mayors. The first named mayor is William Derling, who was in office in 1207, but two years earlier there was another who it has been generally assumed was one Martin Prudume; that year, on 19 June 1205, national government wrote to an unnamed mayor requiring him to provide a vessel for the defence of the country. The office of mayor changed in 1345 with the introduction of new regulations which created a council of 12 men to oversee administration and finance. No individual was to be elected mayor for two successive years. In the following century the number of councillors increased to 24 and then in 1497 it was decided that councillors were to hold office for life unless they were removed for any justifiable reasons. The great reforms of the 1830s changed this and many other aspects of local political life.

For some six hundred years, until 1835, another year of great local government change, each mayor began his term at Michaelmas, the 29th of September. In 1836 a new system took effect: the mayor was elected in November. This continued until 1948 when the mayor's election first took place in May. The Chronicles reflect the mayoral year rather than the calendar year: the events are noted as those taking place in the mayors' terms. Therefore they run from September of one year to the September of the next.

The means by which mayors have been elected have also greatly changed. Until 1496 the retiring mayor nominated two electors and the city's citizens chose two men. These four men then elected the new mayor. For a few years afterwards the mayor appears to have been directly elected by his fellow councillors but by 1500 the councillors offered two candidates and one of these was chosen by the city's freemen to be mayor. This practice of self-election continued until 1835 when the system was criticised for being a closed shop: from the following year onwards the councillors were elected from a wider body of voters and the mayor was thus chosen from a greater cross-section of citizens. For the first time men who were not followers of the Church of England were elected. In 1882 regulations were changed again; ordinary citizens, and not only councillors, could become mayor.[11] From 1973, yet another year of great change of local government, the new mayor has been elected exclusively from the body of councillors.

The mayoralty has continued to evolve. The first woman to become a mayor was Minnie Nichols in 1966 and in 2002 Queen Elizabeth II granted the city the status of having a Lord Mayor. The office of mayor has often in the past been seen as being onerous or financially burdensome. Men, as the Chronicle shows, have frequently preferred to pay a heavy fine than serve as mayor.

Semper Fidelis and the Exeter Salt

The Chronicles shed interesting light on the city's motto, a part of the history of Exeter which is murky at best. It is a local tradition that the motto was given by Queen Elizabeth. This is generally thought to have happened in a letter from her in which she expressed her thanks for help given against the Armada in 1588. This attribution is first mentioned in published form in 1677 by Richard Izacke but it also appears seventeen years earlier on the title page of his manuscript of 1660. Unfortunately that letter does not appear to have survived; it has yet to be found in the city's archive at the Devon Record Office nor has any copy of it been located in the National Archives. Interestingly, in 1590 John Hooker also neglected to mention it either in his Chronicle or in any of his other manuscript accounts of the city. A letter of such importance should have been retained and it is likely that Hooker, or another city official then or later, would have made a copy. Hooker's listings and collection of manuscripts on Exeter contain copies of nearly every important city document but there is no mention of this Elizabethan letter.

The motto was not included in the city's arms which were granted on 6 August 1564 and, curiously, fifty-six years later, when the Herald of the College of Arms visited Devon, the motto was not mentioned. The origins of the motto can first be traced to the Restoration period.

It is possible that in 1660 the city adopted a motto on its own initiative. This was legally possible because permission is not needed from the College of Arms. 'Ever Faithful' would be an interesting choice to make at the Restoration given the city's history during the Civil War. At the start of the war, in August 1642, the city had been cool to a visit by the king's emissary, Henry Earl of Bath, and then it firmly declared for Parliament. It subsequently was besieged by the Royalists and surrendered to them in September 1643. The king, queen and Prince Charles visited Exeter and then Princess Henrietta Anne was born in the city in June 1644. In April 1646 the city was retaken by Parliament and the following month the king himself surrendered the war. He was executed early in 1649 and Charles II came to the throne eleven years later.

It is then, in 1666, that the motto first appears. Six years earlier, in the summer of 1660, Exeter presented the new king with a silver salt, now one of the nation's treasures. Could the adoption of the motto be part of the city's attempt to lay to rest its disloyal part in the Civil War? When the members of the council chamber heard the news of the king's imminent return it proclaimed it throughout the city on the 11th of May. A loyal address was sent ten days later to him and the council voted to spend up to £600 on silver plate as a gift. One of the city's MPs, Simon Snow, was later given £700 for his full costs.[12] Curiously, Snow was a member of the city's 'godly' faction, a Presbyterian,[13] but presumably was given the responsibility for purchasing the gift because of his familiarity with London. He was also a merchant and had been mayor in 1653. Not long after he arranged the purchase Snow refused to take an oath of allegiance to the king.[14] The Exeter Salt, this extravagant piece of silver which stands eighteen inches high and is encrusted with some 73 jewels, is still part of the Royal Collection and is now housed at the Tower of London with the Crown Jewels.[15] The Salt has a second name; it is also known as the State Salt. This pre-eminence is probably what the city had hoped for. During the Commonwealth period the Royal collection of plate had been sold and when Charles II came to the throne he was in need of pieces to replace those of his father's which had been lost to the family. It was only natural that a suitably elaborate salt would find a prominent place on the royal table. Exeter's gift would have been a continual reminder to the king of the city.[16]

Eleven years later the new king revisited Exeter. It was then July of 1671 and nearly sixteen years had passed since he had hastily retreated from Exeter from a Parliamentarian army. On his arrival he was presented with a gift of £500 from the council. The king sent to the city a portrait by Sir Peter Lely of his sister, Henrietta Anne, who had died two years earlier in 1670, as a gift to hang in the Guildhall. It could be said that, like the Exeter or State Salt, it was also a very visible public reminder of his family and of their time in the city amidst the uncertain and changeable loyalties of its people.

It was during these years that the city designated a sword, now thought to have been acquired in the 1570s, as a 'Mourning Sword' to be carried to mark the anniversary of the execution of King Charles I. This sword is still housed in the Guildhall. It was also at this time that the city began a more public association with General George Monk, the Devon man who was widely credited with arranging for the return of Charles to the throne. An enormous portrait of him was also placed in the Guildhall, in size it rivals that of Princess Henrietta, and he was chosen to be the city's High Steward in 1662.[17] There were several highly visible signs of Exeter's loyalty to the crown on show in the early years of the restoration.

But was the motto actually given by Queen Elizabeth? The evidence for this has slightly changed over the centuries. In 1677 Izacke himself wrote in his introduction that 'Queen Elizabeth gave it this motto', in 1806 Jenkins noted in his history of Exeter that 'the Queen, in a letter, returned her most grateful thanks and granted them the honour of bearing the motto, *Semper Fidelis*, for ever, under their city arms, and appointed John Carpenter Esquire to be their muster master',[18] in 1861 Reverend George Oliver thought in his history that 'to this city, so renowned for its loyalty, she assigned the honourable title of *Semper Fidelis*' and in 1936 Lloyd Parry, Town Clerk and Honorary Lecturer at the University College of the South West, wrote it 'is said to originate with a description of the city in those words by Queen Elizabeth'.[19] Interestingly, the College of Arms, clearly having no record of it, cautiously noted in 1874 that 'the motto is said to have been given or suggested by Queen Elizabeth in a letter addressed to the citizens in 1588 thanking them for their exertions against the Spaniards and in allusions to their former zeal, loyalty and deserts.'[20] Yet strangely, the city's four chroniclers fail to specifically identify the motto within their chronologies of the city's history. Also, the city was not particularly distinguished in its support during the Armada crisis: Exeter was asked to provide three ships towards national defence but debated this with national government and asked that nearby parishes situated in the Exe Estuary should contribute to the costs. Within the city itself the wealthier citizens and the poor were at loggerheads over who should pay taxes for the ships.[21]

Could the motto have been invented by the city? They would not have risked ascribing it to King Charles I, who might have mentioned any thoughts towards Exeter at some point in the Civil War to his son Prince Charles nor to James I, the grandfather of the young prince. If the city were to fabricate a story then it had to be attributed to an earlier monarch. Queen Elizabeth never met any of the future Stuart kings and would have been a safer bet. This would allow the city to claim that until her reign it had consistently been loyal, always faithful except for the unfortunate business of the Civil War. The Chronicle by the elder Izacke of 1666, in which the motto first appears, very carefully ignores earlier instances when the city was decidedly not Ever Faithful towards the crown. It might well be that the city found it expedient in the 1660s to employ what became a very useful earlier letter. The finding of this Elizabethan document would settle the origins of the motto.

The Contents of the Chronicles

Each Chronicler used the same format. Following the date of each mayor appears details of what happened in that year. The topics range from war, pestilence, harvest failure, piracy, invasion, crime and even illicit romance. Hooker's accounts are particularly informative for the sixteenth century but also for his notes of the early documents of the city. The subjects for the later writers partly reflects their interests as well as the information they were able to glean. They were all sensitive to political realities.

Each of the Chronicles appears as they were written in their original forms. John Hooker's text is reproduced in its entirety except for the lines of Latin which have largely been omitted or where included they appear in italics.[22] The omissions are principally references from documents referring to the wills of citizens. Richard Izacke's Chronicle has been taken from the original manuscript and is much more extensive than that which was printed in 1677. His son Samuel's additions are reproduced separately. Any and all additions by Richard Crossing are noted as such within the chronicles.

Notes

1. *Rotuli Litterarum Clausarum* (Record Commission, 1833), vol. 1, 39; The document is held by the National Archives.

2. W. G. Hoskins, *Two Thousand Years in Exeter* (Exeter, 1960), 32; The date for Winchester is 5 April 1200: information supplied by Hampshire Record Office.

3. B. Wilkinson, *The Medieval Council of Exeter* (Manchester, 1931), ix.

4. Devon Record Office, ECA Books 51, 53 and 54; Samuel Izacke, *Remarkable Antiquities of the City of Exeter* (London, 1724).

5. Wilkinson, *Council*, ix.

6. Todd Gray (ed.), *The Lost Chronicle of Barnstaple* (Exeter, 1998), 8-10.

7. Mark Stoyle, *From Deliverance to Destruction* (Exeter, 1996), 74

8. Historical Manuscripts Commission, *Report on the Records of the City of Exeter*, 1916, 172, note.

9. Walter J. Harte, *Gleanings from the Manuscript of Richard Izacke's Antiquities of the City of Exeter* (Exeter, no date given), introduction.

10. Stoyle, *From Deliverance to Destruction*, 88, 140.

11. H. Lloyd Parry, *The History of the Exeter Guildhall and The Life Within* (Exeter, 1936), 18-19; N. S. E. Pugsley, *Mayors of Exeter from the 13th century to the present day* (Exeter, 1964). Although the pamphlet is printed under the name of Mr Pugsley, it was written by Margery Rowe.

12. George Oliver, *The History of the City of Exeter* (Exeter, 1884), 133-4; Devon Record Office, ECA, Act Book 1652–1663, meetings of 25 June and 7, 28 August 1660.

13. Stoyle, *From Deliverance*, 48; Stephen K. Roberts, *Recovery & Restoration in an English County* (Exeter, 1985), 20, 159.

14. J. J. Alexander, 'The Exeter Council of 1662', *Devon & Cornwall Notes & Queries*, XX, 308.

15. The Exeter Salt is largely unknown within Exeter itself. One of the earlier references is the catalogue for the marking of the 300th anniversary of the Restoration which was held in 1960: DRO, catalogue by Margery Rowe, 1960, pages 41-2

16. C. Blair (ed.), *The Crown Jewels; the history of the royal regalia in the jewel house of the Tower of London* (London, 1998) II, 385-6.

17. John Allan, *Exeter Guildhall* (Exeter, 2000), 35, 19.

18. Alexander Jenkins, *Jenkins's Civil and Ecclesiastical History of the City of Exeter* (Exeter, 1841), 127.

19. Parry, *Guildhall*, 167.

20. Copy of the Arms by the College of Heralds, October 1874, in the Guildhall.

21. Wallace T. MacCaffrey, *Exeter, 1540–1640* (1975), 236-40.

22. I am grateful to Mrs Margery Rowe for her translation of John Hooker's Latin.

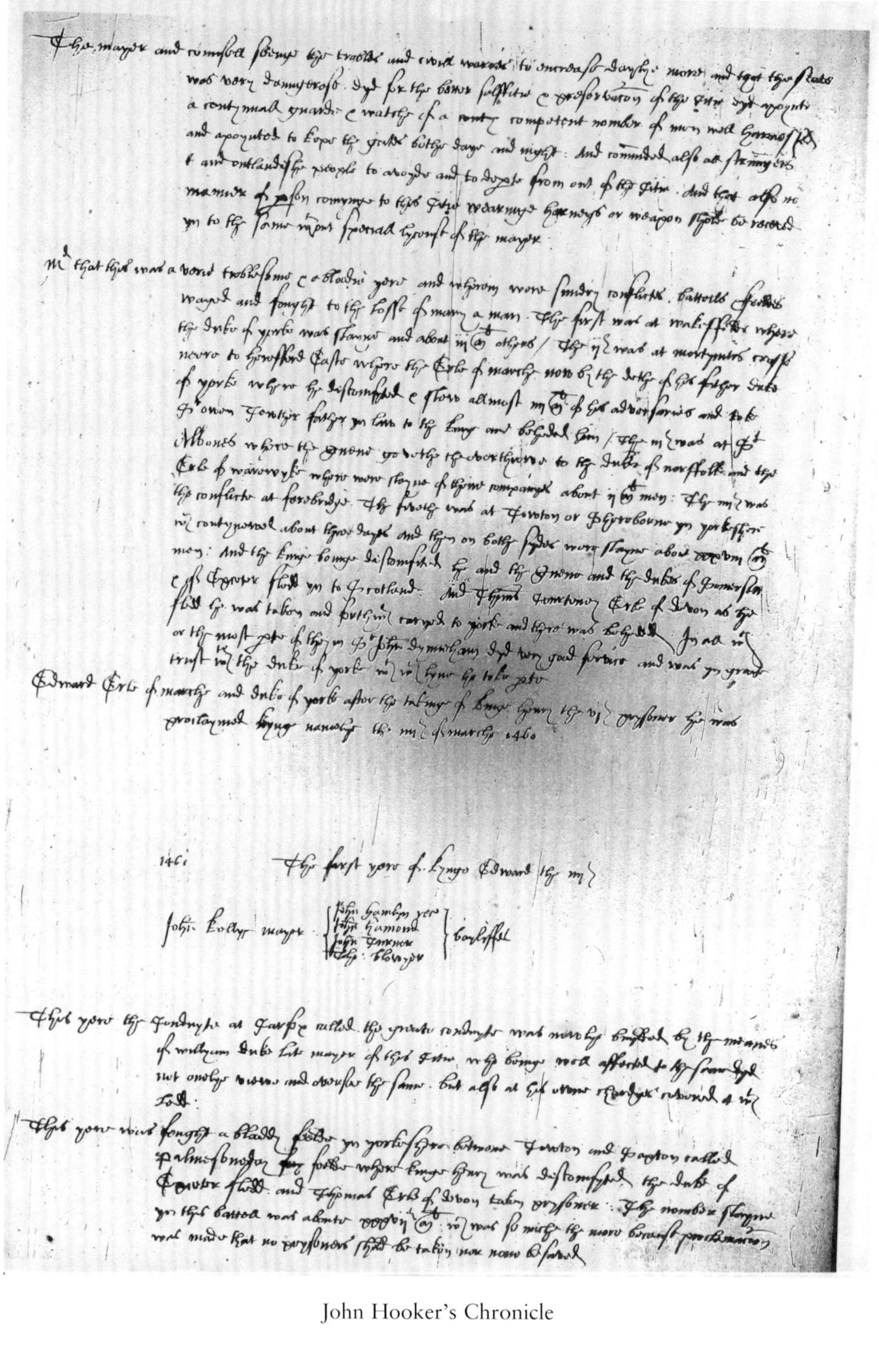

John Hooker's Chronicle

PART ONE

John Hooker 1216–1590

Here follow the names of all and every of the Kings of England from the time of King John, who died in October, *Anno* 1216, until the time of the reign of Queen Elizabeth, and of her years. And the names of the mayors and head officers in every of the said several kings' times, together with a copy of all the records of the city for and during those kings' reigns as be extant and remaining. And here understand you that from the time of the Conquest until the 14th year of King Edward the First [1285–6], there is extant one roll of record making a short mention of the three years in the time of King Henry the 3rd, viz. the 48th, 49th and 50th years of his reign [1263–5], that is to say for 217 years no records remaining but only one, which whether it by the iniquity of the time, the uncertainty of the government, civil wars intestine, rebellions or negligence of officers I refer it to others to think what they list. Further in the end of every particular mayor's year there is subnected and written a brief abstract of some such things as were done in that year and especially in these west parts.

1216

The first year of King Henry the third [Walter] Turbert

In the beginning of this year King John died at Newark and was brought to Worcester and there buried. Of the manner and kind of his death there are sundry opinions but the most common and received report [is] that he was poisoned.

After the death of King John his son Henry was by the nobility of the realm brought to the city of Gloucester and there proclaimed and crowned king by the name of King Henry the 3rd.

In this time the chief and next officers under the mayor for the government of this city were according to the old and usages in the times of the Saxons and Danes before the Conquest and in the reigns of the Norman kings after the Conquest, were named *Prepositi* within the Saxon tongue or the *Portegreves*, named in English portreeves, who were officers in those days of great credit and authority, as may appear by the common laws of the realm collected and published by King Canute, as also by the entomology of the word, which signifieth the lords or ancients of any city or town.

1217

Roger Fitzhenry

This year and the year before were very troublesome and bloody about the expulsing and removing of Lewes, the French king's son, whom the actions in the time of King John had slocked [to draw or lead away] and procured into England for their aid against the king and to whom they had sworn homage and fealty but in the end and in this year he was discharged and all things were pacified.

1218

Walter Gervys the
elder

This year the king deviseth to have a privy seal and maketh an officer for the same, within course of years was assigned to men of great credit and honour and became honourable office.

1219

Walter Turbert

All things being settled in quietness and the realm in peace. The king is crowned the second time.

1220

Walter Turbert

1221

Roger Fitzhenry

1222

Roger Fitz-Henry

The king kept his Christmas this year at Oxford at which time sundry young gentlemen upon a sudden in the night fled from the court and rebelled against the king but it was soon appeased. The chiefest of them was William de Fortibus, Earl of Anmark or of Albarania in Normandy, a man of great personage and honour and very valiant in all feats of arms. He married the Lady Isabella, sister and heir to Baldwin de Ryderere, the 5th earl of Devon, the son and heir to Baldwin the 4th, the son to Baldwin the third, the son of William Deveroan the third son and heir to Baldwin the first, son to Richard the first and the first Earl of Devon and Lord of the Isle of Wight. They had no issue between them. She over-lived him and continued sole and a widow all the days of her life being named after her husband Isabella de Furtibus, Countess of Albemarle and of Devon.

1223

Walter Gervys

1224

Walter Turbert

In this year died Symon de Apulia, Bishop of Exeter, and was buried in his own [?church]. There remaineth no mention of any good thing done by him. He was an Apulyan born and placed by the pope in whose causes he was very diligent. He was successor to Henry Marshall who impropriated Woodbury to the vicars choral of St Peters of Exeter. Successor to John, successor to Bartholomew Ichanus, successor to Robert Warewest, successor to Robert Chichester, successor to William Warewest founder and canon of Plymouth, successor to Osbertus, successor to Leofricus, the first bishop of Exeter and the last of Crediton or Kyrton. There were before this Leofricus 12 bishops of this diocese containing in itself the province of Devon and Cornwall of whose doings and times and places it is before in the catalogue of the bishops declared.

In the end of this year Richard, Earl of Cornwall, passed over into France with 44 ships well appointed and prevaileth much against the French.

This year were the parish churches within this city and suburbs first limited and appointed from the number of a few unto 19. The persons and number of every of which were chiefly maintained & had their livelihoods by the execution of the former decrees of Pope Innocent and Pope Honorius.

This year were very great tempests of winds, thunders, lightnings, rains and hail. And some hailstones were as great as a hen's egg and four square. And with them many cattle were slain and much corn destroyed. Likewise, many birds contrary to nature carried fire in the air in their bills and many houses thereby burned with fire.

Also this time was Joseph Icanus, or Joseph of Exeter, so named because he was born in this city or as some say a minister or a priest in the cathedral church of St Peters. He was excellently well learned in all good letters but especially in poetry. And for his excellence in the Greek and Latin tongues he was said to excel all others in his time.

Likewise christened Alexander Narkann, a man excellently well learned being a very good philosopher, a notable Christian, and a deep divine, who after that he had travelled through Italy and France and having read openly to his commendation in the universities of both those countries he returned into England, and that he might the better apply his studies he became a monk, and was made prior of the monastery of St Nicholas in this city. He wrote many books, the most of them were of divinity.

1225

Walter Turbert

This year William Brewer was consecrated bishop of Exeter at Canterbury by Stephen Langton then Archbishop there, who first made the chapter of 24 prebendaries.

This year was the wardship and marriage of young inheritors given to the king.

The king's brother was dubbed & created earl of Cornwall.

1226

[Roger] Fitzhenry

This year Bishop Brewer according to his devise and determination in ths year before did now exert and establish a dean and 24 prebendaries in his cathedral church of this city. And upon the third Sunday in Advent he installed Serlo, the archdeacon of Exeter, to be the first dean of his church, unto whom & unto his successors for their maintenance of hospitality he impropriated Brampton and Colaton Raleigh. And for his prebendaries he purchased so much lands as out of in every of them have yearly £4.

This year the king granted that the city of London should have two sheriffs and also he granted unto them the fee farm thereof, and a free warren and to be toll free through England.

A great discord fell between the king and his brother Richard, Earl of Cornwall, concerning the manor of Barkhampstead which the said earl took from one Wakeram and whereof wars were to have ensued, had not the same been prevented.

A great army of 40,000 men was appointed to go out of England into the Holy Land against the infidels of over whom this bishop and the bishop of Winchester were made the two General Captains who at the city of Aron met the Emperor Frederick.

The king held this year after Christmas a parliament at Westminster, at which came one Otho, Cardinal of St Nicholas in Carrere Tulhago and a legate from Pope Gregory the 9 and he demanded to have for the pope sundry pensions of the clergy as out of every conventual church within the realm two marks of money in the name of a proxy and out of every cathedral church two prebends and out of every religious house two portions of two monks, and out of the whole clergy to have the tenth. All which was denied and an answer made by the Archdeacon of Bedford.

1227

Walter Turbert

The king appointed a true and certain standard for weights and measures and reformed his coin according to the standard of Stockholm.

The cities of London and of Northampton were set and taxed to great ransom for aiding of Lewes, the French king who was now deceased.

1228

Walter Turbert

This year Richard Earl of Cornwall and brother to the king was sent over into Guyan for the recovery of certain holders delivered to the French King Lewes and had with him a great supply both of ships & of men out of this country.

1229

[Roger] Fitzhenry

This year a parliament was holden at Westminster in April, at which came one Stephen, a chaplin and a nuncius of the pope and required to have for the maintenance of his wars against the Emperor the 10th part of every man's goods both spiritual and temporal. The clergy yielded unto it but the temporal lords and lay utterly denied it. The king levieth a great sum of money of his prelates towards his journey into France and exacteth from the Jews the third part of their moveables.

1230

Roger Fitzhenry

The king towards the maintenance of his wars in France had granted unto him a whole fifteen of the laity and an escuage of the nobility, which was three marks of every one which holds a barony or a foreign knight's fee.

   The king resumeth this year sundry castles and forts within this realm in to his own hands and namely the castle of Exeter, which was then the inheritance of Robert Courtenay, then vice count of Devon by lineal descent. He being the son and heir unto Hawyst the daughter and heir unto Maude, the daughter and heir unto Alice the daughter and heir unto Adele, the sister and heir unto Richard de Briono the son and heir unto Baldwin of Briono and of Albreda his wife the niece unto William the Conqueror who gave the said vice-countship unto the said Baldwin & Albredo and to their heirs forever. And thus the Courtenays who had enjoyed the same in their own name of three descents were now disposed thereof.

   Richard, Earl of Cornwall, married the Countess of Gloucester, the widow of the Earl Robert Clare and the sister of William Marshall Earl of Pembroke.

1231

Walter Gervis

The king called a parliament and demanded a great subsidy for the supporting of his charges and relieving of his want but it was denied him. Whereupon by the advice and counsel of the Bishop of Winchester he calleth the chief officers who were grown to great wealth and riches unto an account and by that means he got great riches and masses of money and especially by the shifting of the Earl of Kent his chief justice. This earl was committed to the castle of the [?]Vyes to be safely kept for whose true imprisonment the Earl of [?] was one surety.

1232

[Walter] Turbert

This was a very troublesome year of storms, thunders, lightnings, great winds, strong sights in the air and earthquakes whereof followed great dearth of victuals, death of people and murrain [plague or pestilence] of cattle.

1233

Hilary Blond

[This] year the two bishops Peter of Winchester & William of Exeter who were the generals captains of the 40,000 English men which went to serve and fight against the infidels for the recovery of the Holy Land returned home again and now recovered with great joy.

   The king and his barons fell at variance but are reconciled again.

1234

Martin Roff

This year was a great plague of pestilence in this city.

   This year the Lady Isabella, sister to the king, was sent over the seas to be married unto Frederick the Emperor who had sent his ambassadors the archbishop of Colleyn & the duke of Loveyn but she was delivered to the custody of the bishop of Exeter who did conduct and present her to the Emperor at Worms whereby they were married and the said bishop very honourably entertained.

1235

Roger Fitzhenry

The king married the Lady Eleanor, the daughter to the earl of Provance. Also this year appeared strange sights upon the earth and many signs in the air, much thundering, lightning and tempests with great inundations and many people destroyed by the same.

1236

Walter Turbert

The king this year confirmed the charter and liberties of the city.

1238

Martin Roff

The pope sendeth his legate Otho into England and demanded to have 300 of the best benefices within this realm for 300 Romans, and forbiddeth any collection of any spiritual living to be had or allowed until this demand were performed. The clergy grudging much at this demand make suit unto the king who forthwith wrote in their behalf to the pope but he was not heard, and thereupon by his own authority did forbid the same as also all other things being prejudicial to his crown and dignity to be paid to the pope.

1239

Walter Gervis

This year for some months together was continually great storms and foul weather whereby the corn in the ground was destroyed and the cattle perished. In July the king's eldest son was born and named Edward. The Jews this year caused a Christian man's son to be circumcised as also secretly committed a murder; for which they some were some imprisoned, some punished and executed but all the residue were generally ransomed and paid the third part of all their goods and chattels. At a council holden this year at Paris, it was concluded and determined that no spiritual person might have any more than two benefices.

1240

Martin Roff

This year was the weather very variable & uncertain, first great storms, tempests, thunderings and lightnings. Then continued dry for three months together, after that continual rain for three other months whereby ensued great dearth of corn and victuals and death of people. All which were said to be the effects of the great comet which appeared the year before.

The king by the means of Richard Earl of Cornwall dubbed Baldwin Earl of Devon knight and made him earl of the Isle of Wight. He married Lady Agnes, daughter in law to the said earl, that is to say the daughter of Gilbert of Clare, Earl of Gloucester and Hereford, who being deceased this Richard, Earl of Cornwall, had married the Lady Isabella his widow. Not long after this marriage of her daughter the said countess died being great with child.

This year appeared a blazing star and whereof followed a very unseasonable time.

The earl of Cornwall being crossed for the Holy Lands taketh journey towards the same being attended by the most chosen company of the gentlemen in these west parts and passing through France, Provence, and other countries was very honourable received and entertained but when he came to the city of Marrella to embark himself and his company the pope by his legates forbade and inhibited him to proceed any further in his journey and enterprise. But the earl listened not thereunto, but took the seas and had a prosperous passage and landed at Acon at his will and pleasure whose safe arrival there being advertised into England, William de fortibus, Earl of Albamarling followed him with a chosen company of lusty young gentlemen. But being not able to brook the seas nor to eat any meat he died at the seas in Mediterranean Sea.

Gilbert Long and John his brother, sons of one Walter Long, a citizen of Exeter, founded and builded the hospital of St Johns within the East gate of the city of Exeter and endowed the same with all their livelihoods and lands. And after their death left the mayor and citizens of the said city to be founders and patrons of the same.

1241

Martin Roff

This year the earl of St Alexis which was the house where now is that which is named St Buryans, being a place of and for two monks, was removed and united to St Johns within East gate.

Richard Earl of Cornwall having concluded peace with the Soldanes redeemed the captives and set all things in good order he returned from out of the Holy Land home and landed at Sicillia upon which he took occasion in his homewards to visit his brother in law the Emperor Frederick and after certain months spent with him he came into England and was received in great joy and honour.

1242

Martin Roff

This year was an earthquake in this west country and much hurt done thereby in houses and buildings which were overthrown and hurled down and likewise great storms and foul weather at the seas at which time the Earl of Cornwall being at the seas was in great danger and at length cast a land at Scilly.

1243

[Martin] Roffe

Richard Earl of Cornwall married at Westminster the lady Cyncia, daughter to the Earl of Provence and sister to the Queen of England.

1244

Adam Ryfford

This year a permuation was had and made between the mayor and citizens, founders of the hospital of St Johns within the East Gate, and the bishop, founder of the hospital of the lazar [lepers] house of the Magdalen without the South Gate, of the said city. The cause of which permutation is this: the lazar people did upon every market day come into the market with a clap dish and went from man to man to beg corn and all other victuals as was to be sold in the market with liberty they claimed from and by the grant of Bishop Brewer who by his two letters patent *Anno* 1163 granted to the said sick people a certain toll of corn sold in the market of this city upon Thursdays and Saturdays which were then the market days for corn. Also toll for bread sold upon and in the Saturdays, and a toll of bread and corn sold upon the fair days. Also that they should collect the alms of all the citizens upon Tuesdays and Thursdays. The poor people having received this the bishop's blessing and persuading themselves that it would be very profitable and beneficial unto them began forthwith to put the same in execution and came in to the markets with their clap dishes and asked the toll appointed unto them. But the people which had not been acquainted with any such custom and not brooking the ugly faces nor liking the thrusting of the sick folks in among them some of them gave them rough speeches, some of them shunned them and some of them forbade them of the market. And all were straight laced and hard girded [to wear] for small and little was it with the poor lazars could have at all. Which things grieved the bishop very much. But in the end for appealing of the matter this permutation was made that the bishop and his successors should from thenceforth be patrons of the hospital of St Johns within the East Gate of this city and the mayor and commonality should be patrons of the hospital of the Magdalen for the lazars without the South Gate. Which things from thenceforth was accordingly observed.

This year upon the 24th of October William Brewer the bishop died and was buried in the middle of the chancel of his church under a marble stone.

The King of Denmark not liking well of the pope and of his outrageous exactions challenged unto him

6

the supremacy of the clergy within his own realm and forbiddeth any tenths, payments or exactions to be made unto the pope out of his realm. He alloweth and permitteth his clergy to marry and have wives.

The pope by his new nuncio, named Martyn, exacteth such payments and intolerable sums of money of the clergy of this land that the bishop and the abbots and religious persons are in such a perplexy as they know not what to do. Whereof they sought and sue to the king for redress and remedy. Who in their behalf writeth to the pope, sendeth his ambassadors unto him but to no purpose until that they threatened the pope to his face that he should have no more exactions out of England.

1245

Martin Roff

Richard Blondye was consecrated bishop of Exeter at Lambtide by Bonefarins, archbishop of Canterbury, in the month of November being the calendar of December.

Baldwin of Rydeverse, the 4th earl of Devon and of Wight, died this year of whose death great sorrow and lamentation was made.

1246

Adam Rifford

This year Boneface, archbishop of Canterbury, obtained & purchased of the pope a grant to levy and gather within & through his province the sum of 10,000 marks toward and for the payment of his debts.

The pope requested a new exaction and tallage of the clergy of England and also made a decree that all such spiritual persons as died intestate within England their goods should wholly remain & to be to his only use. But both these his demands were denied, neither would the king and nobility suffer the same to take place.

Queen Isabella, the king's mother, died this year.

1247

Martin Roff

In this year was a great earthquake from Bath into these west parts and whereof men were more afraid than hurted.

Also this was a continual year of rains, storms and foul weather.

The king calleth a parliament and requireth a subsidy which was not only denied but the king himself also was charged and reproved for his covetousness, unthankfulness and breaches of his promises, whereupon the king for lack of money was driven to sell his plate.

Earl of Cornwall for avoiding to deal between the king and his barons leaveth the court and liveth in this city and in Cornwall out of the way.

1248

Walter Hastement

This year a long controversy depending in suit of law between the mayor and commonality, plaintiffs, and the dean and chapter of St Sidwell's, defendants, for and concerning the fee and liberties of St Sidwell's without the East Gate of the said city, was ended by composition at Launceston before Richard, Earl of Cornwall, Peter, bishop of Exeter, Roger Tynkellry, Gilbert Preston and John Cotham, the king's justices of the Assizes. The special points and articles of which composition are as followeth.

Also the tenants of the dean and chapter dwelling within the city and suburbs of the same and which do occupy any art, trade or traffic shall at all taxes and tallages be assessed and taxed with the citizens so that the said taxation be most & indifferent.

Also the bailiff of the said dean and chapter shall levy, gather & receive up the said bailiff becomes negligent and slack then the mayor and his officers shall and may levy and collect the same.

Also that an indifferent man shall be chosen by both the said parts to be the common bailiffs for them both. And he upon his oath shall yearly and from time to time gather, preserve and collect of all the said dean and chapter towards the customs of balagavel [payment to superior], brothergavel and chapgavel and the same being truely gathered shall truly & indifferently divide & deliver the same between the said dean and chapter and the mayor & commonality.

Also all plaintiffs and actions entered against any of the dean and chapter's tenants within the city shall be tried, ended and determined before the mayor and bailiffs.

Also all plaintiffs and actions against any of the dean and chapter's tenants dwelling within the fee of St Sidwell's shall be determined before the bailiff of St Sidwell's.

If any of the tenants of the said dean and chapter being bakers or brewers are to be punished for breach of the assize in the pillory or tumbrel. The same upon request unto the mayor to be done within the city.

All pleas of the crown to be always determined before the mayor.

All traitors, murderers, felons, thieves and like offenders as shall be found within the said fee to be apprehended by the bailiff there and by him to be brought and delivered unto the mayor.

This time one Richard Fishacre born in this city of Exeter was a famous and an excellent scholar as those days required. He professed divinity and wrote sundry books thereof. He was buried in Oxford.

1249

[Martin] Roff

The earl of Cornwall went in ambassador from the king unto the pope who then was in France and from thence he went to Rome with him where he was very well honourable entertained.

The king setteth forth a new coin named groats of which four make [?].

1250

[Adam] Ryfford

In this man's year namely after Easter *anno* 1252 Walter Gervys died and was buried in the chapel upon Exe Bridge in one of the pillars of Exe Bridge and upon which the said chapel was builded. He was a worthy and a notable good citizen and was so well bent to the care and benefit of the common wealth as that he left nothing undone which might be for the furtherance and he so uprightly and in such wisdom and uprighteous govern the common wealth as none like before him and few better after him. In his time there was no bridge of stone over the river of Exe but only certain clappers of timber which serveth to pass over on foot in the summer time and which in therefore winter were for the most part carried away with the great floods. And the common passage was by boat and the same in the winters when the floods were great and high was very dangerous and many perished and drowned thereby. Wherein this good man being moved and taking some great care how he might remedy so great an evil useth sundry conversations with his friends and by them it was so thought best to have a bridge to be builded. Which was the one and only remedy in this behalf. But when they had cast their accounts of the great and excessive expenses and charges and saw how unable they were to compass the same they were utterly dismayed and discouraged. Nevertheless, this good man being of a good courage and mind shrinketh not at the matter but hoping of a good success advanceth the matter and as determined to make a general collection throughout the whole realm. And God so blessed his doings and he found such favour among all men both high and low that in a few years he had collected and gathered as it is written near about £10,000. And this money was so well husbanded and employed that he did not only build a very fair bridge of stone but also procured, provided and purchased certain lands for the perpetual maintenance of the same and such lands as he had of his own did also enfeoff and give unto the same as may and doth appear by his last will and testament dated Anno 1251. Some do hold opinion that he was a tailor or a hosier but who so looketh in to his doing shall find that he was a gentleman born and of a worshipful house and family.

1251

Adam Ryfford

This was a year of great rains, inundations, storms, winds and tempests.

The Earl of Cornwall foundeth the abbey of Hayles and caused it to be dedicated with much honour and solemnity.

1252

Martin Roff

The king giveth his daughter the Lady Margaret in marriage to Alexander, King of Scotland, at York where the king dubbeth him knight.

This was a very dry year whereof ensued a great murrain of cattle and death of men.

The king investeth his son Prince Edward with the Duchy of Aquitaine notwithstanding he had before given by his patents to his brother the earl of Cornwall.

1253

Adam Rifford

The pope offereth unto Richard Earl of Cornwall the kingdom of Naples and of Sicilia but he forecasting the slights and subtleties of the pope and considering sundry other inconveniences doth resist the same.

This year died a most famous, good and a learned man named Robert Capie or Robert Groteshed, bishop of Lincoln. He was a very sharp inveigher [a denouncer] and a bitter writer against the pope and his court for their insatiable covetousness, great pride and abominable life. He wrote sundry good works among which one was written in French mitre or verse very raw to be had entitled The banishment of love with all her family. The principal point whereof are these, the great simonies and outrageous covetnouse of the pope and of his court of Rome, the great and intolerable exactions of kings upon their subjects by means of flatterers and of evil counsellors, the fruits & livelihoods of the holy church were bestowed upon unfit persons and spent in pride, power and vain glory, that religion was quenched through hypocrisy, envy and a wicked life, that the natural love between the parents and children and between neighbour and neighbour was extinguished by the much love of worldly wealth and riches, that merchants by fraud, forswearing, usury, deceit and treachery gained their riches and wealth, that by these wicked means and outrageous greediness the seven sisters of mercy, that is to say piety or godliness, natural love, chastity, true purity, humility, truth and peace with all their trains and families were exiled & banished out of the world. The pope was marvellously incensed and offended with him and did excommunicate him and meant his utter destruction but the lord prevented it.

The king pretending a voyage unto the holy land obtained a subsidy of the clergy of the tenth part of all their revenues for three years and an escuage or three marks of every knight's fee of the temporalty for one year, for which gift the king promised to observe and keep the great charter.

Upon the former grant of the king all or the most part of the bishops of this realm among whom was the bishop of this city being apparelled in their *pontefisilibus* did pronounce sentence of excommunication against all such as did break and infringe the liberties of the churches.

1254

John Okeston

The king sendeth his son Edward into Spain where he married the Lady Eleanor, sister to Alphonse king of Spain. After the return of Edward out of Spain with his wife the king his father made him Prince of Wales and Earl of Chester which titles have ever since been invested in the king of England's eldest sons.

1255

Hilary Blondy

This was a very hard and bitter year to all the whole realm as well by the means of the king as of the pope both of them using all the means & practising all the devises they could for scratching and exacting of money. The king called a parliament and demandeth a subsidy but the Earl of Cornwall and all the whole nobility and commons deny the same. Whereupon he falleth out with the city of London, quarrelleth with the Jews and fawneth upon the rich men by means he scratched a great mass and sum of money. The pope likewise sendeth one Rustandue his legate and calleth a synod or Council at London of the whole clergy and there demandeth great sums of money for the aid of the pope in his wars against Mansford king of Sicilia, whose kingdom the pope had given to the King of England for his second son Edward, Earl of Lancaster but Sevallas, Archbishop of York, and Fulco, Bishop of London bitterly inveighed against the pope. The like also did after them other the bishops and abbots saying that the pope was the head of the church for the defending thereof and not for the pilling and poleing [to plunder or rob by stripping bare] of the same. And further that subsidies were to be given unto him for the recovery of the Holy Lands and to withstand God's enemies and not to be spent in wars against Christian peoples. Nevertheless, in the end they relented and will they nill they the pope would have & had somewhat.

1256

Philip Dyer

Richard Earl of Cornwall was chosen and elected king of Romans and very honourably was conducted out of England unto Collen where he was crowned by the archbishop there.

1257

Hilary Blonde
alias Whyte

This year died Richard Blonde, bishop of Exeter, and lieth buried in his church who left a very small memorial behind him.

Walter Bronscombe, a citizen born of this city of Exeter, being archdeacon of Surrey, was elected bishop of this city and consecrated upon Palm Sunday by Bonefacis Archbishop of Canterbury.

This year upon Palm Sunday being the 19th of March, Walter Lodeswell, Chancellor to Richard the last deceased Bishop, Richard Sutton, his Register, and John Fitzherbert, his official, did open penance in St Peter's church for false contriving, disposing and conveying of sundry spiritual livings of the church under the bishop's seal without his consent while he lay sick and past hope of recovery.

Also in this year the [king] called his parliament at London and from thence advanced unto Oxford, many things were devised for the reformation of the lands and 12 peers of the noble men chosen to see those orders executed which in the end came to small effect but rather the cause of great troubles and therefore called the mad parliament.

1258

Hilary Whyte
alias Blond

At this time there were but two officers named *Prepositi* or *portegreves* joined with the mayor in government but this year the number of them was increased to three and their names altered the from henceforth being no more named *preposita* or *Portegreves* but *Senescalli Senescheds* or Stewards which words or names though they have in them some differences and discrepancies yet in the order of government they are used indifferently. And taken in our sense and signification but in the common speech borrowed of the Norman tongue they were called provosts and the court of them kept called the Provost Court.

1259

Philip Dyer

The earl of Cornwall and now king of Almayncan over into England and at Canterbury he was sworn and took his oath to see the statutes made at Oxford to be kept and observed.

The king had granted unto him by act of Parliament a task called Escuage which is 40s of every knight's fee whereof by inquisition it was found that there were 40,000 [?marks] in the r[?] and the greater part of them was in the hands of the spirituality.

This year died the famous and worthy citizen Walter Gervis, founder of Exe Bridge.

1260

Walter Okeston

In this year the king not allowing the statutes made at Oxford and for the keeping whereof he was sworn and had given a corporal oath did procure from Pope Urbanus an absolution for the said oath and persuading himself to be dispensed thereby caused the same to be openly read at Paul's Cross at a sermon whereof ensued the dissention and wars between the king and his barons.

This year a long suit and controversy between the mayor and citizens of the one part and the prior of St Nicholas of the other part for and concerning certain liberties was by common consent of both parts referred and compromised to the determination of 12 indifferent citizens to be returned and sworn for the same.

1261

Hilary Whyte

1262

[Walter Okeston]

1263

Nicholas Ilchester

An order was taken that henceforth there should be yearly chosen 4 seneschals or stewards of which one to be the receiver of the city's rents and revenues for that year.

1264

Philip Dyer

Richard, Earl of Cornwall and King of Romans, being yet as indifferent between the king and the barons, after that the Londoners taking part with the barons had spoiled and burned the said Earl's house he became a mortal enemy to the barons and to their side and sent unto them under his hand and seals his defiance.

Henry, the son of the said earl, taking part with the barons, was taken prisoner by the king's soldiers. But not long after both he and his father and King Henry his son were taken all prisoners at the battle of Lewes and the said king of Romans was sent prisoner to the Tower of London. And his son Henry sent to the castle of Dover.

1265

Walter Okeston

At a parliament holden at Winchester the city of London was deprived of their liberties and the mayor and chief citizens were cast in prison until at length they were redeemed upon grievous fines.

1266

William Dyrlinge

Walter Bronscombe, bishop of Exeter, foundeth the college in Penryn in Cornwall and endoweth with great livelihoods. Also he gave the land of Rookesdone and at St Mary Clyst to St John's in Exeter.

1267

Nicholas of
Ilchester
Walter Chawe

A composition was made this year between the abbot and convent of Sherborne of the one part and the mayor and commonality of this city of the other part concerning the passage and ferry at Exmouth and then was ordered that the said abbot should disclaim his title and interest to the same reserved and exacted a free passage to and from the said passage and ferry in the city's passage boat to the said abbot and convent and to all their man and families servants to pass to and from without paying anything with a proviso that if the city's passenger be not ready nor their passage boat in place to whaste them over that they then are at their liberty to take any other boat for that present time.

Nicholas Ilchester the mayor aforesaid died in his mayoralty and Walter Chawe chosen in his place.

1268

William Okeston

An inhabitant of this city (for so the story goes, and twill hardly persuade credit] being a very poor man, and having many children, thought himself blessed too much in that kind, wherefore to avoid the charge which was likely to grown upon him that way, absents himself seven years together from his wife, and then returning again, and accompanying her as formerly, she was within the space of a year thereafter delivered of seven male children at one birth, which made the poor man think himself utterly undone, and herby despairing, put them all in a basket, with a full intent to have drowned them; but Divine Providence following him, occasioned a lady (then within the said city, and thought to have been the countess of Devon) coming at this instant of time in his way, to demand of him what he carried in his basket, who replied that he had therein whelps, which she desired to see, purposing to make choice of one of them, who, upon view, perceiving that they were children, compelled the poor man to acquaint her with the whole circumstance, who, when she had sharply rebuked for such his inhumanity, presently commanded them all to be taken from him, and put to nurse, then to school, and so to the university, and in process of time being attainted to [?]'s estate, and well qualified in learning, made means and procured benefices for every one of them. But such like Eleemosynary Acts in this our age (therein the charity of too many is waxen cold) are almost vanished.

1269

Alfred De porta
alias Dewporte

Edmond Crochebaker, second son to King Henry married the Lady Averialla, sole daughter and heir unto William de fortibus, Earl of Albarnurlia or Anmerle and of Holderness; and unto Lady Isabella, daughter and heir unto Baldwin, Redeverse, 4th Earl of Devon & Lord of the Isle of Wight. And by that means the said Edmond should in her right be Earl of Anmarle, Holderness, and Devon, and Lord of the Isle of Wight. But she died in the same year without issue.

1270

Martin Dyrlinge

1271

Martin Dyrlinge

Prince Edward being crossed for the Holy Lands and among others of the nobility and noble men of this realm he taketh with him his cousin German Henry, the eldest son unto Richard Earl of Cornwall, which Henry in his return homewards through Italy was slain in the city of Viterbe by Guy Montefort, son to the Earl of Leicester.

Earl of Cornwall died this year, after whom his second son Edmond by the death of his elder brother was Earl of Cornwall.

1272

Martin Dyrlinge

King Henry the 3rd died this year upon the 16th of November 1272. Prince Edward his son being not yet returned from the Holy Lands. The Prince Edward was proclaimed king forthwith but not crowned until the next year following.

Here understand you that although King Edward was proclaimed king in the first quarter of this mayor's year yet the title of the same is in the name of the King Henry deceased because he was living at Michaelmas when this mayor was chosen and began his office.

The first year of King Edward the first

1273

Richard le Geythen

In August the King returned being towards the end of this man's year, Anno 1274, and was crowned at which Edmond Earl of Cornwall and others in a bravery when they alighted of their horses did leave them to such as would and did catch them.

Walter Bronscome bishop of Exeter about this time built his house at Clyst Sacheffeld now called Bishop's Clyst and after this annexed Cornish Wood to his barton but how and by what policies he gained this one from the lord of the same and the other from the dean and chapter it appeareth in his life.

1274

Martin Dyrlinge

The king deviseth wholesome laws for the assize of bread and ale.

1275

Alfred Deporte

The king by his letters patent dated the 10th of March the 3rd year of his reign granted to this city a collection of all manner of wares brought to be sold within this city towards the paving of the streets, repairing of the walls and maintenance of the city.

In these west parts upon the 10th of September was a great earthquake and many were destroyed thereby.

1276

Alfred Deporte

An inquisition was taken this year at Exeter for inquiry for the king concerning liberties and lands concealed. And it was found by verdict that Croldyche or Lammas Fair was the one half between King John and the commonality of the city. And that King John resumed or took the whole in to his hands and gave it to the prior and convent of St Nicholas but *it does not stand in law*.

1277

John Fenneton

This year at a parliament holden at Westminster was made the statute of mortemain [the condition of lands or tenements which is that they are inalienably held by an ecclesiastical or other corporation].

1278

Alfred Duporte

A great execution was done upon the Jews for clipping of money for which offences were 280 put to death.

1279

John Feneton

1280

Alfred Dewporte

Walter Bronscombe, bishop of this city, died and was buried in the Lady Chapel of his own church in a very fair tomb of alabaster. Of his doings look before in the catalogue of the bishops.

1281

Alfred Duporte

This year was no election of any new officers known or remembered in any writings and therefore these two years are reckoned as one.

A composition was made this year by consent and confirmation of the king and of Edmond, Earl of Cornwall, between the mayor and commonality and the bishop, dean and chapter for inclosing of the churchyard and shutting of the gates thereof at night.

1282

Martin Dyrlinge

Peter Quyvell was consecrated and installed bishop of Exeter and in the 6 and 7 years of his consecration 1287 he kept a synod of all his clergy in which he made notable canons and constituions among which one was concerning the manner of making of testaments and the order of the petition of the dead men's goods into reasonable portions which is very like order as by act of parliament is granted & conferred to the city of Exeter *in the fifth year of Queen Elizabeth from the register of the said Peter Quivell, 1283, 14 Edward I, 1287*

1283

Alfred Duporte

The east church not bearing the intolerable pride of the pope forsaketh the west church.

1284

Alfred Duporte

In this mayor's year upon St Mark's day 1284 was born at Caerenarvon in Wales Edward, the king's son, who after his father was king of this land. In the beginning of this mayor's year upon St Martin's Eve's even the 9th of November Walter Lychlade, Chancellor of St Peter's in Exon, was slain as he came from matins in the morning which was want to be said about one or two of the clock in the morning and murderer escaped at the South Gate which were left open that night.

1285

David Taylor

In this year the first recorder of this city began which follow in order here under written as they be extant and remaining in the chamber of the city.

The mayor was chosen this year upon the Thursday after Ash Wednesday.

This year the king and queen at the request of Peter of Exeter came to this city and here kept their Christmas upon occasion of the killing of Walter Lychelade, Chancellor of this church, upon the inquisition of whose death Alured Deport, late mayor, and the porter of the South Gate was indicted, arraigned and hanged because the said South Gate was that night left open by which means the murderer escaped.

1286

David Taylor

King Edward came this year to the city for the injury of the death of Walter Lychlade the late Chancellor and kept his Christmas feasts in the bishop's palace and at a sessions holden for the said inquiry it was found that the porter of the South Gate with the assent of Alfred Duporte later mayor of this city suffered to be opened the South Gate immediately after the murder done and suffer the murderers to escape whereupon the said porter was arraigned and executed to death and also the mayor himself.

[crossed through] King upon the occasion of the foresaid murder called a parliament in this city and made the statute of the coroners.

The Gray or Franciscan friars who had their house or monasteries in [?], now called Friernhay, by the suit of Humphrey Earl of Hereford, who had married the Lady Elizabeth the king's daughter and then was lodged with the said friars, made unto the king and by the king unto the bishop, they obtained to remove and place their houses in some more and convenient place where they could best find out in or about the city. The bishop yielded to the king's request notwithstanding contrary to his promise after the king's departure did deny the performance of this promise and would not suffer them to proceed therein so long as he lived.

The Merchant Strangers having obtained to dwell & to occupy in several houses of their own were found to use great deceit in counterfeiting of their wares and in using of false weights wherefore they were grievously punished, imprisoned and set to ransom.

Peter, bishop of this city, erecteth the office of the subdeanery in his church and doth impropriate towards his living, maintenance & keeping of hospitality the rectory of the church of Egloshalye in

Cornwall. The said bishop also impropriates the rectories of Paignton and Chudleigh to the dignity of the chancellorship in his church.

A great part or piece of Exe Bridge through foul weather fell down this year and was forthwith new builded.

This year a composition was made between the bishop, dean and chapter of the one part and the mayor and commonality of the city of Exeter of the other part in the consent of the king and of Edmond, Earl of Cornwall, for the enclosing of the churchyard and building of certain gates there as doth appear by the letters and writings thereof. Dated the Monday next after the feast of the Annunciation of our Lady, 1286.

1287

John Sooche

Memorandum a composition was made this year between the bishop, dean and chapter of the one part and the mayor and citizens of the other part with the consent of the king and Edmond Earl of Cornwall for enclosing of the churchyard.   .

1288

John Sooche

1289

Richard Allen

Peter the bishop after that the chancel of his church begun by William Warwest the bishop of this church about the year of our Lord 1112 was full finished and ended. He to enlarge the same to some bigger proportion beginneth to lay the foundation and to build this body of this church from the chancel downwards. Towards this doing and performance he had gathered great treasure and provided things meet and necessary towards and for the same.

Ryse or Resius, prince of Wales, was taken and carried to York where he was beheaded.

1289

John Sooche

Memorandum Inquisition was taken at Exeter the day of the decollation of St John the Baptist the 18th year of King Edward the First, Anno 1290, before Malcolyn Harleigh, General Escheator of the king, on this side Trent. Before whom the jurors of the hundred of Wonford among other things upon their oaths say that Isabell de fortibus, Countess of Devon, hath cast and made a great purpresture or nuisance in the river of Exe by leaving and raising up of certain wears in the same. And that the said river and the whole course thereof doth appertain unto the king, by reason and in the right of the city of Exeter, that is to say from Chekeston unto the bridge of the said city, to the great nuisance, hurt and damage of the said city and of the whole adjoining.

Memorandum one other inquisition was taken at Exeter the day and year before said before the foresaid Malcolyn of Harleigh, Escheater General of the king on this side of Trent. Before whom the commonality of the city of Exeter and upon their oaths said that the city of Exeter is of the crown and doth appertain to the crown and is so old and ancient hath even been and that the same is immediately holden of the king. And further they say that the King Henry, father to the King that now is, gave the said city to his brother Richard Earl of Cornwall and to his heirs. And that the citizens of the said city do hold the same city in fee farm of the said earl as before they held the same by the king yielding therefore yearly to the said earl £14 9s. And further they say concerning purprestures that whereas the water and river of Exe for ever of old time doth appertain and was wont to appertain to the said city so since and unto the port of Exmouth. And the fishing in the said water and river is and ought to be common unto all men which list to fish therein. Nevertheless Isabella, Countess of Devon, now about 6 years past hath made and raised at Topsham certain weir overthwart the river of Exe and which is of such a height that the fishing and taking of salmons and of all other fishes is virtually taken away and decayed as the said weir to the great damage and annoyance of the said city and country. And further they say that whereas in time past boats & vessels were wont to pass to and from the said haven to the bridge of the said city laden with wines and merchandises to the great commodity of the whole country, now no boat nor vessel can so pass up unto the said city by reason of the said weir to the great danger of the said city and country. And further they say that all lands and tenements within the city of Exeter be legable and may be given and bequeathed by testament as well as any other goods and chattels even in like manner as it is used and accustomed in the city of London.

1290

John Sooch

1291

William Gattepathe

Memorandum that all the records of this year are lost and wanting.

Memorandum in this mayor's year the king, upon the death of Queen Eleanor his wife, did cause Charing Cross to be builded.

Quivel Bishop of Exeter died being the year 1292 by drinking of a syrup whereby he choked or strangled and was buried in the said chapel of his own church. The Franciscans or Gray Friars blasted it abroad that he died of God's misjudgement because he favoured not them neither would he suffer them to build their new house notwithstanding he had promised to the king the contrary.

Memorandum that this mayor and Richard Pollymor, Herbert de pyne and William Le Sparke, knights, were testes to a deed of one Ongarus de Sancto Milone, a citizen of Exeter, in which he gave unto the dean and chapter of St Peter's his wood of Stoke now called Stoke Wood and united the same to their memory of Stoke called Stoke Canon.

1293

Richard Tantyfor

Thomas Bitton was elected and consecrated bishop of Exeter Anno 1293.

Henry Courtenay, the second of that name, was this year made Earl of Devon as heir general to the Lord Rydeverse Earl of Devon, that is to say the son of him the son of John the son of Robert and Mary the daughter and heir to William Rydeverse named William de Verona the son to Baldwin the first the son to Richard Rydeverse the first Earl of Devon created by King Henry the first son to William the Conqueror.

1294

John Sooche

Memorandum this year the king kept certain miners in work at Martin Stowe in certain silver mines there which were very rich and yielded unto the king great treasure for in this year he had in clean fined silver 321 half pounds. In the next year he had 521 half pound weight. In the 3rd year following he had 704 weight. In 4th year he had also great abundance.

1295

John Sooche

1296

Walter Tantyfer

1297

Walter Tantyfer

Memorandum that the king came this year in to Devon and visited the house of Plympton.

Memorandum a composition was made this year between the mayor and citizens of the city of Exeter of the one part and the friars preachers of the same city of the other for and concerning one void place or piece of ground lying between the house of the said friars and the canons of the church of St Peters in Exeter in breadth and extendeth in length from the street there called Stryke Street unto the walls of the said city.

The king giveth his daughter Lady Elizabeth in marriage to John Earl of Holland she with great honour is conducted over unto the said earl.

The king calleth a parliament and demandeth a subsidy which was granted unto him by the Temporality or laity but altogether denied by the clergy or spirituality whereupon the king discharged them out of his protection, who in the end submitted themselves and gave the fifth part of all their goods.

The Pope Boniface the 8th made a law and a constitution forbidding and inhibiting upon pain of excommunication that no sovereign prince should demand or exact any tax or talling of any of the clergy.

1298

Walter Tantyfer

1299

John Horne

1300

William Gattepath

Memorandum that in the year of this mayor's year in the month of October being the 29th year of the king's reign Edmond Earl of Cornwall died *sans* issue and by that means the earl reverted to the crown and came again to the king's hands. The Countess after the death of her husband was endowed for her dowry with five hundred pounds [?]land.

1301

William Tantyffer

Memorandum the mayor of this city was chosen this year by the voices of 12 citizens upon their oaths.

Memorandum that this year was a great contention between the dean and chapter of St Peter's of the city of Exeter of the one part and the warden and friars preachers named the Black Friars of the other part for and concerning the burial of the dead corpse of Henry Raleigh knight which corpse the dean and chapter required to be presented at St Peter's Church before it should be buried and which being by the friars denied the dean and canons did fetch the corpse from out of the friars' church and carried it to the St Peter's and there the same being presented they brought again back to the friars' house but they made fast their gate and would not receive it. By means whereof the said corpse lay so long unburied that it stank and the canons driven to bury the same in St Peter's Church.

Memorandum the king this year made & proclaimed his son Prince of Wales and Earl of Chester, and which honours and titles have ever since been invested in the King of England's eldest sons. The Welsh men were most miffed hereof.

1302

Roger Boynym

Memorandum that this year was a great contention between the mayor and commonality of the one part against the tenants of the Lord of Kenton and Wyke then being Earl Marshal of England for denying to pay murage [a tax levied to repair town walls] for their wares and merchandises.

Memorandum an inquisition was taken and found against Philip of Okehampton, town clerk, and William Bykleye, his under clerk, for putting and enforcing a false roll among the records.

Memorandum an order and an agreement was made between the dean and chapter of St Peter's of the one part and the prior and friars preachers of the other part, that no person within the said city and suburbs should henceforth be buried within the church or cemetery of the said friars but that he should be first presented at St Peter's Church.

Memorandum that about this time flourished one Walter of Exeter so named because he was born in this city. He was a monk of the order of St Bennet and dwelled in a little cell in Cornwall called St Caroke near about Lostwithiel. He was seen in histories and did at the request of one Baldwyn, a citizen of Exeter, write the history of Guy of Warwick.

1303

Roger Le Wheton

Memorandum that sundry persons did take and break ground in Crosdytch for standings [a market stall] before the time limited for Lammas Fair for which they were attached to answer the mayor and commonality.

Memorandum there was a controversy between the mayor and commonality of the one part and the tenants of Kenton for and concerning certain attachments made upon the water of Exon. Likewise the like controversy was between the tenants of Kenton against the men of Lympstone and Pratished.

Memorandum that William of Exeter, warden of the Gray Friars or Franciscans, having provided all things necessary for the building of their new monastery do now build the same without South Gate.

Memorandum that this year a certain knight in Italy named Peter Cassiodorn not liking the intolerable pride, tyranny, covetousness and impiety of the pope did write his letters to the whole realms and lands of England and the church of the same inveighing most bitterly against the pope and Church of Rome and most godly persuading the church of England to shake off the yoke of the very anti-Christian state and utterly to renounce him and his usurped jurisdiction.

1304

Roger le Wheton

Memorandum it was ordered and ordained that no merchant nor other person should go to meet with any merchant or any person or persons coming with any wares, merchandises or victuals to this city to sell the same before and until the same merchant become and have brought the same to this city upon pain to forfeit of all the goods so bought and of imprisonment. Also, that no manner of merchant or other person bringing any wares or merchandise by water to this city shall unlade or put the same to sell before the custom due for the same be paid and satisfied upon pain of imprisonment.

Memorandum that one Roger of Highhampton and Agathe his wife now attached and arrested to answer to the mayor and commonality for a trespass because they did sue William Petre and others before the stewards of Crosdych Fair in a matter determinable before the said mayor contrary to the liberties of the city.

Memorandum that this new inquisitions by the king writs were taken through the whole realm by the verdict of the most substantial men against all manner of officers that had misused themselves in their offices by extortions, barberries or otherwise. And who so were found culpable were punished by fine or otherwise according to the offence.

1305

[blank] Beynym

The king commanded the prince his son to ward & to put in him in prison for making of a riot and breaking the park of the bishop of Chester.

1306

[blank] Beynym

Memorandum the custom of the city of Exeter and of London is that when any man hath entered his action against any inhabitant, the defendant shall be first summoned, and if he make default then shall a distringas go out against him. And if he have nothing whereby to be destrained then shall his rents if he have any be destrained in the tenants' hands. And if the defendant do make default for one month then the said cost shall be destrained from time to time and from year to year & be kept in the bailiffs' hands until the party defendant do [?]fy himself. ['Nonsense'. in another handwriting]

Prince Edward by the mediation and means of Pope Clement was allied unto the Lady Isabel, daughter to Philip le bean King of France.

King Edward after he had reigned 34 years & half died the 6th of July Anno 1307 at Burroughe upon the sands and was buried at Westminster. His son the prince was forthwith proclaimed king but not crowned till February following.

Thomas Bytton the bishop died the 11th of the calendar of October being St Mathew's Day the 21st of September and was buried in his own church in the middle of the chancel.

The first year of King Edward the second

1307

William Gattepathe

King Edward sailed over in to France in January and at Bulleyn he married the Lady Isabella the French King's daughter and in February then following he returned with his wife and queen in to England and both were crowned at Westminster.

Peers Gaveston was made Earl of Cornwall and married the king near the daughter of his sister Joan of Arres by her husband Gilbert of Clare, Earl of Gloucester, and is made Lord Deputy of Ireland.

Walter Stapledon was consecrated bishop of this city of Exeter by Robert Minchelsby, Bishop of Canterbury.

1308

Roger Beynym

Walter Stapledon in the feast day of the Translation of St Edward being the 20 of June 1308 was consecrated bishop of Exeter, who when he came west to the city and being come to the East Gate he alighted from his horse and went on foot until he came to St Peter's Church all the streets whereupon he went being covered with cloth which as soon as he was passed was taken up and given among the poor he was intronyzated [to enthone] or installed with great pomp and solemnity but about his feast and the service thereof there fell some controversy between him and one Hugh Courtenay the son and heir of Hugh Courtenay knight who then used to be steward of the said feast by reason he held the manor of Slapton of the said bishop by that service. At length the said controversy was ended and compounded in manner as followeth:

First that the said Hugh and his heirs being of lawful age and holding the same manor of Slapton shall be stewards at the feast of the installing or intronzation of every bishop of the see and church of Exeter.

Item, they and every of them shall at the first coming of the bishop to Exeter meet the said bishop at the East Gate of the said city of Exeter when he alighteth from his horse and then going a little before him at the right hand shall keep the throng and press of the people from him and bring him in to the Quire of the Cathedral Church there to be installed.

Item the said Hugh Courtenay & his heirs shall at the feast of the said installing serve the first mess at the bishop's own table.

Item in consideration of which service the said Hugh and his heirs shall have to their own use for their fee four silver dishes of those which he shall serve to the bishop at the said first mess or service. Also two salt cellars. One cup of them which the bishop shall drink himself at that meal, one salter, one wine pot, one spoon and two basins which the said bishop shall at that time wash in and all which vessels shall be of silver.

Provided nevertheless that if the said Hugh or his heirs being of lawful age be not present and in place to do and do the said service that then they shall not have the foresaid vessels of silver nor any other things for that time belonging or appertaining to them by reason of the said service expect the said Hugh or his heirs being of lawful age be sick so that they cannot be present and attend the said feast or that they be but by virtue of the king's writ and by the procurement of the said bishop or his successors. That they it shall be lawful for them to substitute and appoint some one other worshipful knight to come in their behalf to do the said service which said knight bringing the letters patents of commission of the said Hugh or of his heirs shall swear that his foresaid lord in whose behalf and for whom he is come is so sick that he cannot in his own person come and do his said service. That then the said knight shall be admitted to do the service and shall have to the use of his lord all the whole fees and manner aforesaid.

And if the said knight do allege that his lord is by the procurement of the bishop served with the king's write and thereby let that he cannot come in person and will depose and swear this to be true in his conscience he shall likewise so be admitted to do the said service unless the bishop himself will precisely swear the contrary. In which case the said knight shall depart without doing the said service or receiving anything for the same for that time only.

After the said Hugh and his heirs shall do all other services to the said bishop and to his successors for the foresaid manor of Slapton as doth to the same appertain for evermore. And furthermore of the heirs of the said Hugh and their successors be of lawful age or not at the time of the feasts of his intronization and do not come and do the service aforesaid and in manner aforesaid that then they shall not have any of silver vessels nor any other things due for the said service for that time of reason of their said affair nor any other person in their name or behalf demanding the same.

And also it shall not be lawful to the said Hugh, his heirs and assigns at the feast of the intronization of any bishop of Exeter for the time being to put in or to put out any person or to do any other thing or things what so ever by him or by any others belonging to the said feast by reason of his office or that he shall demand or require any more or other things then as is before declared.

And furthermore the said heir and his heirs and the knight as is aforesaid which shall to this foresaid service for them shall have hay and provender for their horses and for their servants' horses attending upon him and also his livery of wine and candles as is meet and convenient.

In consideration of which the promises to be hereafter had without any denial or contradiction for evermore. The said Hugh for him and for his heirs hath quietly claimed, consigned and released to the said bishop and to his successors all other exactions, demands or quarrels for and concerning the said office fees or any other things belonging to the said office of Stewardship for evermore.

Given at Newton Plympton under the seals of the said bishop, dean and chapter the morrow after the feast of St Thomas *Anno Domini* 1308 and the second year of King Edward the Second, William Martyn, Philip Courtenay, Thomas Chichester, Stephen Haccombe, Roger Novent, Thomas Wishdeakene, John Burton, John Troyagn, knights, Robert Stokehays, John Battlesgate, Robert Upex and Henry Buckwell with others.

1309

Roger Beynym

Memorandum this year there fell a great controversy which bred great troubles between Hugh Courtenay the 4th Earl of Devon and the mayor and commonality of this city. The occasion whereof was this: the earl upon a certain market day set his cater [a buyer of provisions] to this city to buy fish at which time there were only three pots of fish in the market. The bishop's cater likewise came and either of them thinking the whole to be too little for any of them were at some contention about it. The mayor of his part also tendering that the commons also might be served and have the benefit of the market decided this strife and delivered one pot to the earl's cate and one other to the bishop's cate, and the third part he reserved for the market. The earl being advertised hereof thought himself much injured by the mayor in that he could not have the whole fish. And without further hearing or considering of the matter is offended grievously with the mayor giving and out breathing threatening words that he would be revenged. Not long after this the said earl came to the city and lodged himself in his own lodging within the house of the black friars. And further sent for the mayor to come to speak with him. The mayor, who was a retainer unto the said earl and being advertised of the earl's displeasure and knowing his disposition and therefore mistrusting the worst, calleth all his brethren & honest commoners unto the guildhall. Before whom he declared how the earl was offended with him and wherefore. And that he sent for him which he feared to do unless they would accompany him and help him if need were which they promised and were contented to do. Then said the mayor 'masters I know the earl will fall out with me and as he hath threatened with revenge of me and therefore I am to put you that for as much as the displeasure is against me for the city's cause and for doing my office, I am to pray you to accompany me and to stand by me and when I am before the earl if you do see that I do there tarry and be stayed any long time then in any wise do is break open the doors and perforce fetch me out, for else I shall be in great peril and danger'. After these and sundry oaths likewise thus they all departed and together to the house of the black friars where as soon as they were come the mayor was received in and went unto the earl being in his lodging but the door was made fast and shut after him. The earl, as soon as the mayor was come, began to be in great storms and would not be pacified whereof the mayor seeing none of his excuses nor answers would be received, suddenly took off the coat which he wore of the earl's livery and then delivered and yielded the same up unto him wherein the earl was so grieved that he grew to be in a very great heat and choler. And so hot that the mayor missed what would might become of him that the commoners and people who were now without the door remembering what the mayor had said unto them and doubting what was become of him because he was so long with the earl, they knock at the door and require to have the mayor, which being not in long time and after sundry demands granted, they give ladders and other stuff to rip open the house and to break open the doors which when the earl, misunderstanding what might ensue of the commoners had not their request, did by the advice of his friends fall into entreating of the mayor that he would pacify the commons and other people, which he did and so quietness they departed. But the earl notwithstanding his good countenance then to avoid of the fury of the people, he could never after brook the city nor any citizen. Upon this order was taken by the mayor and the common council that no free or franchised man of the city should wear any man's livery, cognisance or badge except of a freeman's and this order was enforced and put in to the oath of every free man which is kept to this day.

1310

Walter Tantyfer

About this time flourished one Godfrey of Cornwall, a doctor of Cornwall and Paris and prebendary of St Peter's, and did very much good in both these universities. He was very well s[?] up & skilful in Aristotle and in the master of the sentences wherein he was more affected and more skilful than in the scriptures. And being acquainted with making of a subtle syllogism then in the explaining of the text. He wrote sundry works about the number of 30 books.

1311

Walter Langedon

Peers of Gaveston, Earl of Cornwall, was first banished into Flanders and being very shortly returned was taken of the barons and beheaded at Warwick.

The sect of the Templers at a council holden at Vienna under Pope Clement the first were condemned and thereupon banished out of England.

Memorandum that Hugh Courtenay, the 3rd Earl of Devon, his displeasure being first turned into anger and now in to malice doth most maliciously destroy the haven of this city, whereupon sundry bills of complaints were exhibited against him and divers inquisitions taken but it little prevailed for might overcame right. And by reason of certain carelessness of the king in his government, law had no course and justice small execution.

1312

William Gattepathe

Memorandum that this year the king by his writ named the mayor and bailiffs justices of the peace.

1313

Roger Beynym

Memorandum the custom of Shortford is this: when any lord who holdeth freely any land or tenement within the city and suburbs of Exeter, if his fee went unpaid and behind and nothing remaineth or can be found upon the said land whereof he may take distraint and levy his rent. Then he must go to the said land or tenement and a stone from the house or a turf of the grounds or some one other thing and this is called a glebe and the same he must bring at the court of the guildhall and present it to the court requesting that it may be there entered of record how that he hath brought the said glebe from his such or tenement for which is due unto him a certain rent and there can no distraiff be found whereby he may levy his rent so unpaid. And this must he do seven quarters of the year at which the rent ought to be paid. And then of the party who is to pay the rent do not willingly or refuse to come in to the court & satisfy the court with the arrears which were unpaid the gavelake shall be adjudged unto him. That is to say, proclamation shall be made that forasmuch as the tenement nor other person for him doth come into the court to answer and pay the rents due for such a tenement for which seven glebes are brought into the court that therefore it is considered and adjudged by the court that the said lord shall have the said land delivered into his hands and possession. To have and to hold for one whole year and one day then next following. And this is called gavelock. And if after the day and year so expired the tenant or any for him do not come and make full satisfaction the foresaid rent and arrearages then the lord is to come to the court and to pray that according to the custom of the city the said lands or tenement may be adjudged unto him as his own. And the tenants & all others holding or claiming by him & from him before discharged & acquitted, for all manner of claims or interest unto the said lands. And this custom is called Shortford which is very agreeable as the order of the common law. By which it is provided that when any lord is unpaid of his rent for two whole years together and can find no distraff upon the land whereby to levy his rent then he should have a writ named [?] *per* [?] which he shall have and recover the seisen of his land.

1314

Roger Beymyn

The old and ancient customs of this city of Exeter concerning the admission of any person to the freedom and liberties of the same are these: first, the mayor of his own free gift may admit any one person to the liberties of his own gift or disposition. Also the court may likewise admit one other at their will and pleasure. Also, the heir to any free or franchised man may by patrimony claim his freedom whether the inheritance do descend from the grandfather, father, uncle, brother or any other person being a free man by whom he hath any inheritance. Also, all such as have served as apprentices under any franchised for the space of 7 years or at the request of the master and upon the testimony of him that he hath truly served his years is to be admitted freely paying the fees of the court. All other persons are to be admitted by way of redemption and upon such time as by the mayor and court shall be set and assessed. All these things do appear in the course of the common rolls of the reigns of King Edward the second, King Edward the third and King Richard the second.

1315

Philip Lovecocke

1316

Philip Lovecoke

Memorandum the earl of Devon, Hugh Courtenay, the 3rd, his displeasure against the city of Exeter being grown into anger and from anger unto an extreme malice and hatred did this year begin to utter his fury and by way of revenging to satisfy his wrath, devising all the ways he might do hurt, annoy and indomage [variant of endamage – to inflict damage] the whole city by intruding upon their liberties, destroying the haven, building of a quay at Topsham, taking perforce from them the fishing in the river of Exe and vexing them with all forces, power and injuries. The mayor and commonality exhibit a bill of complaint against the said earl unto the king whereupon the king returneth his writ unto the sheriff of Devon dated the 20th of March & the 10th year of his reign for one inquisition to be held and taken. And albeit an inquisition were accordingly taken yet it was never returned whereupon the king sendeth his second writ unto the sheriff of Devon dated the 12th of June the year aforesaid and commandeth him to take an inquisition and to return the same, which he did. And notwithstanding the said inquisition was taken against the said earl yet there followed no redress. Look more hereof before in the traverse between the said earl and the city.

Bishop Stapledone founded and built in Oxford a college named then Stapledon's Inn but now Exeter College and did impropriate to the same the rectory of Ernestcome.

1317

Roger Beymyn

Memorandum that the bakers of this city were found guilty for their bread which was light and not according to the assizes. Whereof they were amerced of whom 17 dwelled in the bishop's fee and therefore they claimed to be exempted from the mayor's jurisdiction but it availed them not.

1318

Philip Lovecocke

Memorandum the king preparing a great army against the Scots who had marvellously and gotten in England did rate and tax every city within the realm to aid him according to their tenure and portion, at which time this city did set forth 30 soldiers well appointed and furnished with money, armour and all things necessary.

This year was one John Poydras or John Powderham, a tanner's son and born in the city of Exeter, named himself to be the son of King Edward the first and that he being in his cradle was by a false nurse stolen out and that the king that now is was put in there in his place but in the end he confessed the truth and how that he did so say by the motion of a familiar spirit which he kept in the likeness of a cat but in the end his spirit failed him and he was hanged. Some write that this should be done in the eighth year of this king's reign but the writings of others of the better credit do refer it to this year.

1319

Roger Beynym

1320

Philip Lovecocke

Memorandum that Walter Stapledone bishop of Exeter was in great favour with the king and made one of his privy council and Lord Treasurer of England.

1321

[blank] Wotton

Memorandum that this year there was granted to the king towards his wars in Scotland a subsidy of the sixth penny of every man's goods.

The sun appeared this year as red as blood.

This year was the barons' wars in which Thomas Earl of Lancaster was taken and after beheaded at Ponscot.

1322

Robert Wotton

Memorandum this year were two *nisi prius* tried at the castle of Exeter before John Stomer and Richard Stapledone, knights, and the king's justices at the assizes. The one Hugh Courtenay, the 3rd earl of Devon, plaintiff, and the mayor and commonality of Exeter, defendants, for and concerning the manor and suburbs of Exe Island without the West Gate of the city which the said earl claimed to be ancient demeanse and parcel of his barony of Okehampton & clearly exempted from the city and no part of the suburbs of the same. The other *nisi prius* was between the said earl and the prior of St Nicholas of the said city, plaintiff, against the mayor and commonality of the said city, defendants, for and concerning the liberties, privileges and customs of Lammas Fair, in both which actions the mayor and commonality had verdicts against them. The whole process hereof you may see at large before, in the discourse of the earl of Deovn, his injuries against the city.

1323

Robert Wotton

Queen Isabella being attended upon by Walter Stapledon, bishop of Exeter and sundry others, noblemen, went and sailed over into France to the French king, her brother, taking her young son the prince with her for the entreaty of a peace between the two kings.

The king is altogether carried and ruled by the two Spencers and Sir John Baldcock, which very shortly turned to the utter ruin of the king and of themselves. For the queen, by persuasion of the barons of the realm by their letters unto her, provided an army beyond the seas and at the time appointed returned into England and with their help prevailed.

1324

Philip Lovecocke

Bishop Stapledon secretly departeth from the queen without any leave and returneth into England delivereth all the secrets and doings of the queen joineth with the Spencers and make preparation to prevent the queen's attempts.

Pope John the 23 writeth his letters to the Christians in Greece persuading them to submit themselves to the church and to acknowledge him to be the only head of Christ's Church and the immediate vicar of Christ upon earth but they not abiding his intolerable pride returned their answer very sharply saying 'thy power we know to be great, they pride intolerable and the covetousness insatiable and which we are not able to satisfy, the devil therefore be with thee and God be with us.'

1325

Philip Lovecocke

Memorandum that out of the great roll of this year there are cut out the first 9 rolls.

1326

Philip Lovecocke

In the beginning of this mayor's year the king being advertised that the prince his son was allied unto the Earl of Honalder's daughter and that the queen had by the aid of the said earl and the help of the most part of the lords and barons of England had provided a great army and was landed within the realm setteth towards Bristol leaving Walter, Bishop of Exeter, to be Custos of London, whom the Londoners took and beheaded in Cheapside and buried his body in a sand hill (as the most certain report of the writers is) in his own house without Christian burial; but which after six months was taken up and brought to Exeter where he was buried in his own church very honourably.

The king being hardly pursued was taken at Bristol together with the Spensers he was sent to Kyllingworth Castle and from thence removed from place to place to sundry other castles and in the end namely the 16th of September 1327 was murdered but the others were executed to death.

Prince Edward, aged about 14 years, was upon the 25th of January 1326 proclaimed king of England by the name of King Edward the 4th.

After the death of Bishop Stapledone James Barkeley was consecrated bishop of Exeter in March 1327 and died in June following.

The first year of King Edward the 3rd

1327

Richard Seler

The king upon the 24th of January married at the city of York the Lady Philip daughter to William Earl of Henanlde. John Grandisson being at Avinion with Pope John the 23 at the death of Bishop Bakeby was made bishop of Exeter and consecrated the 8th of October 1327.

1328

Philip Lovecock

Memorandum that this year there was a parliament kept at Salisbury when the king made his brother John of Eltham Earl of Cornwall.

Memorandum that the porter of the West Gate was sharply punished because he did open the West Gate late in the night and suffered men to go in and out without the knowledge and license of the mayor.

1329

Philip Lovecock

Memorandum this year great inquisition was made for the inquiry of the death of Bishop Stapledon by order of a synod holden at London before Simon Archbishop of Canterbury. They were all executed as were privy or consenting to the same.

Memorandum the king by his patents dated the 10th of March in the third year of his reign gave and granted unto the city a certain custom called murage towards the building and maintenance of the walls.

1330

Martin Leken

Memorandum that about this time was one William named William of Exeter, and a canon prebendary of St Peter's in Exeter, a man very well learned who joined himself with Nicholas of Casena, William Okenham and John Walsingham with others who then did preach and publish that Christ and his apostles were but poor men and had no temporal possessions nor dominions upon the earth and that kings, emperors and the laity were not subject to the pope nor to any ecclesiastical jurisdiction but only in matters of religion. But when he heard that Pope John the 23 had condemned this opinion and excommunicated all such as held the same for heresies he shyly shrunk from his companions being afraid to be deprived of his livelihoods. And to keep himself in credit with the pope he wrote certain conclusions against his companions.

Memorandum that this year the Guildhall of the city of Exeter was builded.

1331

Philip Lovecocke

Memorandum that this year Simon Moxham, Archbishop of Canterbury, sent out his process that he would visit the diocese of Exeter and begin the same his visitation in St Peter's Church. And accordingly upon the Monday next after Ascension Day he came to Exeter for the same purpose but Bishop Grandisson appealed from him and with force withstood the archbishop, not suffering him to come within the church nor cloister.

Memorandum that this year there was a writ of right directed to the dean and chapter for certain lands within the fee of St Sidwell's but because they could not hold plea of land the same was returned before the mayor and his court to be decided.

1332

Martin Le Ken

1333

Thomas Gervys

Memorandum that this year by a jury of inquisition John Mathew, under clerk to the town clerk, was found guilty for convening away all the rolls of the records of 8 courts and had put in others for them.

1334

Mathew Le Ken,
Thomas Lychfeld

Mathew Le Ken the mayor died this year in March & Thomas Lychfelde was chosen mayor for him.

1335

Henry Hughton

John of Eltham, the king's brother and earl of Cornwall, did great good service in Scotland where in the month of October he died at St John's Tower but buried in London.

1336

Henry Hughton

Memorandum that this year the king at a parliament holden at Westminster in Lent made a Duchy of the Earldom of Cornwall and gave to his son Prince Edward surnamed the Black Prince and sent his letters therefore unto the mayor by the name of the mayor of his honourable city of Exeter as also sent a writ for the proclaiming of the same and made this city parcel of the said Duchy as before it was parcel of the Earldom, for this city is holden of the said duke as parcel of his Duchy by the farm of £20 by the year.

1337

Thomas Gervys

The people in these days were so new fangled in apparel and waxed in such excess therein that a parliament was kept at Westminster for redress thereof.

This year Bishop Grandisson founded the college of Ottery St Mary.

1338

Hugh Hughton

The king was this year made vicar general of the empire. And making title to the crown of France quartereth the arms of France and of England. And not long after he proclaimed himself to be called King of England and of France.

1339

Thomas Lychefold

Memorandum that Nicholas Godoscot, late Receiver General of this city, refusing to make his account was arrested for the same where he did forthwith put in bail or sureties promising the next Monday following to do the same but contrary to his promise he went and fled unto Topsham where he kept himself until further order was taken.

This year the mayor's pension being but £4 was increased unto £5.

This year the French men burned the towns of Southampton, Hastings and Plymouth and did marvellously spoil all the coasts and coast towns in Devon and Cornwall until Hugh Courtenay the 3rd and Earl of Devon, being aged about 80 years, did with the help of the knights and gentlemen of the country assemble a great power and giving an assault upon them slain five hundred of them and made the rest to flee to their ships and to leave the country.

1340

Henry Hughton

About this time there flourished one John of Bampton so named because he was born at Bampton in Devon. He was a monk of the order of the Carmelites and a student at Cambridge, a man very well learned in his days. He read openly the works of Aristotle in the university, after that he professed divinity and made doctor of the same. He wrote sundry books which are not now extant.

1341

Henry Hughton

Memorandum the old and ancient custom of the city of Exeter when the chief lord in fee cannot be answered of the rent due unto him out of any tenement and no distress can be there levied for the same is this: the chief must come to the tenement and must there take a stone or some other dead thing of the said tenement and must bring the same to the guildhall court before the mayor and this must he do seven quarters together and this kind is called a glebe or gleba. And if in the said seventh term no person do come to satisfy to the lord for the rent with the arrearages so behind then the said tenement shall be adjudged to the said lord to hold for one year and a day. And this is called Gavelake. And then forthwith proclamation shall be openly published and made in the court that if any man do make or pretend any title to the said house or tenement that he do come within the year and day then following and then and there to satisfy the lord in chief as for as well for the rents then due as also fro the arrearages of the rents due out of the said tenement. And if no body do come or do come but doth not, cannot or will not satisfy & pay unto the lord the rents with the arrearages due then the chief lord shall come again to the court and pray that according to the custom of the city the said tenement be adjudged and delivered unto him freely and in fee as his own demesne according to the equity of the law in the like cases which is named Shortford and this custom in the city is named Shortford but in French forelock and in this case the lord shall have from thenceforth the said tenement with the appurtenances in pure fee for ever absolutely and without any denial or visitations for ever more.

Memorandum that this year was a truce made between the king of England and the king of France and the whole controversy should be and was referred to the deciding and determination of the pope. And that both kings should send their commissioners to Rome for the same purpose. In the mean time both kings were sworn to keep the truce for which peace to be firmly kept the said kings swore by their deputies in France the 19th of January 1342.

1342

Thomas Le Furbor

In this mayor's year according to the composition of the truce made the year before between the king of England and the French king ambassadors were appointed by order of the parliament holden at Westminster to go to Rome unto the pope for the same namely John Grandysson bishop of Exeter, Henry of Lancaster, Earl of Derby, Hugh de le Spencer, Lord of Glamorgan, Ralph Lord Stafford and others whose commission was dated *20 May in the 17th year of King Edward.*

1343

Thomas Le furber

Memorandum also that this year the king was advertised but untruly that there was and should be a great rout and riot made by a certain number of lewd and evil disposed persons within this city of Exeter and therewith the matter and information was so enforced that the king being otherwise encumbered with the care of his foreign wars removed the worst and forthwith his commission of oyer and determiner, dated 20 August Anno Regni 18 was sent and directed to the mayor and bailiffs of the said city straightly charging and commanding them to have a special care and regard both for the staying of the said tumult and riot as also for the punishment of the offenders according to their quantity and quality of the offence.

At a parliament holden at Westminster the king created his son Edward Prince of Wales who before was one but Duke of Cornwall and Earl of Chester.

1344

Henry Hughton

Memorandum that in this mayor's year the king instituted the most honourable order of the garter.

1345

Henry Hughton

1346

Thomas Le Furbor

Memorandum this year was the battle of Cressen where the king of England had a great victory against the French king.

Also the king besieged Calais which in the end he took. In the meantime whereof the king invading England was taken prisoner.

1347

Henry Hughton

Memorandum that this year was a great contention within this city for and about the election of the mayor and officers and whereof great troubles were like to have ensued had not the same been foreseen and provided for, whereof it was ordered by a common council of the mayor and commonality that from henceforth none should be sworn nor admitted to be a mayor except he were a wise, grave, sober and honest man and had been tried a steward of the city for one whole year. And further also that he were able to dispend of his own freehold £5 at the least of the year and further that he should be chosen only by a triple jury that is by 36 who upon their oaths so make their election according to this order.

This year the plague began in this city and continued for almost three years.

Memorandum that in the Easter term this year at Westminster it was found by verdict that the passage, lastage and quay of Pratteshed at Exmouth and all the profits coming & [?] were & parcel of the fee farm of the city holden of the Dukes of Cornwall as member of the manor of Lydford by the yearly rent of 20s.

1348

Nicholas Halberton, Robert Noble

1349

Robert Brydeporte

Memorandum in the end of this mayor's year being the 24th year of the king's reign one William Thorpe, being Lord Chief Justice of England, being vehemently suspected for bribery and corruption, was arrested that he had taken monies and bribes for repriving of a certain felon which had been indicted, arraigned and condemned before him for which the king was so grieved and offended that he caused the said Thorpe to be apprehended and to be put to his trial who was indicted, arraigned and condemned to die but his execution upon earnest suits to the king was stayed as doth appear in the records of this year remaining in the tower.

1350

Robert Brydeport

Memorandum that the custom of the city of Exeter that all forestallers and such as do buy fish at Alphington and elsewhere and do sell the same at and in the market at Exeter at higher price and be thereof indicted and convicted shall for the first, second and third time be committed to prison and make fine and for the fourth offence he shall abjure the city.

Sir John Carew, baron Carew of Mohunsottery, was made Lord Deputy of Ireland.

1351

Robert Brydeport

1352

Robert Brydeport

Memorandum the pasture of Croldyche now called Southinghay was set to rent for 5 shillings by the year.

1353

[blank] Spycer

This year was a continual dryeth from the months of March unto the end of July by means whereof grew great scarcity of corn & victuals. Likewise by the means of the same dryeth there increased a marvellous & an infinite number of caterpillars which wasted, devoured and consumed the corn and all other fruits upon the earth.

1354

John Spicer

Memorandum one John Wekes was made Recorder of the city and had allowed for his fee £3.

This year was a great riot in Oxford between the townsmen and the scholars.

1355

Robert Brideport

Memorandum this year John Wekes, the first Recorder of this city and chosen the year before, was chosen again this year and so was he from year to year as was the mayor and other officers.

1356

John Gyste

Memorandum that this year Baylick, King of Scots, resigned his crown and kingdom unto King Edward whereupon the king invaded Scotland and did so afflict the same.

This year also was the battle of Poitiers in France where Prince Edward surnamed the Black Prince had a great victory and took King John and many of the noble men of France prisoners.

The king and his son being determined to follow the wars the one in Scotland and the other in France. And mistrusting what might or could be done by the adversaries at the seas, prepared a great fleet and navy for the seas and as he had sent unto all towns upon the sea coasts for preparation to be made in this behalf, so among others he sent his letters patent under the broad seal of England unto this city bearing date the 25th of March *Anno Regni* 31 and required thereby to be furnished of three ships well appointed and in every of them 60 mariners and 20 archers which the mayor and commonality did at the charges of the city and delivered the same to one Gervyse Aldelary, then Vice Admiral of Devon, who conducted & whisked them to Sandwich and there delivered them to John Monte Gomer, then Lord High Admiral of England.

1357

John Spicer

This year Prince Edward brought over into England John, the French king, and sundry his noble men, and landed in Plymouth and from thence came to this city and were very honourably received and entertained. And so were conveyed from thence to London.

1358

Robert Noble

1359

John Spicer

1360

John Spicer

Memorandum the king this year besieged Paris where he dubbed 400 knights but in the end a peace was considered and the siege raised. And the French king then being prisoner was set to his ransom which was at three millions of scules every two scoules valued at one English noble or 6 shillings 8 pence sterling.

This year the disease of the pestilence began through the whole realm and whereof this city was much infected. Also there fell great storms, tempests, which many churches, houses and steeples were overthrown.

1361

[John] Gyft

1362

[John] Gyft

Memorandum that the bakers had secretly concluded, agreed and compared among themselves that because they could not bake after their own pleasure and at their own assize, that therefore they would not bake at all. By means whereof the city for two days together was destituted of bread, whereof they were all indicted and put to their fines 36 shillings eight pence.

1363

[John Gyft]

1364

[John] Gyft

Memorandum that this year there came three kings, viz of France, Scotland and Cipies, into England to visit the king who were most honourably entertained.

1365

[Nicholas] Taverner

1366

[Nicholas] Brydastowe

Memorandum that Richard Archbishop of Armarhe did write certain invectives and conclusions against the hypocrisy and sect of the Franciscans or Gray Friars.

1367

[Nicholas] Brytteston

Memorandum and be it known that this year was a *nisi prius* to be tried at the castle of Exeter before John Mowbrey & Edmond Choley, justices of the assize, between the Dean and Chapter of St Peter's of the one part and John Gist, late mayor, and the bailiffs and commonality of Exeter of the other part, at which time the said dean and chapter either doubting of the equity of their cause or failing of their processes or instructing some other things and therefore not wanting to proceed did for the stop thereof use this prevention: they exhibited unto the king a bill of information advertising that the mayor by his proclamation made before the time of the said assizes commanding that every citizen and inhabitant at the then next assizes should attend him in arms or with their weapons unto the castle of Exeter and they shut fast their doors and at the time appointed the said mayor should accordingly repair unto the castle and there inhibit the said justices to proceed in the said jury and threatened the said dean and chapter very much. By means whereof the jury could not be taken at that time. The king not liking hereof directeth & sendeth out his commission to John Montague & four others for the examining hereof. But before the said commissioners did or could sit upon the matter the foresaid two justices & one Sir Guy de Bryon were come to the court where they were examined for and concerning the foresaid riot, who when they had testified and justified that there was no such matter. The king sent his inhibition to the foresaid commissioners inhibiting them to proceed therein, which bore date 12 February *Anno Regni* 40.

1368

[Warren] Bayliff

The king forbiddeth any more monies to be paid to the poor by the name of Peter Pence.

1369

[Roger] Plente

1370

[Martin] Batteshill

Memorandum this year died John Grandesson, bishop of Exon, and lies buried in a tomb of lead within the chapel built in the west wall of his cathedral church. He was a man of a noble parentage and descended from Otho the Great and Duke of Burgundy. He was according to that time well learned and wrote two books, the one entitled *Conciones* and the other *de vitis sanctorum*. He was a special and liberal benefactor to his church which he enriched it great possessions, buildings, ornaments and treasure. He founded the college of Ottery St Mary and left many good memories behind him. He seemed to foresee to foretell of some ruin to the clergy which whether it were by the observation of the stars or by some secret spirit or by mistrusting the greedy & inordinate covetousness of the pope much maligned at and that the temporal princes seemed to envy at the great encroaching of temporalities of the clergy. He built at Bishop's Torrington and impropriated the parsonage of Radway to the same for his successors to the end as he writeth in his last will and testament . . .

This was a year of great sickness through the whole land, after which by reason of great inundations followed great dearth of corn and victuals.

1371

[Roger] Plente

This year by the good favour of the king Thomas Brentingham was consecrated bishop of this city. He then refusing the bishopric of Hereford unto which he was also then chosen. Also one Roger Presell was excommunicated because he had beaten one John Carbonel a priest. The prince named Edward the Black Prince in February being very sick came out of France with the princes, his wife and Richard their son who afterwards was king and arrived at Plymouth and came to this city and were very honourably received and entertained.

Memorandum there is due to the city for fetching of the rolls of record 3s 4d.

Memorandum also this year at a Parliament holden at Westminster was made the statute of prominence against the clergy.

1372

[John] Gyste

About this time was one Walter Parker born in Devon and much residing in this city. Very famous for his learning and much commended for his preaching. He sharply rebutted both clergy & laity for their loose and sinful lives. And he wrote three books which were greatly accepted for his learning and deep judgement.

Memorandum that this year John Wytcleff did openly preach at Oxford against the pope and his doctrine and defended certain conclusions against him wherewith the clergy was much offended.

1373

[Roger] Plent

This year through the great & immoderate heat the sickness and plague was in this city.

1374

[Robert] Wylfford

1375

[Robert] Wylfford

Prince Edward, worn out with continual travels and consumed with sickness which followed, died in June 1376 and was buried at Canterbury.

1376

[John] Gray

In this mayor's year King Edward the third, having reigned 50 years & 3 months, died the 21 of June 1377 and was buried at Westminster after when Richard his nephew proclaimed and crowned king.

The pope sendeth by Edmond Stofford (who after was bishop of Exon) 3 bulls against Wytclyff, one to the king, the other to the University of Oxford and the 3rd to the bishop of Canterbury and of London.

The first year of King Richard the 2nd

1377

[Robert] Wylfford

The king shortly after his coronation made choice of such wise and grave men as were thought most meet to be of his privy council and to govern the realm under him, of whom the chiefest was William Courtenay, then bishop of London, and Edmund Mortimer, Earl of March, with sundry others both of the laity and clergy as of whom the commons liked well. Among whom was Thomas Brenthingham, bishop of Exeter, was one and who shortly after was made Lord Treasurer.

The French men understanding that the whole realm was now busied about the settling of the new king and seeing orders for the good government of the land, do with a great fleet occupy and possess the seas and invading the south coast do take the Isle of Wight and burn the most part of the haven towns, namely Dartmouth, Plymouth, Fowey and others. The Scots do the like at the land.

This year the city builded a balinger [a small sea-going vessel], for and towards the service of the king against France which being advertised to the king and council by Thomas, Bishop of Exeter, at the parliament the king confirmed the charter of the city and enlarged the same with certain new liberties & privileges.

1378

[Robert] Wylsford

This year the earls of Arundell and of Salisbury long grieved with the injuries and brags of the French done the last year past prepared a navy and a fleet to scour the seas and mustered a company of the most piked, lusty and chosen gentlemen of the whole realm namely of the gentlemen in Devon, Somerset and Cornwall. Among whom were two young sons of the earl of Devon named Peter and Philip. The one of them in fight at the seas was slain and the other hurt to death, by means whereof the wife of one of them being sister to King Richard was widow and after married to the Earl of St Paul but some write that this lady was the widow of Hugh, Courtenay, Earl of Devon.

This year also the Duke of Lancastow at a Parliament prayed some portion of the subsidy then granted to the king and in consideration thereof he would scour the seas and defend the same from the French nation which was granted unto him. And thereupon a great navy was prepared but the duke so lingered the time to take shipping according to promise that the noble men and gentlemen which were appointed and lay in their ships in readiness were grieved both with the long lingering of the duke and also that they daily saw their enemies ranging and triumphing upon the seas and none to resist nor encounter them. Wherefore the most part of them hoisted their sails and entered into the seas and they had not so soon chased the seas of the French nation but that they met with the Spanish fleet, between whom was a cruel fight and the Englishmen had the worst side. Many fled, some were slain and some were taken prisoners, among whom the said Hugh Courtenay was taken and carried away prisoner.

1379

[?] Wylsford

Memorandum that at a parliament holden this year at Westminster there was granted a certain tax to be paid unto the king that is to say every duke & archbishop to pay ten marks, every earl, bishop and mitred abbot 6 marks, every abbot for his monks 3s 4d, every justice, knight, esquire, parson, vicar and chaplain to pay according to his living.

Memorandum that John Hull was chosen this year to be Recorder of the city of Exeter.

Memorandum that about this time flourished one William Slade, who was born in Devon and brought up at the school in Exeter and from thence sent to Oxford where he proved and became very well learned especially in Aristotle whose work he did read openly in the school to his great commendation. In the end he professed monkery and was so well liked that after the death of the abbot of Buckfastleigh he was made abbot of the house. He furnished the house with fair buildings and adorned the commonwealth with his learning leaving behind 13 books of his own penning.

The king gave his sister Joan Courtenay, the widow of the earl of Devon, in marriage to William Earl of St Pauls in France.

1380

[John] Graye

Memorandum that this year William Bronelham was indicted because he arrested one Peter Hadleigh without the South Gate in the High Street and carried the party to the bishop's gaol.

This year at a parliament holden at London Bishop Brentinham was discharged of his office to be Lord Treasurer and one Robert Holes appointed in his place.

1381

[John] Nymet

Memorandum this year was very troublesome by means of sundry rebellions in sundry parts of the land vide Jack Cade, Wat Tylor & others. In which Symon of Sidbury Archbishop of Canterbury being Lord Chancellor was by the rebels taken and beheaded.

1382

[Robert] Wylsford

Memorandum that Sir Philip Courtenay the fifth son of Hugh Courtenay the 4th earl of Devon & of the Lady Margaret his wife, daughter to the Lady Elizabeth wife to Humphrey Bohun, earl of Hereford, and daughter to King Edward the first, was made Lord Deputy of Ireland.

The Recorder's fee for every freeman is 12d.

1383

[John] Talbot

1384

[Robert] Wyllsford

About this time William Courtenay was of great authority and in credit. He was a very good scholar according to the time that then was which was the more commended by reason of his nobility and parentage. He being a young son to the Earl of Devon and brought up in bearing whereunto he was well affected. He was first a prebendary of the cathedral church of Exon and after the death of Lewes Charleton, Bishop of Hereford, he was Bishop of Hereford, and then Bishop of London and lastly

Archbishop of Canterbury. He was very sharp and bitter against Wyckleff which was a great part of the cause of the variance between the Duke of Lancaster and him.

This year a great part of Exe Bridge by means of high waters and continual rain fell down and sundry persons were destroyed therewith.

The Lord Mayor of London named John Northampton was banished from out of London and sent in to Cornwall to the castle of Tintagel and there was kept prisoner.

1385

[Adam] Scut

William Courtenay, Archbishop of Canterbury, falleth into the king's displeasure and secretly conveyeth himself from the court.

John Wykelyff died this year in December.

This year was a great earthquake, tempests, lightnings and storms whereby great harms were done.

The merchants of Dartmouth and Portsmouth set their ships to the seas against the French men and took 4 ships and drowned other 4 all laden with wines.

1386

[Robert] Wylsford

This year by act of Parliament sundry officers were removed from the king and it was ordered that 12th of the most gravest and wisest personages of the whole realm should be and were appointed for the oversight and good government of the realm under the king of which number Thomas Brentingham, Bishop of Exeter, for his wisdom and great experience, was one.

1387

[Richard] Bozomm

That this year the cordwainers and curriers of this city were first incorporated.

This year Robert Vere, Marquis of Dublin, and Michael de la Poole, Earl of Suffolk, by the King's Commission raised an army to withstand the king his uncles the Duke of York and Gloucester, and came to this city of Exeter and here stayed until that the said dukes did so hardly pursue them that they [were] driven to flee in Scotland and from thence into Flanders. Polydore.

1388

[Robert] Wylsford

John Holland, the king's half brother, being newly returned out of Spain was created Earl of Huntingdon.

1389

[Richard] Bozomme

Memorandum that in March this year happened a terrible tempest of lightnings and winds whereof followed great hurts, not long after followed a great plague of pestilence whereof died infinite numbers of people in every place throughout the whole land and lastly followed great scarcity and a dearth of corn and victuals.

1390

[Robert] Wyllsford

Memordandum this year a Portugal ship laden with beans and corn arrived at Exmouth and there did unlade the same before licence had of the mayor wherefore the said goods was seized and forfeited but upon a fine of £4 at the request of Edward, Earl of Devon, it was released.

1391

[blank] Bozonne

The king and his council being at Stamford it was ordered that every gentleman who might dispend yearly £40 in lands should be made knight.

1392

[Robert] Wyllsford

In this year the king directeth and send his commission under the broad seal of England dated 19 September *Anno Regni* 16 unto his uncle Edmond Duke of York & Thomas Duke of Gloucester to make inquiry of evil government of the city of London, but in the end by mediation of the said dukes the city recovered the king's favour and their liberties.

1393

[?] Bozomme

1394

[Robert] Wyllsford

This year died Thomas Brentingham, bishop of Exeter, in December 1394 and was buried in his own church.

1395

[Simon] Grendon

This year Edmond Stofford the 20th of June 1395 was consecrated bishop of Exon being before Lord or Keeper of the Privy Seal.

1396

[John] Talbot

This year died William Courtenay, archbishop of Canterbury.

1397

[Adam] Scutt

Memorandum the king this year created John Holland Earl of Huntingdon and Duke of Exon.

The king exiled and banished Thomas Arundell, Archbishop of Canterbury, being then the Lord Chancellor and in his place Edmond Stofford, bishop of Exeter, was made Lord Chancellor who at the great parliament holden at Westminster did make the sermon and his theme was *One king to all*.

1398

[Simon] Grendon

This year being 23rd year of the king's reign he made a voyage into Ireland in whose absence Henry Duke of Hereford and of Lancaster by the good will and favour of the Lords and Commons of the realm came from beyond the seas and obtained the crown by the resignation of King Richard himself who was committed to prison.

John Holland, Earl of Huntingdon, was this year created Duke of Exeter and he attended the king in his journey and voyage into Ireland.

The first year of King Henry the 4th

1399

[John] Grey

Memorandum that this year a certain citizen in his last will and testament gave and bequeathed to a parish church within this city a piece of land to certain intents and purposes for ever; with a proviso that the parson for the time being should be always a secular priest but in no wise to be a gray friar or a black friar or a professed monk for then he willed his foresaid gift should be void.

This year began to be troublesome, for both the French nation and the Scots [?denoma] wars against the king and some of the king's own subjects conspire against him.

1400

William Willsford

Memorandum that John Holland, Duke of Exeter, being half brother unto King Richard the 2nd by his mother's side who was Countess of Kent and named Joan the daughter and heir to Edmond, Earl of Kent, son to King Edward the First, and brother-in-law to King Henry the 4th for he married the Lady Elizabeth the sister notwithstanding in respect of the said marriage the king had received in to a special favour yet he was one of the confederates which conspired the king's death whereupon he was taken at Plashey in

Essex and there beheaded. He had two mansion houses in this West Country, the one was the Castle of Exeter which was sometimes a very fair and a princely house but now destroyed and scarcely any monument left thereof. The other was at Dartington besides the town of Totnes.

The town of Plymouth was spoiled by the French men.

1401

William Oke

This year was sent an honourable ambassador into France of sundry noblemen among whom were Edward Courtenay, Earl of Devon, and Ivan Lord Fitzwarren of this country who concluded for the continuance of the peace and also for the sending home of Queen Isabel, the widow of King Richard, unto her father King Charles of France.

1402

William Wilsford

This year the Lord of the Castle in Brittany came with a fleet of ships unto Plymouth and lodged himself and all his company in the town all night and, notwithstanding his good and friendly entertainment, he robbed and spoiled the town and country and carried the spoils away with them in revenge as it was supposed of the French men who under the conduct of the Earl of St Paul were discomfited at the siege of the castle of Mark by Callais.

Richard Izacke added: In the parish church of Budleigh in the county of Devon a stone sheweth this inscription *orate pro anima Radulphi Node*. This (as tradition delivers) was the sepulchre of one that presumed to fly with artificial wings from that tower, and so falling, broke his neck, which phaetonical fact of his hath well deserved the name of Node, be the inscription what it is, who being a native of this city, gives me here an occasion to mention him. Bladud, a British king, who for his love to learning went to Athens and brought from thence four philosophers, and founded the first University at Stanford near Oxford, which was afterwards translated to Oxford, he was the first discoverer of the hot Bath in Somersetshire and being a famous magician, and practicing that art, by attempting to fly, Node like, under-went even in the like manner the like destiny. Not unlike to either, have I read of an active Turk in Constantinople, having openly published that he would fly the space of a furlong, and for that end being mounted on the top of a high tower, showed himself to the people without number assembled, girded in a long and large white garment, gathered into many plaits and foldings, to take advantage of the wind. The foolish man, vainly persuading himself to have hovered in the air, as do the birds upon their wings, and thus a great while standing as ready to take his flight, the beholders still laughing, and crying out 'fly Turk fly, how long shall we expect thy flight?' Who having a long time thus deluded the expectation of his spectators; at length finding the wind fit (as he thought for his purpose) with his arms spread abroad, committed himself with his vain hopes unto the air, but instead of mounting aloft, this foolish Icarus came tumbling down with such violence as that he broke his neck, arms and legs, with almost all the bones of his body. I have likewise read of another person having the like mind to fly (the truth of poetical reports, 'for tis said, that the first writers were poets, so were their writings but fictitious) tied wings to his hands and feet, and taking his rise from a tower did fly near a furlong, which is the eighth part of a mile, till something failing him, down he fell, and brake both his thighs, 'tis pity but that Icarus like he had fallen into the water and then *Nomina fecit aquis*.

1403

Henry Hull

The Britains [Bretons] the second time under the conduct of the Lord of Cassyls came with a great fleet and landed at Plymouth and spoiled and burned the town whereupon one William Wilsford to revenge the same maketh a great preparation and passeth over into Brittany and there he took about 40 ships laden richly with wines, oils and other merchandises as also did burn a great part of the country upon the sea coasts.

1404

William Willsford

In the end of this mayor's year the Admiral of Brittany, together with the Lord Chastell came with a great fleet before Dartmouth minding to have entered the town and to have spoiled the same. But being resisted they hoisted their sails and returned back unto a place two miles off called Black Pool and there landed. But the people of the country and the women so besetted them that there they were overthrown and which the Lord Chastell were slain and many taken prisoners. Wherein the Britons were so grieved that afterwards of such English ships as they took they killed or hanged all the merchants and mariners.

1405

Simon Grendon

This Simon Grendon was a good and well-disposed man and well inclined unto the poor for whose relief he built an almshouse within this city which he named the ten cells but since and yet is commonly called Grendon's Almshouse. He purchased certain land and endowed the mayor and commonality therein for the weekly relief for ever of ten poor women dwelling therein; the same house since and of late hath been endowed with other lands namely by one Alice Hethe, widow, William Herne, priest and parson of St Petrocks and David Henson, Parson of Kenn and John Haydon of St Mary Ottery, executor to the said parson of Kenn.

1406

William Wilsford

1407

Adam Scutt

1408

William Willsford

Memorandum that this year the waits were first received and entertained in the city of Exeter.

It was an usage in these days and first begun by the grant and gift of Bartholomew, sometimes bishop of Exeter, that the lazar people of the Magdalen without the south gate of the city of Exeter shall with a clap dish [a wooden dish with a lid carried by lepers and others to give warning of their approach] upon every Wednesday and Friday through the year gather a certain toll of all the bread and corn brought to be sold in the market in this city. And upon every Tuesday and Thursday gather the alms and good will of every man thought the city but this order for sundry causes was in the end taken away. And yet nevertheless it is continually observed that the proctor of the Magdalen shall come weekly upon every Thursday to the church of St Peter's and there gather the alms and devotion of every of the canons.

Memorandum that Sir William Bonvill, knight, after that he had finished his almshouse in the come row in the city he made his testament dated the 24th of March 1408 and by it gave all his lands within the city of Exeter, his mansion house excepted, and fifty marks in lands towards the maintenance of 12 poor men and women in the said almshouse.

1409

Richard Bozome

Memorandum that at a parliament holden at Westminster this year the king among others did advance and create his brother Thomas, being Earl of Dorset, to be Duke of Exeter which duchy was now in the king's hands by the death of John Holland, the king's brother in law, who was attainted and beheaded as is before written in the second year of the king. This Thomas was half brother to the king, both sons to John, Duke of Lancaster. The king being born of the body of Blanche, the first wife, and this Thomas by

Katherine, the third wife. This Thomas died without issue after whose death John, the son of the foresaid John Holland, was restored to the title to be Duke of Exeter by King Henry the 4th in the 24th year of his reign.

1410

Adam Scut

1411

William Wilsford

1412

William Willsford,
Henry Hull

Memorandum that in this year the 19th of July William Wilsford mayor died and in his place was chosen Henry Hull to supply the residue of the year.

Memorandum that this year died Simon Grendon, who was a very good citizen and had been mayor three times, and left behind the memories of his good government and virtuous disposition as partly before is touched in the 7th year of this king.

Memorandum also this year died upon the 20th of March 1413 died King Henry the 4th and forthwith the prince was proclaimed king by the name of King Henry the 5th and upon the 9th day of April then following was crowned king and upon Trinity Sunday then following King Henry the 4th was buried at Canterbury.

Memorandum it was found for the city of Exeter this year by verdict that the passage and ferry of Exmouth and the lastage, stallage and the petty custom of all wares and merchandises landed and discharged within the port of Exon were parcels of the fee farm of the city for the cost of £20 to be yearly paid to the Duke of Cornwall.

The first year of King Henry the fifth

1413

Peter Scurte

Memorandum that in the testament of Richard Prall contained in the 44th roll of this year is contained the old and ancient usage and custom of this city concerning the reasonable part and portion of every dead man's goods due to his wife and children.

Memorandum also in this mayor's year, in the year 1413 being the 2nd year of this king's reign, in April was called a High Court of Parliament at Leicester town, there were 3 bills put in. The first that the temporal lands given to the church and by the churchmen and very disorderly spent – might be seized in to the king's hands for the increasing of nobility and maintenance of the king's honour and common wealth. The second was that the king having a just title to the crown of France should make claim thereunto. The third was that the king should make an entry into Scotland and by conquest unite the same to the crown of England. The Duke of Exeter taking in hand to speak unto the second bill, did so pithily and wisely handle and discourse the same that he prevailed and his judgment was allowed, and not long after wars were proclaimed between England and France. The first bill was thought to be put in by Sir John Oldcastle, then Lord Cobham, who was a follower of Wytcleff and an earnest professor of the gospel and altogether enemy to the pope and all popish religion. For which cause the bishops and clergy did so malign at him that they never ceased until they had got the mastery of him and condemned him both of treason and of heresy, for the one he was hanged and for the other burned in St Giles Field the 14th of December 1417.

1414

Thomas Eston

Memorandum that in this mayor's year the dauphin of France sent an ambassador to the king who presented unto him in scoff a ton a tennis balls to play withal, which was taken in grief, and whereof followed the wars in France.

1415

Peter Scutt

This year the king passed over into France and took Harfleur town in Normandy, where he appointed the Duke of Exeter to remain and be captain, and unto him he did join and associate in commission Thomas Baron of Carew, a gentleman for his gravity, wisdom and valiantness much commended. The foresaid Thomas Beauford, Earl of Dorset, at a parliament holden at Westminster in the 4th year of the king's reign was made or created Duke of Exeter, who had assigned unto him yearly out of the Exchequer one thousand pounds and £40 of the farm of the city.

1416

John Batyn

Memorandum that one John Roke, a grey friar, was accused for the carrying away of the wife of one John Perott and his goods and for his unchaste life with her.

1417

John Coke

Memorandum that it is an old and an ancient custom in the city of Exeter that every person which hath any house, lands and tenements within the said city and suburbs of the same shall throughout all his own lands carry his own water and all fall down water in gutters of his own that it do not fall nor descend upon his neighbours' lands to their annoyance.

Memorandum that this year upon the 14th year of December, Sir John Oldcastle, Lord Cobham, was by the tyranny of the pope and his clergy hanged and burned in St Giles Field at London.

1418

John Batyn

1419

Thomas Eston

Memorandum that in September 1419 Edmond Stafford having been bishop of Exeter about 23 years died and was very honourably buried in the Lady Chapel of his own church in a sumptuous tomb of alabaster. He was born of a noble parentage and descended of the Lord Stafford who lived in the time of King Edward the Confessor and was made or rather restored a baron in the time of the Conqueror. Of this man descended Ralph Lord Stafford, created Earl of Stafford by King Edward the third, which Ralph was brother to this bishop, a man no more noble than learned and no more learned than grave and wise, for which he was very well accounted generally of all men but most specially in favour with the king and nobility. The king was very zealously affected unto him and received him to be one of his privy council, made him Lord Privy Seal and in the year 1397 was made Lord Chancellor, his government tended very much to the benefit of the commonwealth. He was a great favourer and a further to good learning and for the increase thereof, increased two fellowships in Stapledon Inn now called Exeter College in Oxford, a singular man he was in that age and who left many good memorials behind him.

1420

John Batyn

Memorandum that John Catherick, bachelor of law and bishop of Chester [sic], was at Florence with Pope Martin the fifth which news was brought of the death of Bishop Stafford and then and there by the pope was proffered to this bishopric but he never enjoyed it for very shortly after he died and then another chosen.

Memorandum that Edmond Lacy, bishop of Hereford and a professor of divinity, was removed or translated from Hereford to this city and made bishop of the same.

The Duke of Exeter in the end of this mayor's year laid siege to the great town of Meaux in France.

1421

John Cooke

Memorandum that one William Jurden for a licence to unlade and discharge his ship at Colpole gave for his fine £5.

Memorandum also that Roger Batyn being arrested at the suit of Richard Crinell in an action of debt for £6 for two tuns of wine was admitted to do his law for the same which 3 hands according to the custom of the city.

Memorandum that by the custom of the city if there be not sufficient citizens or inhabitants of freehold to be returned in a jury for any trial, that then a return may be made of other citizens which have moveable goods sufficient.

Memorandum that a parliament holden this year at London concerning a confirmation of the clergy, Bishop Lacy was then made Lord Chancellor who in the Convocation House made a most excellent oration. The king being then present and which was so well liked that the king was determined to have followed the same if he had lived.

Also this year the mayor's pension from £5 was increased to £6 13s 4d upon condition that the mayor should not thenceforth ask any further allowance for his diet.

Also in this mayor's year upon the last of August 1422 King Henry the 5th died and his son aged 9 years was proclaimed king.

1422

Thomas Eston

Memorandum that Thomas Duke of Exeter was this year made guardian and keeper of the king his person.

The first year of King Henry the 6th

1423

John Batyn

Memorandum it was ordered and decreed by the mayor, bailiffs and common council that the son and heir of the eldest son of any free citizen should not nor shall be admitted to the freedom of the city by patrimony and by the right of his father during his father's life, nor that any apprentice shall be made free of the city for his service until he were bounded by indenture and have served truly seven years at the least according to the same indentures by good proof and testimony.

Memorandum also that no ship coming within the port of Exeter can or may discharge the same without licence but only at the quay of Topsham and note the custom at full declared.

1424

John Cooke

Memorandum it was ordained by the mayor and common council that henceforth every mayor for the time being shall have annually against the feast of Christmas 6 loaves of bread at 1d the piece and 12d in money and the like also he shall have against Easter. And that every Steward shall have at every of the said feasts 3 loaves and 6d in money at the costage of the city.

1425

Robert Veysye

Memorandum that by the custom of Exeter a man seized of any land in Exeter in the right of his wife may make a suit thereof for a town term of 29 years reserving a reasonable rent.

Memorandum also that this year Thomas Duke of Exeter died and was buried in St Edmunds Bury. He was the son to John Duke of Lancaster by his third wife the Lady Katherine and after the attendance of John Holland he was created Duke of Exeter and not long after this man's death the son of the aforesaid John Holland was restored to the said duchy.

1426

Thomas Eston

Memorandum it was proved in open court that the mayor of this city for the time being had the charge and government of every free man's child being within the age of 21 years and is to appoint guardians for the said orphans as well for the good government and bringing up of him as also for the preservation and good ordering of the goods left unto him.

This year died the Lady Elizabeth, sister to King Henry the 4th and Duchess of Exeter the first wife to John Holland Duke of Exeter and after to Sir John Cornwall Lord Fannehope.

1427

John Hall

Memorandum it was ordered by the mayor & common council that if any of the 24 being lawfully warned by the sergeant to come before the mayor & common council do refuse and do not come at the time appointed shall pay for every default 3s 4d except he have some reasonable excuse and cause of absence.

1428

John Shillingford

1429

John Shillingford

Memorandum this year was traversed an action in the Guildhall before the mayor of annoyance for carriage of another man's water.

Memorandum also the king being aged about 17 years was crowned at Westminster the 6th of November.

Memorandum that in the end of this year Philip Duke of Burgundy instituted the order of Knights of the Golden Flesh following very much the Order of the Garter in England.

1430

John Hull

Memorandum that the custom of the city that in every action wherein any foreigner is to do his law in a court of Pie Powder may do it by his own hand only.

This year the worthy and good man William Wonerd Esquire and Recorder of this city finished and ended his hospital or almshouse without Southgate named by him God's House but now commonly walled the Wenerds, which he endowed with lands, livings and revenues for the maintenance and relief of 12 poor, needy and impotent people for ever. And which lands he did so ensure to that use that it was in those days it could not be amended. He made, set down and ordered sundry good and godly orders and constitutions for the good governance of the said house and people. In his last days he yielded and resigned all his livings and lands unto his son and spent and lived the residue of his life among the poor in this his house and hospital. A man he was of great worship and reverence, very well learned in the laws of the realm and who did much good in his country and common wealth, and left many good precedents thereof to his posterity. A great pity that in so honourable a city he left so few followers.

1431

William Cooke

Memorandum it is recorded that if any man at the suit of any person be condemned in the court and be then and there present in the court he shall be committed towards and remain in execution until he have made said satisfaction.

Memorandum also that by the custom of this city no person coming with any wares and merchandises within the port of the same ought or may unlade and discharge the same but only at the place accustomed without several licence of the mayor.

Note that this year the king was crowned at Paris with great solemnities unto whom all the nobles and peers of France did homage and swore fealty, at which John Holland Earl of Huntingdon was present and did many good feats at arms in the triumph there.

1432

Thomas Coke

Memorandum that this year John Holland Earl of Huntingdon and son to John Holland Duke of Exeter was sent into France with a great army where he did many great exploits and good service.

1433

John Salter

Note that this year an order was taken by the mayor and common council of this city that no person dwelling within the same should keep any dogs within the city upon pain to pay 12d for every dog so kept. And further that the watchmen which after the watch charged did find any dogs in the streets and out of any man's door they should kill him.

1434

William Coke

Memorandum that by an order taken at the council of Basil an entreaty of peace was then appointed to be made between England and France and one of the chief commissioners for the king of England was John Holland Earl of Huntingdon, man in sundry respects as well for chivalry as for his wisdom, worthy of great commendation.

1435

Thomas Coke

1436

John Cutler

Memorandum that this year there died two queens in England, Katherine mother to the king and Joan grandmother to him.

1437

John Hull

Memorandum that this year that the butchers of this city had made an order among themselves that they would not henceforth keep any shops nor standings in the shambles but only in their own dwelling houses. And accordingly one John Smithe and one John Taylor the two chieftains of them began the matter. But the matter being had before the mayor and common council the said butchers were committed and sent to ward where they remained until they had renounced their former order and paid the fine assessed upon them.

Memorandum that in the end of this mayor's year being the 17 of King Henry the 6th John Holland Earl of Huntingdon and Chief Steward of Gascoyn was sent into Gascony with a great army and by his policy saved that whole country which was in readiness to have revolted to the French king.

1438

Benet Drew

Memorandum that this year the bishop of Exeter claimed to have recognisance of pleas in his court of his fee.

Also this year a large controversy between the mayor and commonality of this city and the dean and chapter of St Peter's concerning St Sidwell's Fee was by Act of Parliament ended and determined and the bonds and limits of the same set down as appeareth by the exemplification of the same dated *the 4th of May the fifteenth year of King Henry the 6th*.

1439

William Coke

Memorandum this year Edmond Lacy bishop of Exon did begin the building of the Chapter House in his own church which is a very fair and sumptuous house.

1440

William Upton

Memoprandum that every foreigner in an action of debt before the mayor shall do his law within his own hand only but every citizen & inhabitant with two hands besides himself.

Memorandum that in the end of this mayor a controversy between the mayor and commonality of Exon and the dean and chapter of St Peter's concerning two parcels of land lieing at the Broadgate in and at the house then William Willford's but in the year of 1596 Christopher Spicer was compounded and ended and concluded under the city's deed & common seal by . . .

1441

Thomas Coke

Memorandum that in the end of this mayor's year being the 21st of King Henry *Anno* 1442 the Earl of Arnynate offered the daughter in marriage to the king and offered to give with her all his towns and castles in the Duchy of Aquitaine besides a mass of money to recover what the French king or any others kept, for which Sir Edward Hull knight with others were sent over and concluded the marriage, which notwithstanding was after undone.

1442

John Cuttler

Note that by the old and ancient customs of the city of Exeter every inhabitant within the same which is a tippler and soldeth ale or bread within the liberties of the city being not free of the same shall pay quarterly to the mayor and commonality to the use of the city 7d ob.

Memorandum that John Holland Earl of Huntingdon was made lieutenant of Aquataine and in the days being troublesome he did with great care and his wisdom govern the same.

It is entered among and in sundry of the records of this city that all the clerks of the Chancery, their servants and ministers are privileged persons and not to be served in any other court then in this Chancery against their good will for any matter whatsoever except in causes of freehold, felony or appeals.

1443

Hugh Germyn

Memorandum that this year a peace was concluded between England and France in which John Holland Earl of Huntingdon being then in great credit and Lieutenant of all Aquitaine was a dealer. And who after the said conclusion of peace was created and made or restored Duke of Exeter as his father was before him being the 23rd year of the king's reign 1444.

1444

John Shillingford

Memorandum that John Shillingford being elected and chosen to be mayor for the year did refuse to be sworn and to take the office upon him whereupon advertisement was made unto the king and council. And then a writ under the privy seal was directed and sent to the said John requiring and v'ding him upon the pain of one thousand pounds to take the office upon him and to execute the same who accordingly upon the Monday next after the feast of St Valentine at two of the clock of the afternoon came to the Guildhall and there was sworn and though at the first with an evil will yet in the end did perform it very well.

This year King Henry by the persuasion of the earl and after marquis of Suffolk contrary to the promise made before unto the Earl of Arnynake by Sir Edward Hull and others did marry the Lady

Margaret daughter to Richard Duke of Anjou named King of Sicily, Naples and Jerusalem having much with the first and taking nothing with the last.

1445

John Hull

1446

John Shillingford

Memorandum that one Emett the wife of Robert Webber was prosecuted for a scold and speaker of slanderous words against one John Lucas who was punished for the same notwithstanding the ordinary cited her and claimed the jurisdiction but the mayor would not have it.

Memorandum that John Holland Duke of Exeter died in this mayor's year Anno 1447 and was very honourably buried at Saint Katherine's near the Tower Hill at London. He served very well of his prince and commonwealth for he was a very wise man and a good councillor in civil and political matters and very expert and valiant in all martial affairs and was very well tied in both to the good liking of the king to the benefit of the commonwealth and to the greater commendation of himself.

1447

John Shillingford

Memorandum that Hugh Germyn late mayor was served upon an act of false imprisonment for keeping of one in prison when he was mayor.

Memorandum that this John Shillingford the mayor was a very wise man and learned in the laws of the realm, bold and sturdy. And in his government very just and upright and so well he directed the same to the benefit of the commonwealth of this city as few before him did it before. In his time was the long and troublesome suit between Edmond Lacy the bishop and the Dean and Chapter against the mayor and commonality of this city concerning their liberties which suit this Shillingford did follow very carefully and diligently and by the means thereof and also by reason of his acquaintance with the Lord Chancellor and the Council his suits were the better considered. The same at length was referred to arbitraiance and then to be finally and for ever ended. In this mayor's time Exe Bridge was in great ruin and decay, the stone work being much foundred and the higher part being all of timber was consumed and worn out. And this man being of good credit and acquaintance with John Kempe, then Archbishop of York and Cardinal and one of the executors to Henry Beauford Cardinal and Bishop of Winchester who for his wealth was called the Rich Cardinal. To this John Kemp the Archbishop, John Shillingford made an earnest suit and supplication for some relief and contribution towards the new building of Exe Bridge and was promised the same. But before the money was paid John Shillingford died and the money never received.

1448

John Cutler

Memorandum that John Kelley, one of the common council of this city, was returned in a jury for trial of an issue between party and party and thereupon he brought forth and exhibited the king's letters under his seals patent by which he was privileged from all juries as also discharged to be a mayor, bailiff, sheriff or other office against his will.

Note that in a plea of debts for wines the defendant is to do his law with 3 hands.

Memorandum that this year the bishop of Winchester, Thomas Earl of Devon and John Lord Sturton came to this city the 3 day of August and brought with them a writ from the king unto the mayor for the loan of a piece of money to be levied upon the inhabitants for the victualling and furnishing of three ships for the whafting of certain soldiers into Brittany. Which thing was performed.

Also a long suit and controversy between the bishop and the city concerning their liberties was by order of the council committed to the arbitrance of Thomas Courteney Earl of Devon and Sir William Bonnevill knight who by the advice of the learned council of both parts determined the same, in under their seals dated the 12th of November the 27th year of the king's reign.

Note that in the end of this mayor's year being 28th year of King Henry all Normandy was lost and all the towns therein did yield themselves to the government and subjugation of the French nation.

1449

Hugh Germyn

Memorandum that this year John Holland Duke of Exeter after the death of his father John Holland who died *Anno* 1447 was Lord Great Admiral of England and having certain ships of war at the sea, in one of them named the *Nicholas* of the Tower, the constable of the Tower was then Captain. And he met with a ship in which was William de la Poole Duke of Suffolk who then was to transport himself over into France and after a small fight took the same and the duke therein; who he brought immediately into Dover and there he was forthwith beheaded.

Note that this year was the rebellion of Jake Cade in Kent who named himself Mortymer.

1450

William Crymell

Memorandum the stewards heretofore named Seneschals began this year to be first named ballin or bailiffs.

Note that this year the mayor's pension was increased to the yearly sum of £8 in consideration that he should yearly keep two dinners for the 24 and all his officers, the one upon Monday after his election when he taketh his oath and the other upon the Monday when the new mayor is chosen.

Memorandum in the end of this mayor's year being the 30th year of King Henry the 6th 1451 the Duke of York came out of Ireland and consulted with his friends concerning the title which he made to the crown among whom Thomas Courteney then Earl of Devon was one.

1451

Hugh Germyn

Memorandum that this year the king made a progress and having passed through many shires he came to this city upon Monday at the afternoon being then the feast day of St Kenelm. And the 16th of July being accompanied with a great train of noble gentlemen and others. And in this manner he was received, at his first coming into Devon he was received and lodged in the abbey of Ford and he stayed one night at the costs of the abbey. From thence he came to Ottery St Mary and there was received with great solemnities and lodged in the college two nights. Then upon the Monday aforesaid he came to Exeter and by the way was met first by the most part of knights and gentlemen. The mayor and commonality of the city being above three hundred persons and every one apparelled in the livery of the city met him at Honiton Clyst. The next company which met him was the clergy and the first were the Grey Friars and the Black Friars, the one being of St Francis' Order and the other of St Dominic's. And these met him at Livery Dole. Then came the prior of St Nicholas and the prior of St John's and all the curates, priests and chaplains of the city being ravished and clothed in their copes and vestments and two crosses before them and met him at the cross without the Southgate. And when they incensed the king with their frankincense and perfumes and that they had kissed the cross the mayor delivered him the keys of the gate and rode in before the king bareheaded carrying the mace before him and brought him through the streets which were richly hanged with silks and tapestry unto the Broadgate where the bishop, the canons and choir apparelled in their copes received him with a procession. Where he alighted from his horse and followed them on foot into the church and so into the high altar where when made his prayers and oblations he was brought into the bishop's palace and there lodged. It happened that the next day after the king's justices, by virtue of a commission to them directed from the king by the means of the Duke of Somerset, did sit in the bishop's hall and before there were two men indicted, arraigned and condemned for treason and should have been executed to death for the same, but the bishop and chapter found themselves grieved herewith and went unto the king and declared unto him that his justices had sat in commission within their sanctuary contrary to the privileges of their sanctuary and orders of the holy church. Wherefore the king to appease and satisfy them pardoned the two condemned persons and so upon the then next Wednesday he returned back and lodged at Honiton and all his charges while he [was] in the city were [met] by the bishop and city.

1452

Walter Pope

Note this year fell a hateful controversy between the Duke of York and the Duke of Somerset which was never ended until they were both consumed.

This year was all Aquitaine lost which had continued English about 300 years and in the last conflict there Sir Edward Hull who was elected to be knight of the order was slain at the Battle of Chastilion.

1453

Hugh Germyn

Note that Nicholas Radford was this year chosen Recorder of this city.

About this time was invented and devised the art of imprinting. Monsteras writeth that it was first invented by a gentleman named Catenbergins who practised it first at Mentes. Gasnerns writeth that it were two citizens of Mentes the one named John Faustus alias Goodman, the other Peter Sphesarins. Polidorus sayeth that it was a knight named Enthonbergins but whosoever devised it the invention was notable and nothing is there which hath more enclosed knowledge in divine and human letters than imprinting and some are of the opinion that this was fore-prophesied by St John in his revelation under the type of the angel which passed through the heavens with a scroll or a book in his hands meaning that imprinting hath dispersed and carried knowledge throughout the world.

1454

Richard Oronge

Memorandum that this year there was a great fight upon Clyst Heath between the Lord Thomas Courtenay Earl of Devon and the Lord William Bonnevyle Baron of Chutt [Shute] between whom was much hurt done and many hurted. The occasion thereof was as some say about a dog but great displeasure grew thereby unto the city, for immediately after the fight the Lord Bonnevyle came to this city and was received and also rescued, with the earl conceiving it in evil part thought it had been done of some displeasure against him.

Also this year John More of Colhampton, a man well learned in the laws, was chosen to be Recorder of this city about whose election was much trouble.

Memorandum that this Richard Orenge was a gentleman of a good house and parentage and descended of the family of the Orenges which dwelled in the countries of Annowe and Mayne and came over at such time as Sir John Falstaff Governor of Annoye and Mayne did recover the castle of St Owen Destayes from Sir William Orenge then Captain thereof in the 5th year of the king that now is. This Richard gave the same arms as the said William did. He became to be a sick man and infected with the leprosy and notwithstanding his great birth and nobility, his wealth and ability, his worship and credit yet most humbly did submit himself to good pleasure of God and was contented to dwell at the Magdalen without Southgate among the lazar people where he ended his days and there lieth buried in the chancel of the chapel.

Memorandum also that one John Carmynoke, a citizen, went to Dyrherd [Duryard] Wood and did there fell and cut down certain wood and 6 trees which he carried away with him. He was accused for the same but he alleged that he was a free man of the city and one of the Lords of the Wood and therefore might lawfully do it notwithstanding he was committed to prison and paid his fine and ransom for the same.

Memorandum that John Spyne and Thomas Kellye, two of bailiffs for this year, went forth out of the town and were absent from the courts without license beforehand. Wherefore they were committed to war and paid their fines.

Memorandum also William Crymell, late mayor of this city, was called and summoned to come to the common council and refused to come wherefore he was abridged to have any more his common bread and wine money.

1455

Hugh Germyn

Memorandum that this year was a great tumult and riot in London by reason of a quarrel between and English and an Italian merchant. For the appeasing whereof the Duke of Exeter and the Duke of Buckingham were appointed commissioners of oyer and determiner.

Memorandum also in upon the 18 of September 1455 Edmond Lacye bishop of this city died being the 35th year of his consecration and was buried in his own church. He was a professor of divinity and as that age required very well learned therein whereof he gave good by his oration and speeches made in the open convocation house at London in the presence and before the king and the whole nobility of the realm concerning the reformation of the loose and disordered life of the clergy which so liked them all that they promised reformation. He was well disposed and very well given and did good many ways both to his church and otherwise but was so subject to flatterers and drowned in popery that after his death his was taken and reported to be a saint and upon the reports of many feigned miracles great pilgrimages were made to his tomb.

This year John Holland Duke of Exeter because he would not consent that the Duke of York, the Earl of Salisbury and the Earl of Warwick should have the government and rule of the king and realm suspecting what would ensue he went into Westminster and there took sanctuary but they violently took him from thence and conveyed him to Pomfrett but shortly delivered again.

Memorandum that about ten weeks after the death of Bishop Lacy George Nevell 2nd son to Richard Nevell earl was in the end of November then following consecrated bishop of Exeter.

1456

William Duke

1457

John Kelley

Memorandum this year John Holland Duke of Exeter lay at his house of Dartington besides Totnes and upon occasion came to Exeter at the Sessions holden at the Castle where for certain considerations he with the advice and control of the justices of the peace caused and commanded to be proclaimed that no manner of person or persons saving the said duke and justices should use nor wear any sword nor weapon nor make breach of the peace. Not long after the said Duke and all the peers and noblemen of the realm were sent for to come to London where a reconciliation was made between the houses of Lancaster and of York and a general procession made for joy thereof at Paul's. At which the king in his royalty and all the noblemen were present and went two and two one of one faction and one of another but whatsoever the outward appearance was for the time, it appeared in the end it was but a disassembled friendship for all to come to small effort.

This year William Vicecount Bourchier was sent an ambassador into France.

1458

Richard Druell

This year there happened a controversy between the cordwainers and the tuckers the contending which of their companies should have the pre-eminence for going in the mayor's watch upon Midsummer. And then for the appeasement of the strife for that present it was ordered that both companies should march together and that one of one company and one other of the other company should go one with the other. But afterwards upon further deliberation and upon trial and forth of the priority it was found that the Company of the Tuckers & Weavers were the more ancient and thereupon it was ordered that they thenceforth should have the priority which hitherto they have kept.

This year also and at the same [time] happened one other controversy, for the manner in those days was that the mayor and aldermen did use to ride in their robes in every Midsummer watch and John Kelley, late mayor of this city, being warned to attend and to ride with the mayor in the said watch according to the old and ancient customs refused so to do. Whereupon and for which contempt he was annexed and set to pay the fine of ten marks and which he paid. A good and commendable precedent of an upright government when without respect of persons, law and justice are kept ministered and observed. For as the soul is the life of the body, so the keeping of orders and laws is the preservation of all cities and commonwealths. And as the body dyeth without the soul so the commonwealth perish without law.

This year there happened an affray between the king's servants and the Earl of Warwick's men whereof ensued such a variance and a broil that the late reconciliation made in the year past was clean dashed and broken and great stirs and controversies ensued which were never appeased until the one side was overthrown and confounded with the shedding of much blood. And this year was the field fought at Bloreheth in Shropshire.

1459

John Bettye

This year was an affray in the body of St Peter's church between certain young gentlemen and divers of them were there hurt and because the church in common opinion was thought then to be unhallowed and polluted by the blasphemy wherefore the Dean and Chapter caused and commanded the church doors to be shut and no more service to be there used until the same were new hallowed and because delays of time might hinder and hurt their markets and extraordinary gains which did daily grow by masses, dirges, & trentalls and such like they procured and in all haste did send for one Thomas Suffragane [Stillington] then the Bishop of Bath who with his exercises restored the church to his former state.

This year the Eastgate of this city being very old and ruinous fell down in the midday without the hurt of any person.

The fire of discord enkindled the last year past between the houses of York and Lancaster brake out every day more and more into great flames. And the Duke of York distrusting his own case took his younger son the Earl of Rutland and crossed the seas into Ireland. His eldest son being Earl of Marche and the Earls of Salisbury and of Warwick with others their allies came into Devon and by the aid and help of Sir John Dyneham who dwelled then at Nutwell they procured or bought a ship at Exmouth and from thence they sailed into Geurnsey and so unto Calais. This Sir John Dyneham was after Lord Treasurer of England but now he held with the line of York and in the service with them he kept the seas and entered into the town of Sandwich and there took the Lord Ryvers and sundry other persons and took certain of the king's ships there being well furnished with all kinds of munitions and artillery. But in the same service he was then hurted and maimed in one of his legs.

Also John Holland Duke of Exeter being now made Lord Admiral had in commission to keep the seas for the apprehending of such as were the king's enemies and namely for the Earls of Warwick and of

Salisbury which he might well have done if the captains and mariners had not been too much affected to the said earls against whom they would not do any service but still murmured and repined [to complain] against the duke and whatsoever he commanded or took in hand.

In this year also the king kept a parliament at Coventry in which the Duke of York and sundry of his allies and confedereates were all attainted of high treason. But not long after they came over into England and waged battle with the king at Northampton where they took him prisoner and carried him to London.

1460

William Duke

Memorandum that it was ordered by the mayor and common council that if any manner of person do upon any account or otherwise owe anything to the city and do refuse to pay the same he shall be committed to ward, there to remain without bail or mainprize [procuring the release of a prisoner by acting as surety] until he have made full satisfaction.

This year the mayor's pension was increased unto the sum of £10.

The city tendering the king's distress did levy a contribution throughout upon every person and also did set out and appoint 31 soldiers of their own charges well appointed and did send both them and for the better safety and preservation of the city did appoint a continual guard and watch of a competent number of men well harnessed and appointed to keep the gates both day and night. And commanded also all strangers and outlandish people to avoid and to depart from out of this city. And that also no manner of person coming to this city wearing harness or weapon should be received into the same without special license of the mayor.

Memorandum that this was a very troublesome and a bloody year and wherein were sundry conflicts, battles & fields waged and fought to the loss of many a man. The first was at Wakefield where the Duke of York was slain and about 3,000 others. The 2nd was at Mortimer's Cross near to Hereford East where the Earl of Marche now by the death of his father Duke of York where he discomfited and slew almost 4,000 of his adversaries and took Sir Owen Tewther father-in-law to the king and beheaded him. The 3rd was at St Albans where the Queen giveth the overthrow to the Duke of Norfolk and the Earl of Warwick where were slain of their companies about 2,000 men. The 4th was the conflict at Fore Bridge. The 5th was at Towton or Shereborne in Yorkshire which continued about 3 days and then on both sides were slain about 38,000 men. And the King being discomfited he and the Queen and the Duke of Somerset and of Exeter fled into Scotland. And Thomas Courteney Earl of Devon as he fled he was taken and forthwith carried to York and there was beheaded. In all which or the most of them Sir John Dyneham did very good service and was in great trust to the Duke of York with which line he took part.

Edward Earl of Marche and Duke of York after the taking of King Henry the 6th prisoner he was proclaimed king namely the 4th of March 1460.

The first year of King Edward the 4th

1461

John Kellye

This year the Conduit at Carfax called the Great Conduit was newly builded by the means of William Duke, late mayor of this city, who being well affected to the same did not only view and oversee the same but also at his own charges covered it with lead.

This year was fought a bloody field in Yorkshire between Towton and Saxton called Palm Sunday

Field where King Henry was discomfited, the Duke of Exeter fled and Thomas Earl of Devon taken prisoner. The number slain in this battle was about 37,000 which was so much the more because proclamation was made that no prisoners should be taken nor none be saved.

1462

Hugh Germyn

Memorandum that this year the Skinners were first incorporated by the mayor and common council and the first master was named John Macye and the wardens were John Hackeworthy and Simon Carew. And then it was ordered by the said master, wardens and company that no person being of that company should sell or utter any wares pertaining to that art and mystery being a foreigner's goods and not of the goods of some free man of that company upon pain to pay for every offence 20s.

1463

Richard Druell

Memorandum it was ordered this year that every baker of this city shall from time to time grind all his corn at the city's mills only of Duryard and Cricklepit.

Memorandum it was also ordered that every inhabitant within this city which holdeth any tenement within the same for 24 years he shall be returned in juries if the said tenement be worth clearly 40s by the year.

Memorandum the king this year under his letters patents dated 21 July *Anno Regni Tertie* gave to the city all felons goods as also granted unto them the Maudlin Fair.

Memorandum this year was the battle fought at Hexham where King Henry was discomfited and fled but very shortly taken and brought to the Tower of London.

1464

Hugh Germyn

Memorandum this year the king married the Lady Elizabeth Grey, widow, whereof ensued in the end great troubles, first the king himself was expulsed the realm and spent the most part of his reign in civil wars and bloodshed. Then his queen lived a distressed life and in great misery after the death of the king. Her two sons reputed for bastard and both murdered. The Earl of Warwick and his line clean destroyed. The Queen's brother and cousins almost utterly confounded and a number of souls killed and destroyed by the sword.

Memorandum that his year George Nevell bishop of Exeter in the end of this mayor's year was removed from this church unto York and made Archbishop thereof. This man did end and finish the building of the Chapter House of this church. He was a man of a noble birth and parentage, being brother to the Earl of Warwick and to the Marquis Montarte. And being of their confederacy in the troublesome state and civil wars was partaker of the suits thereof for in the end he was sent to Giysens and there for a long time remained a prisoner and in the end died for sorrow and grief of mind.

1465

Richard Druell

Memorandum that it was proved in open that if any person now excommunicated and did stand excommunicated under the sentence of the greater excommunication that then he cannot sue nor stand in any court.

This year John Bothe succeeded George Nevell in the Bishopric of this city and was consecrated by Thomas Burchier bishop of Canterbury the 22 of February

1466

Hugh Germyn

Memorandum this year order was taken for new building of the Guildhall which was then very ruinous and in great decay and forthwith all things necessary for the same was provided and the house builded.

Also this year was a parliament holden at Westminster which began the 3rd day of June 1467 being the 7th year of the king his reign at which Thomas Callwodleigh and Richard Clerke, being then burgesses for the city, procured an act of Parliament for paving of the streets of this city which then for the most part was for want of pavements, very filthy and full of stinking puddles very dangerous for men to travel as all very contagious & noisful.

This year also John Boothe, a bachelor of laws, was made bishop and installed in the same in the end of the month of January.

Memorandum also that this year there fell a controversy between the said bishop and this city for and concerning a tower in the city's walls and behind the bishop's house in the orchard where the bishop's prison was then kept and by means thereof the said bishop claimed to him the inheritance thereof. But in the end it fell in proof to the contrary and the city pulled it down and employed the lead and stuff of the same unto the reparations of the walls.

1467

Thomas Callwodley

Memorandum that after the death of John Holland Duke of Exeter who after the overthrow given unto King Henry VIth at Towton Field fled into Scotland was made Duke of Exeter. He grew in such credit and favour with King Edward that after the death of Henry Bourchier Earl of Essex the king gave his widow to wife to this Duke.

1468

John Hamlyn

Memorandum that this year Humphrey Lord Stofford of Southwark was by the king named Earl of Devon which earldom the king kept in his hand ever since the death of the late earl Thomas Courtney who was beheaded at York in the last year of King Henry the 6th after the overthrow given at Towton Field. This new named earl was commanded to serve against the northern men who were then up in a rebellion. And had the king his letters to the mayor of this city for his provision and furniture in the said service. And being come to this city he was very honourably entertained and was furnished with 30 tall men, well armed and appointed at the city's charges. This Lord Stofford thus well appointed marcheth northwards with 800 archers and cometh to Banbury where he met with the Lord Herbert Earl of Pembroke and there too fell at variance whereupon the next day when the service was to be done, the Lord Stofford departed away and forsook the Earl who by that means was slain and lost the field at a place called Edgecote and then this Lord Stofford fled and came in to Somersetshire and by the king his commandments was taken and apprehended in Brent Marsh and from thence was carried to Bridgwater where he was beheaded.

1469

Robert Smythe

Memorandum that this was a very troublesome year and by reason of the civil wars the course of the laws for a time lay as it were asleep and as the whole realm generally was full of troubles so this city in particular felt some part thereof more than others. For after that King Edward was taken prisoner at Woolney besides Warwick and by means had shifted [a fraudulent or evasive device] and delivered himself out of prison he gathered a new army and then the Earl of Warwick and the Duke of Clarence mistrusting their own parts prepared themselves to pass over to Calais. And first sent away before them the Duchess of Clarence being then big with child, who being accompanied with the Lord Fitzwarren, the Lord Dinham and the Baron of Carew and a thousand of good fighting men, came to this city upon the 18th of March 1470 and she was lodged in the bishop's palace. Sir Hugh rather Sir William Courteney who then favoured King Edward his party hearing that this company was lodged within the city forthwith assembleth all his friends, allies and kinsfolk and with such a power and force as he had gotten he environeth and besiegeth the city. The bridges leading to the city were broken up, the passages stopped and the gates of the city ramparted. By means whereof there were no markets kept, nor victuals brought to the city for 12 days together. Great were the troubles to the whole city. But in greater perplexity stood the mayor and his brethren and being as it were assailed many ways could not find one way how to be eased and relieved. First, Sit Hugh Courteney sendeth his messenger to the city and doth demand the delivery of the keys of the city's gates and of the noblemen within the same areas with sword, fire and famine he will pursue against them. On the other side the Lord Fitzwaron & the residue of the noble and gentlemen mistrusting the mayor and especially the common people who were very impatient and could not abide to endure the wants and scarcity of victuals they required to have the custody of the city and the keeping of the keys. But the mayor by the good advice of his brethren and councillors denyeth the requests both of the one and of the other. And as for the commoners albeit hunger have no ears and a hard matter it is to persuade empty bellies to [?]ens yet the matter was so handled and they so curteously entreated that fair speeches and good words prevailed with them until that at length by the continual mediation, intercourse and entreaty of certain canons of the Close of St Peter's and other good men the matter was compounded, the siege was raised, the gates opened and every man at liberty. The next day after being the 3rd of April the Duke of Clarence and the Earl of Warwick and here for a few [?days] rested and sojourned until shipping was prepared for them at Dartmouth which as soon as it was in readiness they and their wives and whole company rode to Dartmouth and there embarqued themselves for Calais. The king in this meantime prepareth all things in readiness to pursue and follow them and came to this city the 14th of April 1470 with 40,000 men but the birds were flown and gone away but yet being come so near the city he would see the same and the country adjoining. Wherefore being accompanied with all his nobility, namely the Bishop of Ely then Lord Treasurer, the Duke of Norfolk then Earl Marshall, the Duke of Suffolk, the Earl of Arundell, the Earl of Wiltshire son to the Duke of Buckingham, the Earl of Worcester Constable of England, the Earl of Shrewsbury, the Earl Ryvers, the Lord Hastings, The Lord Gray of Codner, the Lord Awdleigh, the Lord Saye, the Lord Sturton, the Lord Dakors, The Lord Monteroye, the Lord Stanebury, the Lord Ferrys and the Baron of Dudleigh, with the whole army, to the city being Saturday [crossed through 'and the next following being Palm Sunday the king in proper procession to the great comfort of the beholders and in princely manner went and followed the procession in the church and according to the order then used. And did here in this city rest and continuing two whole days and until the Tuesday then'] Before whose coming the mayor being advertised thereof took order and gave commandment that every citizen and freeman being of ability should provide and prepare himself a gown of the city's livery which was then red and to be in readiness for serving of the king which accordingly every man did. And when the king was come to the city the mayor being attended with four hundred persons well and seemly apparel received the king without the Southgate unto whom Thomas Dorrishe then Recorder of this city made an oration, in being ordered the mayor delivered the keys of the gates and his maces unto the king and therewith also a purse with a hundred nobles therein which his grace took very thankfully but the keys and maces he redelivered to the mayor. And then the mayor going before the king with his mace bareheaded brought him to his lodging. The next day following being Palm Sunday the king in proper person and most princely and royal manner followed and went in procession after the manner as was then used about the churchyard the view of the people and the beholders being not so great but that their joy and comfort was much greater. For such is the rejoicing of the people especially of such as be far removed from king's courts to see and behold their prince. The king continued in this three days namely until Tuesday then next following who when he had dined took his horse and departed giving great thanks to the mayor for his entertainment as also showed himself very loving and bountiful to the people.

Also in the end of this year in the month of August the Duke of Clarence and the Earl of Warwick with all their retinue returned from out of France and landed some at Plymouth, some at Dartmouth and some at Exmouth. But all met at this city and from hence they all departed and marched towards London who in every place as he passed proclaimed himself King Henry whereupon the King Edward was so troubled that he forsook the realm, took shipping and sailed over into Holland to the Duke of Burgundy.

1470

Hugh Germyn

Memorandum that this year in the month of October immediately after the departure of King Edward the 4th over the seas King Henry was restored and the year named the 39th of his reign and the first of his redemption and King Edward by sound of trumpet was proclaimed usurper but his continued a very short time.

In these troublesome times the mayor and his brethren doubting the sequel thereof took order for the safe keeping of this city and therefore did appoint a guard by the day and a watch by the night of men well appointed for keeping of the gates. And continually they had always espials abroad in every coast and quarter for understanding and knowing how all things happened. And as before this they were driven to give good countenance and entertainment to both parties coming severally to this city so now that King Henry was restored, it was ordered for keeping of his favour and good will that Richard Clerke the Receiver should defray £20 in gold and present the same unto the Queen and to the prince her son.

About this time one Sir William Hankford knight who dwelled at Annery in Devon unto whom the Lord Fitzwarren, Sir John Saintleger and Sir William Ballayn were heirs, was one of the Chief Justices and whose counsel and advice was asked and sought in every doubtful matter especially in matters concerning the crown for which were the continual rebel wars. And this man considering that when the sword ruled the law suffered, and bethinking with himself in what a dangerous case he stood that he in all the councils asked of him he must soothe the parties and speak noblis placentia or be in danger of his life began to wax weary of his life and for the cutting of and shortening the same he used this practice. He called the Keeper of his park unto him and picking a quarrel unto him challenged and chid him that he was careless and sloughful and did not take the pains which ought to do nor did walk abroad nor nor day nor night and by that means thieves came and spoiled his game. And therefore he gave him in charge and commandment that he should be more careful then in times past and especially in the night seasons. And willed him in any wise that if he espied any night rangers in his park, which would not stand nor answer when he spake unto him, that then he should not spare him but shoot him through if he could. This knight having laid this foundation and determined to perform when he had devised for the ending of his doleful day did upon a certain dark night secretly and alone get into his park and walked until at length he came where the keeper was walking. The keeper perceiving a man to be stiring and to be as he thought coming towards him called unto him and asked 'who was there?' Who gave no answer but still was coming forwards. Then the keeper bid him to stand who likewise would not whereupon the keeper nocked his arrow and shot at him and killed him. Thus this knight, otherwise a very wise and a learned man, feared to displace man did displease himself and very disorderly ended his life.

I find it written in an old and an ancient annual of this city that this year there was one John an Earl of Devon who what he was it doth not appear but a commission was directed and sent from the king to the mayor and commonality in the behalf of this earl as doth appear by the said record. The words whereof are these the 14th of April being Easter Eve the 49th year of King Henry the 6th a commission was directed [to] John Earl of Devon and sent to the mayor of Exeter to be proclaimed and so was it done the same day at the afternoon. But the writer is mistaken in the name for it be meant of the earl of Devon then his name at this time was Thomas, but if it be meant of John then it was Holland Duke of Exeter whose name was John and he abiding and dwelling in Devon. Likewise it is written in the same annual by the words as followeth *the 24th day of April in the 49th year of King Henry the 6th, on the fourth of March John Earl of Devon by the assent of the mayor and 24 by the hand of Richard Clark.* About 6 months after this King Edward returned again out of Flanders and having renewed his force and army and in the end near unto Barnett he met with the Earl of Warwick upon a heath called Glademores where they joined the battle in which the Earl of Warwick was slain.

Not long after Queen Margaret she returned from out of France and she having received and repaired her army of goodly lusty and good soldiers landeth at Weymouth in Dorsetshire and came to this city of Exeter. And being furnished with all the powers and strength of this country, laboured and procured by the Dukes of Somerset, Exeter and Earl of Devon they all marched forth and in the end they came to Tewksbury where they entered and waged the battle for King Edward and lost the field.

1471

Richard Geffrey,
Hugh Germyn

Memorandum that the foresaid Richard Geffrey mayor died upon Wednesday next before the decollation [the act of beheading] of St John the Baptist in the end of August and Hugh Germyn was chosen to supply his room for the residue of the year.

Note that King [Edward] having gotten victory over all his enemies bethinketh himself now upon such as were adversaries or had succoured and taken part with them and being advertised both of succours and monies given and contributed unto them out of this city waxed very angry and was of the mind to have been revenged thereof until he was advertised and pacified.

1472

Richard Clerke

Memorandum that this year being King Henry the sixth died or as some merit was murdered in the Tower of London.

1473

Richard Ronnewell

Memorandum that the Duke of Clarence came this year to this city and was very honourably received and entertained.

This year there was a composition made between the Abbot of Sherborne and the mayor, bailiffs and commonality of this city dated 3 August concerning the passage at Exmouth.

1474

Hugh Germyn

Memorandum that this year King Edward the 4th passed over the seas with an army against the French king and in which were slain of the English side but only John Duke of Exeter of name as Polydore and Harding do write But Fabyan reporteth that this Duke was found dead upon the seas between Calais and Dover. And Grafton writeth that the Earl of Exeter was so drowned which must needs be meant of the Duke of Exeter or of nobody because there was no Earl of Exeter at that time nor long before.

1475

John Orenge

That this year there was a great controversy between the mayor and citizens of the one part and the company of the tailors of the other part for and concerning a new incorporation which the said company of tailors had procured from the king whereof ensued great troubles, long and chargeable suits but after two years the king ended the same and delivered his determination under his privy seal unto Dr Peter Courteney, then dean to the Cathedral church of St Peter's of this city, and he delivered the same to both parties. And albeit this was a final end of all suits in law yet the malice and grief which was conceived hereof could not in long time be satisfied nor appeased.

In this year a peace was concluded between King Edward and King Lewes of France, which the French men (though they redeemed the same at their great charges) yet they thought it to be the more honourable because with [?]clyghtes & devices they had compassed the same much by feats of arms by their own confession they could never have obtained and the Duke of Burgoyne the constable of France and the Duke of Gloucester did very much mislike it and were grievously offended therewith.

1476

John Atwell

The king now that he was at peace with his enemies and all things at rest at home he bethinketh how to establish his succession and to deliver the same from the danger of such as whom he feared would after his death impeach his issue of the crown. And being advertised that Henry Earl of Richmond the sole and only heir remaining of the house of Lancaster was now in the Duke of Brittany's court which said duke was also compromised in the league late concluded did send his ambassadors unto the said duke for the having of the said Earl of Richmond pretending a marriage which he meant to conclude between the said earl and the with his eldest daughter Lady Elizabeth a thing by him never meant although in the end by God's providence it came so to pass. The Duke did once grant the king's request but upon a further advertisement he respected the safety of the earl and sent him from his court to a place of his better safeguard.

1477

John Kelley

This year upon the fifth of April 1478 John Bothe bishop of Exeter died at his house in St Clemondes parish without the Temple Barn in London and was buried in the same church. He was descended of very good and noble parentage and very well brought up in good learning and knowledge, he professed the canon and civil laws of which he was a doctor and had very good knowledge in the laws of the realm. A man of very great courtesy and affable to every man, good to the poor and liberal in good causes and albeit he had been bishop 12 whole years and more he lay for the most at London by reason of the continual troubles and civil wars.

1478

William Oblegh

In this mayor's year Peter Courteny, Dean of the Cathedral Church of this city, was by Pope Sextus the 3rd made bishop of this church and upon the 8th of November then following he was consecrated at Westminster. He was a man of noble parentage being the second son to Sir Philip Courteney of Powderham, knight, and of the Lady Elizabeth his wife, daughter to the Lord Hungerfford. He was a great favourer of learned and was well learned himself, very affable and loving to all men and a special peace maker for many and sundry controversies he did compound and a long suit in law between the citizens and the tailors he was a special mediator for ending and finishing of the same. He was a great keeper of hospitality and for which King Richard the third who loved him not because he took part with the Earl of Richmond yet being well and princely entertained in his house at his being in this city when he at that time was fled into France did highly commend him for the same. He was not so well beloved for the sundry and many good virtues while he dwelled in this city but as much was his departure from the same bewailed and lamented when he was removed unto Winchester.

This year the king not forgetting the old grudge between himself and his brother George the Duke of Clarence, the variance between them was renewed and revived, upon a surmised prophecy that G should be king after him which the king interpreted and applied to him because his name began with the letter G which indeed was verified upon Richard Duke of Gloucester. Upon which imagination he was cast into the Tower and made his burial in a butt of malmsey.

This year died Thomas Kyrkbye, Treasurer of St Peter's of this city and Master of the Rolls in the Chancery, a man very well learned and for the many singular good gifts in him much commended.

1479

John Atwell

In this year there was a great pestilence in this city whereof there died very much people.

1480

Thomas Calwodley

Memorandum that this year there was fault found in the accounts of the Customer of Devon and whereupon a precept from the king out of his court of the Exchequer was sent unto the mayor of this city that he should send up a true copy of the collection of the petty or town custom of this city for the year last past which was done and the same was sent by Philip Atwill the king's messenger who was sent for the same and by these rolls the customer's account was controlled.

This year John Boneffant, an attorney at the common law, in the guildhall was greatly complained upon for his sundry and lewd practices and forgeries whereupon he was disenfranchised and clean dismissed to be any more an attorney. And yet he not leaving, the same complaint was made against him unto the king who forthwith sent his letters and commission unto the Lord Thomas Marquis Dorset then his Lieutenant in these west parts to here examine and determine the same. Who forthwith came to this city upon the 28th of March and was very honourably received and entertained. And upon hearing of the matter he found sundry forgeries of deeds and evidences proved against him and they commanded him to be carried upon a horse through the city upon a market day in the said market and with a paper upon his head whereon was written 'for forging of false deeds, evidences and counterfeiting of seals evidently proved'.

1481

Richard Druell

This year the Cordwainers of this city were incorporated or reduced into one fellowship or company under the common seal of the city but since altered and newly made according to the statute by the Lord Chancellor and the two Lord Justices of England.

1482

Roger Worthe

The bakers were this year incorporated by the mayor and common council under the common council and under the city's seal. And an order take that all foreign bakers should sell their bread at the high conduit only.

The Skinners were also incorporated under the city's seal.

This year William Huttersfield, Recorder of this city, being a man very wise and learned was made the King's Solicitor and then was Thomas Hext made Recorder of the same.

An order was made this year that the Receiver of this city for the time being should wear a scarlet gown as doth the mayor & every alderman of the same but without any tippert [a garment covering the shoulders, often made of fur or wool].

This year King Edward the 4th died being entered about five weeks in the 23rd year of his reign.

The first year of King Richard the 3rd

1483

John Atwill

This year King Edward aged about 13 years was proclaimed king but never crowned and long did not enjoy that his kingdom for about 2 months & 11 days after the death of his father he died also being by an untimely death most unnaturally murdered in the Tower of London. And then King Richard who by means had procured himself to be crowned king did possess the crown.

King Richard albeit he were possessed of the crown yet he wanted the quietness of mind which he wished for, he saw and perceived that he was hated and his government misliked which bred him many enemies and he by especial knowing what practices were devised against him for the supplanting of him and for the bringing in of Henry Earl of Richmond whom of all men he most doubted and duly hated, and understanding also that sundry noblemen and gentlemen in the county of Devon were assembled to that effect he caused John Lord Scrope of Bolton with a commission of Oyer & Determiner to come into this country who sat in his commission at Torrington and caused inquiry to be made of all such persons as were considered against the king for the bringing in of the Earl of Richamond and they there were indicted before him for high treason. Thomas Marquis Dorset, Peter Bishop of Exeter, Sir Thomas Saintleger brother-in-law to the king and Sir Thomas Falstaff knight as principals, Sir Robert Willoughby after created Lord Brook & Sir Thomas Arundell knights, John Arundell Dean of Exeter, David Hopton Archdeacon of Exeter, Oliver Abbot of Buckland, Bartholomew Saintleger, William Chelsen, Thomas Grenefeld, Richard Edgecome, Robert Barnabye, Walter Courteney, Hugh Lawrell, John Parker, John Hollewell and five hundred others were indicted as messengers. All these fled and shifted for themselves, some into France, some into Britany and some one way and some another way saving Sir Thomas Sentleger and Sir John Rame who upon a sudden were surprised and taken and forthwith brought to Exeter and there at the Carfax were beheaded. All those things done, King Richard for the better satisfying of his mind made his progress into Devon and came to this city in November, whereof advertisement being before given preparation was made for the honourable receiving of him but he came upon such a sudden that all things could not be provided to receive him in such honourable manner as they could and as unto so high an estate did appertain. Nevertheless they did what in they in lay according to the time and took order with Thomas Hext, Recorder, to make the speech or oration unto the king and in reward gave him a scarlet gown and also made a collection among themselves by way of loan of one hundred marks in money to be given and prosecuted unto the king. And so accordingly when the king came the mayor and his brethren in all their best and most seemly array met and received the king at the gate of the city where the Recorder made unto him his gratulatory oration which done the mayor delivered unto him the maces went to be borne before him and the keys of the city's gates and therewith presented unto his grace 200 nobles in a purse with their services & present he accepted very thankfully and giving them very good speeches delivered back to the mayor the maces and the keys. From thence he was conducted to the bishop's palace where he was lodged. The mayor going before his grave and carried the greater mace before him. He was bountifully entertained in the bishop's palace and all things were plentously prepared for his entertainment as well in plate and furniture of the house as also for abundance of viands and victuals sufficient for the king and his whole train. The king when he saw all things so well appointed called for the bishop's officers and demanded what was become of their master, saying he was a wily prelate and had made him good cheer for which he gave not only thanks but would also consider him for his great courtesy and costages bestowed upon him and so with many good words the king dismissed what was his meaning. For he knew that he upon the indictments was gone out of the way. The noble men and the king's train were all lodged according to their estates in the city and wanted no provision meet for them at the charge of the city with the king when he had did command and give the mayor and his brethren great thanks. During the short time of his abode here he took the view of the whole city and did very well like and commend the cite thereof and when he was come to the castle and had behold the seat thereof and the country thereabout he was in a marvellous great liking thereof both of the strength of the place which was to command both city and country about it as also the goodly and pleasant aspects of the same. But when it was told him that it was called Rugemont he was suddenly fallen into a great dump and as it were a man amazed at length he said 'I see my days be not long' for it was a prophecy told unto him that when he came once to Richmond he should not long live after which in effect fell false out in the end not so much in respect that he had seen the castle but in respect of Henry Earl of Richmond whom as his brother before him he found would be the ruin and fall of him & of his house and so it fell out in the end for a little above a year following Henry Earl of Richmond being newly arrived out of France into Wales, who was then attended with all the gentlemen of Devon before indicted, he landed in Milford Haven and then his forces daily increased more & more as he did march through the country until he met with King Richard with whom he encountered and waged the battle at a place called Bosworth in which King Richard was slain.

1484

Mathew Jubb

This year order was taken for watching and warding of the city both by day and night and also every man was set what armour he should have and keep. And likewise sundry men out of the city armed and well appointed were sent out of the city to the seaside and there to watch and ward for fear of any invasion of the enemy and over them were appointed certain chosen citizens to be their captains.

The king sent his commission to the mayor and citizens for certain soldiers to be sent unto him to serve him upon the receipt of which commandment there were chosen 20 very good and sufficient and able men, well armed and appointed, named Richard Magot, Henry Netherton, John Boncer, William Robyns, William Master, William Osett, Walter Knight, George Singleton, Richard Dabroy, John Sywell, John Leche, John Rudge, Richard Baylye, John Duxton, William Lange, Walter Lever, Stephen Cleve, Robert Lychell, Thomas Coteler and John Segor which men were delivered to Sir Ralph Hastings knight to be conducted to the place of service and to continue in the same for 20 days at the costs and charges of the city and the said Sir Ralph during his being here had very good entertainment and one Byston who was the king's messenger was well rewarded.

Memorandum that this year the forepart of the Guildhall and the Council Chamber was of new builded by the city.

This year there was great murmuring of the citizen bakers against the foreign bakers whom they would have to be utterly excluded from the coming to this city with any bread at all and one special cause was because when they came to this city they would go a hawking with their bread from house to house to their great annoy as they said. And thereupon order was taken that the said foreign bakers should from henceforth have free coming and going to the markets with their bread upon any market day but they should keep their standings only at the high conduit and there only to make sales of the same which order from thenceforth was formerly kept.

In the end of this mayor's time in the month of August 1485 King Richard was slain in the battle of Bosworth being the beginning of the third year of his reign.

The first year of King Henry the 7th

1485

Richard Russell

Memorandum that King Henry after the death of King Richard the 3rd being proclaimed king was also in the 30th day of October then next following crowned king and then remembering his old friends and faithful helpers did then as also afterwards as occasion served, advance and prefer them to honours and high estates, as namely of this country he made Sir Robert Willoughby Lord Brooke and Lord Steward of his household, Sir John Dynnham Lord Dynnham and not long after Lord Treasurer, Sir Richard Edgecome he made him one of his Privy Council and shortly Comptroller of his house and for his better increation, livings and livelihoods he gave unto all the lands, possessions and inheritance of Sir John Bedrogan knight late Sheriff of Cornwall and who was attainted of treason but fled over the seas and never returned.

1486

Thomas Callwodleigh

This year the king married the Lady Elizabeth the eldest daughter to King Edward the 4th by which means the houses of York and Lancaster which had been at division and in civil wars about 70 years were united and joined in one.

The king not forgetting the fealty of Peter Bishop of Exeter did bestow upon him the bishopric of Winchester and in the bishopric of Exeter he placed Richard Foxe his faithful counsellor.

This year in September Prince Arthur the first begotten son of King Henry was born at Winchester.

This Thomas Callwodleye now the 3rd time mayor of this city was a gentleman born & of a good house and he being learned he did the better govern this city to his great commendation & to the benefit of the common wealth. He was severe against notorious & evil offenders and such as escaped corporal punishments paid for their redemption with monies he employed in building the front & chapel of the guildhall. In matters indirect concerning the court he was very precise & upright. Towards the poor he was very pitiful & charitable and the commons being much charged with continual exactions. He departed with his manor of Awliscombe which was purchased of him by John Hooker mayor of this city & others for relieving of them in payments of taxes & tallages and for finding of a chaplain. He died anno 1492.

1487

Robert Newton

This year the Lady Margaret Duchess of Low Burgundy, sister to King Edward the 4th and a mortal enemy to King Henry the 7th, joined herself unto the Earl of Lincoln her nephew and others who by the creafy delusions and devilish devices of one Richard Symon, a priest, were or would be persuaded that one Lambert Symons, his scholar, should be the son of King Edward the 4th who was supposed to be dead and the matter was so followed that rather in despite of King Henry than for any good and true matter this Duchess aided him both with men and money and furnished him with 2,000 Almayne soldiers under the conduct of one Martin Swarde a wily captain. And with this and his own companies the Earl of Lincoln and they went in Ireland where he was received and proclaimed King of England and Lord of Ireland only the citizens of Waterford refused to receive him or acknowledge him. From thence he and his whole train sailed over into England and landed in Lancashire and by journey came to Newark in Yorkshire & from thence to Stoke where in a pitched field after a mighty fight they were all vanquished and all slain for the most part saving this Lambert and his master, the one being made a kitchen boy & the other committed to perpetual prison.

In this year Richard Foxe, Bishop of Exeter, and Sir Richard Edgecome were sent Ambassadors to James King of Scotland for continuing of peace between the two realms.

This year the Barbers of this city were incorporated.

Also ale tasters were appointed for searching that wholesome drinks should be made.

1488

Richard Clerke

Sir Richard Edgecome, a faithful, a grave and wise knight and one of the king's council was sent in an ambassador to the French king for a peace to be concluded but it took no effect.

This year Sir Robert Willoughbye Lord Brooke was sent over into Britain to the aid of the Duke thereof with 8,000 men. And for his better furniture in the service the king sent his letters to the mayor of this city who forthwith furnished him with 20 soldiers appointed.

This year Edward Courtney Earl of Devon was made free of this city as son and heir unto Sir Hugh Courtney his father who was a franchised man of this city. This Edward was of a second house unto Thomas Courtney Earl of Devon who taking part with King Henry the 6th was slain at Tewksbury Field in the 10th of King Edward the 4th and he being deceased without any issue made the Earldom descended unto this Edward being the son to Sir Hugh de Courtney son to Sir Hugh de Coureneye the son to Edward Courteneye Earl of Devon ancestor to this Thomas slain at Tewskbury.

This year was made a statute that all such murderers and felons as were convicted and admitted to have the benefit of his clergy should be burned in the hand with the letter M if he were a murderer and with the letter F if he were a felon.

1489

Stephen Ridgeway

This order was taken by the mayor and common by a commandment from the king & council that every man should be furnished and provided of good and sufficient armour for his own person and for all such as were under his charge and government and every man was rated and assessed what and how much he should provide according to his portion and ability.

This year were delivered to the mayor at the day when he was sworn to the office of the mayoralty a certain roll named the Black Roll & a book in the roll were contained the ancient orders, privileges, customs of the government of this city with sundry things appertaining to the sate of this city and in the book the like was contained concerning the city of London and order taken that the same should be yearly delivered from mayor to mayor. This roll in the time of King Edward the 6th was by one Griffeth Ameredith delivered to Sir William Cirvell knight then secretary to the king and never could again be had. And what become of the book it is not known.

1490

John Hooker

This year it was enacted by the mayor & common council that every person being to be made free of the city by fine or redemption and not exercising the trade or traffic should pay but 20s for his fine.

This year died Thomas Callwodley and by whose means was the manor of Awliscombe purchased for the relieving of the poor inhabitants of this city from payment of taxes and tallages and for finding of a chaplain.

1491

Robert Chubb

This year Charles the French king married Ann daughter and sole heir unto Francis Duke of Britanny by means whereof the Duchy of Brittany came wholly and was subjected to the crown of France and the long wars between France and Britain ended and determined.

Richard Fox, bishop of Exeter, and Giles Lord Danberry were sent in an ambassador to Charles the French king for conclusion of a peace which was obtained.

The Lady Margaret Duchess of Burgundy persisting still in a malicious mind against King Henry the 7th raiseth and setteth up Perkin Warbeck the son of one John Osbote of the town of [blank] of a base birth and parentage. This Perkin by devises she named Edward and [torn] him to be the second son of King Edward the fourth and she so cunningly handled the matter that her falsehood was taken for truth and both kings and great estates were eluded and deceived by her. Great troubles ensued thereof but in the end to the reproach of the said duchess. The slaughter of many men and the confusion of the said Parkyn who according to his deserts ended his life with a halter and was hanged at Tyborne.

This year Roger Holland and Thomas Denys Esquires were made and sworn free of the city of Exeter but because they did not inhabit within the city it was accepted that they should not give any voice to the election of any mayor of other officer.

This year the king's second son who was king afterwards was born and Richard Foxe, bishop of Exeter, was his godfather.

1492

John Atwill

This year Richard Fox bishop of Exeter was removed to Bath and there installed and Oliver King, the king's chaplain, Dean of Windsor and Register of the order of the garter, was consecrated bishop of Exeter in February 1492.

1493

John Colshull

This year in the month of February Richard Fox, Bishop of this city, was removed to Bath and Oliver King, chaplain to the king, was installed Bishop of Exeter by John Moreton Archbishop of Canterbury.

This year died John Hoker, lately mayor of this city, a gentleman descended of a worshipful house and parentage. A man of great wisdom, gravity and council which did well appear in him both in the times when he was in office as also when he was burgess for this city of the parliament in the several times of the three kings Edward the 4th, Richard the 3rd and Henry the 7th. A worthy and a good citizen he was and who in sundry respects deserved well of his commonwealth both for his diligent care of the public government and for ministering of justice when he was in office as for his zeal and readiness in all matters for the commonwealth unto which he did so dedicate himself that leaving his own private causes he would attend the same. He was a favourer of all good and godly men, family and friendly to all sorts of people, a keeper of great hospitality beneficial to the needy and liberal to the poor. And the taxes and tallages to the king's in his days being many and great he did so much tender the poor estates that when in the time of his mayoralty the manor of Awliscombe was purchased for the relieving of the poor citizens and inhabitants for payments of taxes and tallages he was a liberal contributor unto the same as also in his last testament remembered the poor in this behalf and further for a mere benefit to the commonwealth and for the ease of the country people coming to the markets he offered to have builded at his own charges a market place for corn in the southgate of this city if death had not prevented him. In the time of his mayoralty he had a regard to keep the true assizes for bread and drink and visited the bakers more often than they were willing. He was also very severe and sharp against all notorious offenders especially adulterers and whoremongers whom he spared not to punish according to their deserts which thing caused and bred some differences between him and the clergy who claimed the punishment and correction of such offences to be incident only with their charge and office.

The king upon a disturbance between Philip Archduke of Burgundy and king of Romans did remove the mart from Antwerp unto his own at Calais but especially for the malicious and indirect dealings of the Lady Margaret Duchess & Dowager of Burgundy who was the author and maintainer of Perkin's Rebellions. But after a few years, when all those troubles were overrun and the premises reconciled the mart was returned again but Antwerp, who having felt the smart of the want of the same mart were not a little joyful for having gained the same and their general processions, bonfires & great banquets did not come and receive the Englishmen at their return.

1494

William Obley

Memorandum that the Company of the Cappers granted to be incorporated the last year now in the beginning of this year fully incorporated. And here understand you that about this time all the several arts, mysteries and occupations within this city were incorporated and every particular artisan within this city was of some one company or other though generally of that art which he professed, but all within the time of the writing hereof are for the most part all dissolved by reason that the fraternities and brotherhoods which were annexed and appended unto them and contributors to the maintenance of the same are dissolved and so by consequences the others not able to maintain their society are likewise dissolved.

1495

John Collwodley

Memorandum it was enrolled that the custom of this city that all and every of the artificiers dwelling within this city and not free of the same shall pay every Wednesday & Friday ob. for all such wares as they shall set to sale until he be free of the city.

Memorandum also that the liberties of the city for cognisance of pleas to be had before the mayor was allowed in certain actions had before Thomas Bryan & his fellow justices of the common bench being in Easter term in the 11th year of the reign of King Henry the 7th.

In the end of this mayor's year 1496 Bishop King died and Richard Redmon then a bishop of Wales was removed from thence and installed here.

1496

John Atwill

Memorandum that this year there was a great division among the citizens about the election of the mayor and for avoiding of the same it was ordered and considered by the mayor and common council that no man should be mayor or officer nor any election should be accepted as good except the same were had and done according to the old and ancient orders of this city. And that there should be a choice made of 12 of the most best and discretetist citizens and these together with the 24 of the common council and these 36 persons should make the choice of the mayor, bailiffs and of all the other officers as also of the 24 which should be of the common council for the year following.

This year was very troublesome as well unto the king and whole realm in respect of foreign wars and intestine rebellions as also unto this city particularly by two several commotions. For concerning the foreign wars James King of Scotland taking part with the Duchess of Burgoyne assisteth and helped Perking Warbeck who named himself Richard Duke of York second son to Edward the 4th invadeth England with sword and fire but he was withstanded and disappointed of his purpose and in the end by the mediation of Richard Fox, late Bishop of Exon, but now of Durham, a peace and a reconciliation was made between the two kings. Concerning the particular suits and insurrections about this city, the first was by the Cornish people under the conduct of Thomas Flamock learned in the laws and Michael Joseph, a blacksmith, for whereas in the last year past a subsidy was granted unto the king towards his charges and great expenses as well in France as within this realm for the disuse thereof. These Cornish people altogether mislike it and utterly refused to pay the same. And understanding that the Earl of Devon was come to the town of Launceston the last of August in commission about the said subsidy of the said people by the writing of the foresaid two ringleaders assembled themselves to the number of 10,000 men and came first to Launceston where the Earl of Devon had been but newly gone away. From thence they marched and came to this city and would have entered in to it but the gates were shut fast and they were denied to come in whereupon they threatened to besiege the city. In this distraff the mayor by the advice of his brethren advertiseth the Earl of Devon and all the chiefest gentlemen of this shire and admitteth their aid and assistance. But none was promised and none were sent. In the meantime the rebels urged to come into this city and to pass through the same which in the end was granted in this order. That the said captains after afore with their waiting servants should come through the city but the whole troop of the soldiers should go without the city about the walls and meet their captains without Eastgate and under condition that neither the captains nor any other person or persons of their companies should do or offer no wrong nor injury to any body or person whatsoever. Whereupon the said captains with the number appointed unto them came into this city and being come up over against the guildhall where the mayor then was the said captains being offended and angry that they were so long kept out began to quarrel with the mayor and threatened to cut off his head in the same place but yet they quietly departed and went to Taunton where the Lord Awdley met them & became to be their general and they began their tragedy. They killed the provost of Penryn in Cornwall who was one of the Commissioners for the said subsidy. And then they marched from thence from place to place until they came to Black Heath where they were slain to the number of 2,500 persons and their captains were taken and executed to death. For the said James Lord Awdley having his coat of arms painted upon paper and reversed and torn was carried from Newgate to Tower Hill and there was beheaded and the other two, Flamock and Joseph, were hanged, drawn and quartered. The second commotion or rebellion was by Perkin Warbeck beforenamed who in the month of September landed at Whitesandbay in Cornwall having but a small company with him for he depended in a great hope of hope of the Cornish people and being landed with such company as he had he marched towards Bodmin. The common people having no sooner heard of his arrival but in great flocks repaired unto him. When he was come to Bodmin he proclaimed himself Duke of York and undoubted heir to the crown of England. The Cornish people having not forgotten their evil success in their rebellion under their own countrymen Flamock and Joseph and now put in good hope to have a better success were in very short time assembled to the number of three thousand persons and these offering their service to this new captain attended upon him and came to this city the 16th day of the said month of September who when they came to this city and could not be suffered to come into the same they besieged it round about and gave sundry assaults thereunto but they were monstrously resisted the enemy having still the repulse and many of them slain. At length when they saw that no assault nor scaling would serve them then as to their last refuge they did determine to force to burn and break open the town gates and so to enter into the city. Wherefore first they burned the North Gate but by reason that they were to all to up against the hill and that a few within were too good for many without they leave that place and went up to the Eastgate which they broke open and with force entered into the city. The Earl of Devon, the Baron of Carew and the most part of the gentlemen both of Devon and of the shires adjoining being not long before advertised of the king's displeasure against them because they had so altogcthcr tofore suffered Flamacke and the blacksmith to pass through the country without any resistance they were now come to this city for avoiding the same. And the earl being in his lodgings in the house called the Black Friars when the gate was thus broken open and the enemy entered as soon as he heard the alarm issueth out with all speed with all such company as he had and could get and cometh into the High Street within the East Gate where he found the citizens and the enemy in hand struck and forthwith he joineth with the citizens and the fight was for the time very hot & firey. And notwithstanding the enemies were all or the most part of them within the gate and had gained a great part of the street even so far as the castle lane yet they were driven back & with force compelled out of the gates. In this fight among others the earl as he issued out of the lane from his house into the street was hurt in the arm with an arrow but he was so little therewith dismayed that both [he] & his son the Lord William Courteney did the more eagerly follow upon the. The enemy begin thus driven out of the city and in despair to do any good against so great a company departed from hence and & marched towards Taunton and there being advertised that the king was coming with his army to encounter with him the secretly fled from thence to the Sancutary of Bewdlye but it was not long before he was taken & executed as in the Chronicles of England it is at large set down. The king when he understood that Parkins was fled came with his whole army unto this city and he tarried until Allhallowtide then next following in punishing of the rebels and quieting of the country. At his first coming he called before him all the noblemen and gentlemen of the country and much blamed them for slackness and breach of duty in that they suffered the blacksmith and the Cornish rebels to pass through the country without any resistance made against them as also for their unkind dealing with this city who had requested their aid therein but could not obtain it. But they all in such humble and wise manner so answered and behaved themselves that the king considering the same and their good services now done that he was satisfied and convinced and commended them for the same. The like he did also with the mayor and the citizens whom he commended for their [?] and very thankfully did accept their good entertainment among them and did in many things amend the manner of their government especially in the election of the mayor and of his officers as in the year following it may appear.

This John Atwill mayor was the fifth time was a very wise man and of a good government as well of his own person as of the common people which were of this city under his charge. He was a gentleman born as were the most part of the mayors of this city in those days. He gave for his arms argent and sable a pike and chaffron voided. He knew what appertained to his duty unto the king as unto all noblemen and to his equals and inferiors as did appear in the third time of his mayoralty when King Richard the third was in this city and now in this his fifth year of his mayoralty when King Henry the 7th as is before said lay in this city. Both which kings favoured and commended him. The nobility which followed him had that entertainment at his hands that they thought him more worthy to be a governor of some great state than this city. The noblemen and gentlemen of this his country found him so substantial and wise in matters of policy and upright dealings that in all matters of importance they always used his advice and council. And as for the governance of this city not many before him and few after him did pass or excel him. And forasmuch as this man was the last of his name which were mayors of this city it were not amiss to set down how God blessed this man in his posterity. This man had only one son, named Henry, whom he had brought up very well in knowledge and learning and made him his heir. After his father's death he contented himself with the lands and livings left unto him and sequestered himself from all manner of trade of other lives or dealing in any office in the common wealth. His father was no more wise than this man was pleasant and full of many conceits but within the compass of honesty and therefore his company was desired of the best and grateful to all men. This man had only one son named Lawrence and two daughters. This Lawrence gave himself to the traffic of merchandise and dwelled in London and was free of the company of the skinners and for a time did prove well & become wealthy and was in promise with one [blank] Smith who afterwards was Customer of London. Thrice two men howsoever they prospered for the time, yet in the end their unfortunate adventures at the seas and their losses at the land was so great that they both became very poor and this Lawrence was so far driven in debt that in the end he sold all the lands & possessions which were descended unto him and which otherwise he had procured and yet all did not help but he was so far indebted as that he could not as the common proverb is able to show his face. But lived in a poor and in a distressed state. At length it pleased god to raise up some good friends unto him by whose means he grew in to credit and beginning anew his former traffics, god blessed and increased the same in such sort tha the waxed wealthy & rich and did not only recover his first estate but increased the same to a far greater wealth both in riches & in possessions and did carry himself in very good credit and continuance and was one of the principal officers under her Majesty in the Custom House of London. In the end of his latter days he being of a good mind to set in his things in good order did make his last [will] and testament anno 1588. And calling to his remembrance the state of his life past in which he had tasted both of wealth of and of woe did accordingly bestow his goods and lands, for to this good friends and kinsfolk he gave liberal legacies and sundry hundreds of pounds. And to the poor besides moneys and other things he gave all his lands to be employed to their uses. Some he gave to the company of the skinners in London of which company he was free. Some he gave to the hospital in Southwark and to the hospital in London for the relieving of the poor orphans and children. And some he gave to this city namely £12 land by the year which yearly with all the increase thereof to be employed in wool and like things by the discretion of the mayor and aldermen for the continual keeping of the poor people and inhabitants of this city in work from time to time for evermore without impairing of the stock or employing the same to any other use. This man closed up his days in godliness and virtue and made a most godly end whose body though it be buried in the earth yet his virtue and name shall live and remain for ever.

This year William Burgayn was chosen Recorder in lieu of Thomas Hext, late Recorder deceased.

Memorandum that this year was granted and gathered a 10th and a 15th through all the city and suburbs for waging of a captain and soldiers in this troublesome time.

Also Mr Robert Newton was committed to the guildhall and there to remain until he had paid his watch money.

1497

William Froste

Memorandum that in this year there lack two rolls of the record of the court in which are set down and written the manner and election of the mayor, stewards and sergeants made and established by the king himself. For in these days the times were more troublesome than was the manner of the election of the mayor and officers of this city which being advertised which being advertised unto the king and he desirous to have the government of this city quiet & peaceable had the mayor & common council of this city before him. And when he had by them learned the manner of their elections and the many troubles which ensued thereof did of himself devise and set down an order which he did establish to continue and delivered the same & engrossed in parchment under his privy seal which from henceforth hath been duly kept and observed. And to begin this order he named one William Froste to be now the first mayor who had been one of the bailiffs of this city in the year before last past but a servant unto the king. And further to encourage the mayor and citizens to be mindful of their duties and to continue dutiful and obedient subjects henceforth as before they had done: he took his sword which then were about his middle and gave it to the mayor together with a hat of maintenance to be borne before him and his successors as it is used in the city of London.

Memorandum this year upon the 6th of November it was first ordered that the mayor and all such as been and shall be mayors shall have his scarlet gown and his scarlet cloak lined with sarsenet and every receiver to have his gown of crimson in grain and every one of the 24 to have his gown of violet or merry colour in grain.

The king during his being and abiding in this city was continually and his council busied and occupied about the matters of the late rebellions and when the principal and chief ringleaders and offenders were punished and executed to death and then of his goodness minding upon sundry humble suits made unto him to execute his mercy to the residue of the rude and penitent commoners he caused them all so many as were within this city to be brought before him in the churchyard of St Peter's within this city and his grace being lodged in Mr Awstell his house then Treasurer of the cathedral church he came forth out of his chamber and stood in a fair long window newly and of purpose builded towards the said churchyard and then and there before him stood at the foresaid offenders bareheaded with halters about their necks and cried out unto the king and prayed for his mercy and pardon. The king after that he for a while beheld and heard them made a short speech unto them and that ended in hope of their amendment he pardoned them all wherewith the people made a great shout hurled away their halters and cried 'God Save The King'. When the king had done all these things and as he thought had set all things in quiet order, yet by reason that it was advertised unto him that sundry notorious offenders abroad and yet not came in to submit themselves he granted out certain commissions as well for apprehending and punishing of them as also for good government of the country for Devonshire and Cornwall were appointed the Baron of Carew with sundry gentlemen of each shires and for Somersetshire was Sir Amys Powlett and others appointed.

This year was the Lady Katherine Gordon wife to Perkin taken at the mont and not long after Perkin himself was taken and executed to death as also Edward Plantagenet Earl of Warwick.

This year Oliver King, Bishop of Exeter died in February and was buried at Westminster and Richard Redman was translated from out of a bishopric in Wales unto this city.

1498

Richard Undye

This year the Scots came to the Castle of Norham which is belong to the Bishop of Durham and for two days together did view the same. And being then demanded by some of the castle what they meant in so doing they gave great very proud answers and quarrelled so long that in the end they fell to blows and divers of the Scots were in the fight killed. When King James was hereof advertised he would never enforce that this private quarrel was a breach of the peace and forthwith sent his herald to King Henry advertising the same. But not long after he being better advised did secretly send his messengers to Bishop Foxe who lay then in his bishopric of Durham and requested him to come and speak with him. The bishop forthwith acquainted King Henry his master herewith who willed [him] to go to the king and being come into Scotland and after sundry communications passed between them the bishop made mention unto the said king that if there might be a marriage had between the said king's eldest son and his master King Henry's eldest daughter. He thought it could be a means of a perfect and personal peace between the said two kings and their realms which mention the said King James so well liked and the said bishop so well followed the same that twas in the end concluded and brought to pass.

Memorandum Roger Holland Esquire after the death of William Burgoyn was chosen Recorder 13 March.

1499

Nicholas Hamlyn

This year a complaint and an information was made against the merchants of England for concealing of the king's customs. Whereupon commissioners were granted and awarded and sundry commissioners were sent abroad to every port and haven town through the whole realm namely to this city of Exeter. The end whereof was that all the merchant adventurers through the whole realm was for the most part found faulty and made fine with the king.

1500

Walter Yorke

Memorandum this year Richard Fox, first Bishop of Exeter and then of Bath and Wells and after of Durham, was upon the death of Bishop William Wayneflete removed from Durham to Winchester and made bishop of the same and so was thereby made prelate of the order of the knights of the garter. And by the means and mediation of this bishop the marriage between James the 4th King of Scots and the Lady Margaret the king's eldest daughter was concluded as the like marriage also was concluded between Prince Arthur the king's oldest son and the Lady Katherine daughter to Ferdinando King of Spain.

1501

John Callwodley

Memordandum that in the beginning of this mayor's year in the month of October the Lady Katherine the spouse of Prince Arthur arrived at Plymouth unto whom forthwith resorted all the knights and gentlemen in these parts and conducted her unto this city and was lodged in the dean's house and had such entertainment as did appertain to so honourable a personage. While she lay in this city the weather was very foul and windy and full of storms by reason whereof the weathercock which was upon the steeple of the church of St Mary the More which is adjoining to the said dean's house did so whistle that the said Princess could not sleep. Whereupon order was taken that some one man should climb up & pull it down which was done but the said man in great danger. And after her departure the same was put up again where it continued until about the year 1580 the wind blew it down and not long after the whole steeple was pulled down. This honourable lady was by conreys [a company or troop] conveyed to London when in the month of November then next following she was married to Prince Arthur and not long after they both were conveyed into Wales and in April following the said prince there died.

The Lord William Courteney son & heir apparent to Edward Earl of Devon and who had married the Lady Katherine, sister to the queen, and they both daughters to King Edward the 4th, upon a suspicion that he was confederated with Edmond de la Poole Duke of Suffolk who was fled into Flanders, he was committed to the tower where [he] continued all the time that this king reigned.

This year Bishop Redman was removed to Ely and there installed bishop of Ely in September 1501 and John Arundell who had been before dean of Exeter but now Bishop of Coventry and Lichfield was removed to this church of Exeter and here was installed the 15th of March 1501.

1502

Walter Champneys

In this year in the month of June the Lady Margaret the king's daughter before by the means of Bishop Fox allied to James the 4th King of Scotland was very honourably sent and conducted into Scotland and there with great solemnity was married.

In this year John Arundell Bishop of Exeter died at London and was buried in the St Clement's church.

1503

Robert Newton,
John Donester,
William Frost

This year was a great plague in this city in which Robert Newton & John Donester mayors and John Guyfte & John Nordon, stewards, died and many [other] people.

This year in June Hugh Oldom, chaplain to the countess of Richmond, the king's mother, was installed bishop of Exeter.

1504

Thomas Andrew

In this year as it doth appear by the records Inquisition was taken upon the deaths of sundry freeholders within this city & dead in the last plague of all such their lands within this city and liberties of the same which all were & are holden of the mayor, bailiffs and commonality as of their chief lords by socage service and it was found that every of them and every like freeholder is to pay for a relief 2s 6d.

Memorandum that about this time it is noted by Erasmus there was a benevolence granted unto the king but I take it that it was in the 11th year of this king which though it were but small yet the common people who cannot brook nor digest any payments of money found to grudge thereat and namely the Cornish people who as the histories do express it did rebel under Flamack and Joseph a blacksmith who were discomfited upon black heath. The king to prevent the troubles which might ensue hereof made choice of the most noble, principal and grave persons to be his commissioners for the levying of the same throughout the whole realm. And for the benevolences to be had of the clergy in the diocese of Winchester the chief Commissioner was Richard Fox bishop of Winchester who according to his commission caused his clergy within his commission to be called before him at places and time appointed. The clergy men though in ability they differ from the laity yet in this they agreed that they were very loath to pay any money and therefore did use all the means and devices which they could to ease themselves from paying or defraying of money. Of these clergymen which came before him they were of two sorts. The one company were very well and comely apparelled, well mounted upon lusty geldings, and well attended with waiting men, every one according to his estate and living. These being brought before the bishop, he persuaded them the best he could to consider the king's necessity, their own safety & the common state of the realm which was and had been sundry ways molested and troubled, and therefore they should be the more the willing to consider the same and to be the more liberal in so good a cause. These men to save their purses alleged for themselves that they were many ways overcharged aswell in keeping of good hospitality & great families as also in sundry other things incident to the same, and to their own private persons that they were very bare of money and therefore desired his lordship to think well of them and to be good unto them. The other company came very beggarly apparelled in cloaks thread bare and the cost of their apparel very simple and slender, nothing answerable to that decency and cleaness as should be in men of their calling & profession And these answered for themselves that their livings & benefices were so mean & small that they could neither keep that hospitality which they wished nor yet were able to support the continual charge which was laid upon them and therefore most humbly prayed his lordship so to consider of them. The bishop being a very wise man and who did look so far in to the state of the clergy as no man better in his time when he saw their fetches [a trick or contrivance] and devises he preventeth the same and with one pretty and wise delivery answereth them both, saying to the first company 'Sirs my brethren, where for your excuse you do allege sundry reasons of your want of money and inability to satisfy the king's request, I do not find your reasons to hold nor your excuses to be true. For by your devout and seemly apparel, your fair palfreys, your attendance of waiting men, your great hospitality and great families and other like charges which you be at, it doth appear that you are rich and wealthy and are not without some store of monies by your to support such continual charges and therefore what so ever be your words, your actions do declare the contrary and there is not reason but that you should pay.' To the other company he said 'your examples are but vain, for I know in what sate the clergy of this land now lieth, your livings are sufficient and good, and the less that you do spend in apparel and hospitality, the more you do save and the more money you have in store and your monies cannot be better employed than by your free and liberal benevolence unto the king's grace at these present and therefore content yourself you must show yourselves dutiful and you shall pay'. And thus by this witty and wise delivery he reduceth the clergy to the payment of this benevolence and this doth Erasmus write of this man, in his book entitled *Ealesaster* or The Preacher.

1505

William Crudge

In this year there was nothing recorded worth the mention other than the ordinary course of the court.

    This year in the month of January Philip son to Maximilian the Emperor and Archduke of Austria having married the Lady Jane sister to the Lady Katherine married to Prince Arthur and she the elder daughter to Ferdinando King of Aragon and Elizabeth his wife Queen and heir of Castile came from out of Flanders minding to pass through the Narrow Seas into Spain. But through foul weather and great storms his whole navy was dispersed and he with his queen was driven in to Weymouth in Dorsetshire and there he landed which being known Sir Thomas Trenchard and Sir John Carew knights made their repair unto him and in all most humble manner saluted him and also made the best provision they could for the entertainment of so honourable a personage and used all the persuasions they could to request his stay until the king was advertised of his there being which he very unwillingly yielded. And forthwith Sir Thomas Trenchard posted away to the king who then lay at Windsor. And left Sir John Carew to attend the said archduke, which Sir John for the honour of the king and his country he sent both to the principal gentlemen of Devon and to the mayor of this city to furnished with a competent number of handsome and chosen men to attend upon him there which was done of which 30 were sent out of this city. And he so attended the said archduke that he never left him so long as he [was] within this realm and until he had taken his ship to depart. The king as soon as he heard of the said archduke's arrival was marvellous glad thereof and sent the earl of Arundel well accompanied to him and who after the delivery of his letters obtained so much of him that he took his horse and rode to the king at Windsor and very shortly after him his wife Queen Jane did also follow whom King Henry most joyfully received and entertained. And after a few days thus spent the said Archduke and his queen took their leave whom the king commanded to be accompanied by sundry of the chiefest lords of the lands and because the said duke being not best able to brook the seas he road straight to Falmouth where he appointed the fleet and navy to attend for him and the king sent his letters to the mayor of this city for the honourable entertaining of the said archduke according whereunto all things against his coming were prepared and he at his coming to the city was honourably received and entertained. And so from hence he was brought to Falmouth where he as soon as wind and weather did serve took ship and departed returning unto the king most hearty thanks by Sir John Carew who never forsook nor departed from the time of his landing until his departure which Sir John Carew at his return unto this city did deliver the 30 men which were sent unto him at Weymouth with his most hearty thanks to the mayor and his brethren.

1506

Richard Hewet

The king this year granted out his commission unto Richard Empson and Edmond Dudley for the execution of outlawries, recognisances, forfeits, routs & riots & all penal statutes who followed the same with all extremity and thereby greatly enriched the king's coffers and filled their own purses which though it were sweet unto them for the time yet in the end it was to their own ruin and loss of their heads.

1507

John Callwodleigh

In this year Richard Fox, bishop of Winchester, was sent an ambassador to Charles, king of Castile, the son of Philip son to Maximilian the Emperor for a marriage to be had between him and his daughter the Lady Mary which was then promised but not performed whereupon she was afterwards allied and married to Lewes the French king in the 6th year of King Henry the 8th.

1508

John Lympeny

This year concerning matters in law little was done in any of the city's courts of record saving only that William Froste, sometimes mayor of this city, died and his will was proved the 11th of May in the Guildhall before the mayor according to the custom of this city. He was a very wise man and his credit being great to the king great good came thereof to this city in the suit of the Scavage against lands and in other things. This year the king, a little before his death, gave a general pardon to all offenders against his lands except some offences & certain persons and did also extend his liberality upon sundry prisoners in the gaols and in the end upon the 22nd of April 1509 he died leaving to his son Henry the Prince great riches and wealth who immediately upon his father's death was proclaimed King of England.

King Henry upon some advice to him given married the Lady Katherine late wife to his brother Prince of Wales. Which marriage Pope Julius did did excuse with all, notwithstanding sundry of his cardinals did not like thereof. And shortly after this marriage he and she were crowned at Westminster in the 24th of June.

This year also William Huntingdon, one of the Stewards, died and for him was chosen one William Mathew. This William Huntingdon was a gentleman born and of pretty possessions about Plymouth and in this city, a man wise and politic of whom was received a good hope that he would have been a necessary and a good member to this commonwealth if he had lived.

This year Empson and Dudley, the Commissioners of late upon penal statutes, were executed to death.

The first year of King Henry the 8th

1509

John Buckenam

In the Guildhall court and in the provost court there was nothing done this year but only ordinary course of common [?].

1510

Thomas Andrew

This year the East Gate of the city which was very ruinous and in decay and shrewdly shaken in the late rebellion & assaults of Perkin Warbeck was now begun to be pulled down & new builded.

1511

William Wilsford

In this year from the month of May all matters in the Guildhall courts did cease and the court from Monday to Monday was adjourned by reason of great troubles and wars now feared to come as it seemeth by the words set down in the records which are these *by reason of insurrections made for the defence of the land against enemies invading the land of England and this is said* and true it is there were great rumours of wars and which afterwards came to effect.

In this year William Wilsford, the mayor, died who was the last of his name that was mayor of this city before whom sundry of his ancestors had with great [missing word] and great credit borne. They were gentlemen of good livelihoods, worship and reputation. Their lands within this city in every was for the most part divided among all their children whereof the writer hereof being descended of some of the daughters both enjoy some portion hereof, by means of which divisions the revenues of this gentleman was so much the less and yet sufficient and good enough. This man had only one son who contenting himself with the fair lands and revenues left unto him in the country as well as within this city, did altogether dwell in the country at his house called Oxton in the parish of Kenton in the county of Devon who having only one daughter she was married to one Jasper Horsey Esquire and their eldest son named George Horsey sold the said house to William Hurst of Exeter Esquire.

1512

John Simons

This year began the troubles which followed both in this year and in others following. For first being requested of his father-in-law Ferdinando King of Aragon for some help and aid against the moors which the king granted and sent the Marquis Dorset and the Lord Brook who passed the seas with an army unto him well appointed. Then he was also requested by the Lady Margaret Duchess of Savoy Governor of

Flanders and the Low Countries for aid against the Duke of Golders unto whom was sent Sir Edward Poynings and others with a sufficient company of archers and others. Then preparation was made of a fleet to keep & scour the seas aswell against Andrew Barton, a Scottish pirate as also for the invading of France.

The king minding to invade France did sent to this city for 30 soldiers to to attend & serve him in his wars of Franch which was done and a 10th & 15th was levied within this city for the furnishing & setting them forth well appointed. The like letters were before sent for the furnishing of certain voluntary men to attend & serve the Lord Brook which was also performed.

1513

Richard Huet

Memorandum that Hugh Oldom Bishop of Exeter sued one Robert Laskey Bishop who was a condemned prisoner in his gaol for breaking of the said gaol which said Robert the Bishop did acquit, release and discharge upon condition that he would absent and forswear the diocese of Exeter.

The king this year denounced wars against the king of France and prepared a mighty navy at the seas and appointed Captains for every ship of which one was named *The Regent* in which Sir John Carew and Sir Thomas Knevill were captains of seven hundred men in the same. And taking the seas under Sir Edward Haward Lord Admiral they met with the French fleet between whom was a great fight and this *Regent* being then grappled with a mighty ship well appointed called the *Great Carick* of Brest they were grappled and a French gunner distrusting the success set the *Carick* on fire and by that means both ships were burnt with all their companies of the same and so Sir John Carew and Sir Thomas Knevel were both burned.

This year there was given to the king towards his expenses in the wars a certain subsidy after this rate: every knight to pay 20s, every man having £40 in land to pay 20s, £20 land 10s, £10 in land 5s and 40s in land 2s. And every man worth in goods £800 to pay 52s 4d and £400 in goods to pay 40s, and £200 in goods to pay 27s 8d, and every £100 in goods to pay 14s 4d, every £40 to pay 6s 8d, every £20 to pay 3s 4d, every £10 to pay 20d, every £5 to pay 12d, and every man receiving 20s in wages to pay 6d, and every one of the age of 15 years to pay 4d and every Denison to pay double the Englishman.

Also Sir Edmond Carew knight baron of Caew lying at the siege of Tyrowyn and as he sat in council with Sir Charles Somerset, Lord Herbert and Lord Chamberlain in his tent he was with a shot out of the town slain in the midst of them and thus was the last baron of the name.

This year was Sir Thomas Denys knight chosen recorder of this city.

1514

John More

An inquisition was taken this year before the mayor upon the several deaths of Lady Katherine, Countess of Devon, Richard Holier, William Fursedon, John Obley, Anne Wyllsford, John Fortescue and Robert Batyn and by the same it was found that every of the said persons was seized of their lands within this city of their deaths and did hold each some in free socage of the mayor and commonality of every of them 2s 6d for a release.

This John not long after than he had been mayor did together with one Bartholomew Fortescue Esquire build certain almshouses upon the east end of Exe Bridge reserving to themselves for term of their life the nomination and placing of the poor in the said houses but after their deaths the same to remain in the mayor, bailiffs and commonality. And very shortly after these houses so builded he forsake the city and dwelled in Collumpton parish where he was born and was the son of Roger More of Morhayse Esquire. He was a younger son and being an apprentice to a mere merchant of this city he by good haspe did prosper very well and became very wealthy and did very much good in the commonwealth of the city as well in the time of his mayoralty as at all other times.

1515

William Crudge

Sir Thomas Denys knight followed a suit before the mayor and bailiffs against John Cole Tinner in an action of trespass done within the jurisdiction of the Stannary.

This year the custom for paying of the diurnal within this city was tried in the Guildhall.

Also in this year was born the Lady Mary the king's first daughter and she being proclaimed Princess of Wales, Doctor Voysye, then Dean of the Queen's Chapel and of the St Peter's Church of Exeter, was appointed to be under her a Governor in Wales.

1516

John Buckenam

Richard Fox, sometimes Bishop of Exeter but now of Winchester, with the help of Hugh Oldeham of Exeter founded and builded Corpus Christi College in Oxford. This man was a very famous man as few better in his age being well learned, a wise and a grave man and to the king most trusty and faithful. He was sometimes a student in Paris in the time of King Richard the 3rd and at the time of Henry Earl of Richmond came together from Venice to crave and desire help of Charles the King of France for his recovery to the crown of England which he was persuaded and solicited to do by many or rather the most part of the choicest and most principal peers and noblemen in England. And being at Paris he above all others used the advice and followed the counsel of this Richard Fox, for he was a councillor of great judgement and a man of most sound integrity by means whereof he grew into such credit with the king and the whole states of the realm as that in all matters of counsel weight and importance every man did submit himself to his judgement. And therefore for the most part he was the chosen ambassador to all foreign princes with whom by reason of his wisdom and integrity he could & did much prevail. The king was so much affected unto him as to no man more. First he made him bishop of Exeter, then of Bath and Wells, after of Durham & lastly of Winchester and would have preferred him to be archbishop of Canterbury but that he refused it. He was godfather to King Henry the 8th and unto him after the death of the king his father he was a most trusty and a faithful counsellor. There was a great emulation [to strive to rival or equal] between him and the Earl of Surrey after[wards the] Duke of Norfolk. For after the death of King Henry the 7th by means of the Countess of Richmond, grandmother to the king whose care and drift was to advance unto authority such personages as were worthiest and of greatest integrity. By means whereof these two men were chiefly put in trust and had the special charge in the government of the commonwealth. And according to the trust committed unto them they acquitted themselves in all matters whatsoever which either touched the king or the commonwealth. But in the things they differed and lived in suspicion the one of the other. The bishop contented himself with his own possessions being no craver for any more but the earl for the advantage of his own house and the increase of his inheritance seemed to apply himself the more for the attaining thereof. But both agreed in this that they were careful the one at home in matters of counsel and the other aboard in matters of war, and both in all causes of policy, truth and dutifulness to serve the king and commonwealth. And yet their secret emulations did sometimes break out into such jars [discords or disputes] that the Lords of the Council would no suffer it to increase between but used such means that the same were appeased and they reconciled and made friendly. This bishop being a very good man and a great learned man and desirous to have some monument of his zeal and love towards learning and the service of god began to build a college in Oxford about the beginning of the reign of this king and with the help of Hugh Oldham Bishop of Exeter he finished it this year. He first meant to have made the same a house for religious persons but by persuasion of Bishop Oldham he made it a college for learned scholars. In his later days he waxed blind and by that means the more unfit to serve in public affairs and yet such a man he was for wisdom, knowledge, being expedient and truth that he left not his like at that time after him.

1517

Thomas Hunt, baker

This year Nicholas Staplehill the eldest steward died in December and for him John Richards was chosen who also died in March following and for him Mathew Long was chosen who continued the rest of the year.

This year was the evil May Day in London between the Londoners and Strangers whereof did follow great troubles for the time.

In these days it was an usage in this city that the Receiver and Bailiffs did yearly at the time of the election of the new mayor and officers to keep breakfast and dinners for the mayor and officers and all comers and goers which being very chargeable to the said officers and some of them exceeding their ability were decayed thereby. And yet no commodity given thereby to any person. The foresaid Richard Duke now Receiver with the advice of his brethren and [?comptenors] gave over this custom and kept no breakfasts at all wherefore they were assessed to their fines. This order did the Receiver and Stewards keep the next year following and kept no dinner at all whereupon in the next year following Anno 1519 Geoffrey Lewes being then mayor an order was taken by the mayor and 24 that the Receiver and Stewards should as in times past keep yearly their dinners and breakfasts upon pain that who so made default should pay the fine of 40s whereupon some of the said officers thought I far better to pay the fine of 40s than to spend £20 in a breakfast but the more part of them partly standing upon their vain reputation and partly persuaded thereunto continued the custom until the coming of the honourable Lord Russell who was made Lieutenant of this country by whose means counsel and advice and order was made 21 of September in the 4th reign of King Edward the 6th that no more such dinners should be kept but in lieu thereof every Receiver should pay £5 or £4 and every Steward to pay £4 or £3 6s 8d at the discretion of the mayor & 24. And these fines should be bestowed yearly toward the reparation of the town walls.

1518

William Crudge

This year was commenced a great suit between the parson of St Mary Steps and one J. B. tenant to William Peryam for and concerning the diurnals which the said parson demanded.

This year Robert Tooker of this city married Joan the widow of one James Pole who dwelled in Old Durwood and was tenant unto the city. This Robert Tooker being married the mayor would have expulsed him out of the house but he kept perforce from him whereupon there was great questioning and fighting among them and the said Robert Tooker was by one of the sergeants maimed in one of his hands whereupon he made a suit at the law against the party for a maim and by reason the said Tooker had served in Spain under the Lord Brook and had done very good service his case was the better considered and his damages was the greater and having thus given a piece of money he did so employ the same that in process of time he he waxed rich and was in the end mayor of this city.

In the end of this mayor's year in the month of July 1519 the good and reverend father Hugh Oldham bishop of Exeter died and was buried in his own church in a chaple which he builded of purpose for the same. He was born in Lancashire and chaplain to the Lady Margaret Countess of Richmond mother to King Henry the 6th and in great credit with her and by her and by her means he was promoted to great ecclesiastical livelihoods and among others he [was] first a prebendary and a canon of this church of Exeter and then dean of the same and lastly bishop. He was a wise man but very rough and plain and albeit he was not very much learned yet a great favourer and a friend both to learning and to learned men and in his church & diocese he preferred very few or none to any ecclesiastical livings unless he was learned which bred unto him great credit and estimation. He was a special benefactor to the building of Corpus Christi College in Oxford. He built a free school in Manchester and did many other things worthy of memory as is partly touched in the Catalogue of the bishops of Exeter collected by the writer hereof. He was very temperate in all his doings and for his diet as it was according to his estate so was he therein very precise to keep his preferred and accustomed hours namely at 11 of the clock for his dinner and 5 of the clock for his supper and for this purpose he kept a clock in his house and appointed one special man to keep the same. But many times by reason of his business he would break his hour and then must clock keeper frame his clock accordingly for how so ever the day went the clock must strike 10 or 11 or 5 according as my lord was to dine or sup. Whereupon many times some of the household would ask the clock keeper what time of the day it was, he would answer as it pleased my lord and when he was ready to go to dinner or supper, the bishop understanding hereof would of many of purpose ask his said man what was the clock and he would answer him as explaineth your Lord for if you be ready to go to dinner the clock will be a 11th whereat the bishop would smile and go his way.

In his time there was [a] woman dwelling in his town of Kyrton [Crediton] which accused before him of witchcraft and sorcery against whom he was very hard and extreme. It happened that the bishop fell sick and finding small help by the physicians he was committed to send for this woman but he utterly refused it. Nevertheless partly by the extremity of his sickness and partly by persuasion of his friends he was contented and she was sent for. So he of the contrary sides remembering the hard dealings of the bishop towards her denied and utterly refused to come unto him, nevertheless in the end upon many entreaties she was persuaded and went unto the bishop. When she came before him and after some speeches between them she willed him to say after her these words as she spoke them 'Hugh Oldham by they full name, Arise up in God's name' which he did and therewith he arose up in his bed, then said she 'and lie there down again the devil's name', and so he did but what virtue so ever was in her charm he never recovered nor yet rose out of his bed after, which if were so he had his deserts that contrary to God's commandment and his own knowledge he would seek to such persons for remedy.

The French king this year redeemed the city of Turney which upon payment of certain thousands of crowns was delivered unto him.

1519

Geoffrey Lewes

This year an order and an act was made by the mayor & 24 that the receiver & stewards should yearly keep three dinners and breakfasts at the times of the election of the new mayor & officers according to the old custom upon pain to forfeit & pay £4.

This year it was ordered and agreed that every alderman which hath been once mayor of this city shall at and after his death leave his scarlet cloak or robe to the chamber of this city which order William Crudge and John Buckenam late mayors and deceasing this year did perform.

This year the almshouses upon Exe bridge were built by John More late mayor of this city and Bartholomew Fortescue upon consideration that they and every of them during their lives should have the nomination of such poor people as should dwell in the same.

Thomas Slapton who was Receiver of this city this last year being called to make his account did depart out of this city's liberties and dwelled in the fee of St Sidwell's without East Gate and refused to make any account until in the end he was forced and compounded to do it.

This year John Voysie, Doctor of the laws and Dean of the king's Chapel and of the Cathedral Church of this city, was made Bishop of Exeter. A man for his learning, wisdom and good behaviour had in great favour both with the king and council. He was godfather to the Lady Mary, the king's daughter and Princess of Wales. Under whom he presideth of the principality of Wales for sundry years to his great praise and commendation.

William Crudge, mayor, the last year of this city, died this year. He was first a tanner, but being maimed by one that quarrelled with him he sued him at the law for a maim and by that means he received such damages that by the good employing thereof he became very rich and wealthy and was great purchaser of lands and best to his posterity a fair and a large revenue to live thereby as gentleman. He was somewhat self-willed and not easily to be removed from the opinion which he had received which was on occasion sometimes of some disliking between him and his brethren. To the commonwealth he was very about and affected and his purse strings never shortened to do good to his country. His son lived after him in the degree of a squire and gave for his arms which were assigned and given unto him – argent a bend assure between two griffins constant sables upon the bend 3 rooks or ravens.

John Buckenam late mayor & who deceased the last year past was descended of good parentage and born in Suffolk but being a younger brother and brought to this city became to be a merchant and waxed very rich and wealthy. He had been twice mayor of this city and in great wisdom and uprightness did behave himself in those affairs. For which he was greatly reverance and esteemed & so much the more that he kept a very good house and a liberal hospitality. He had no children but he left his goods to a nephew of his own name named William Buckenam.

This year was the evil May Day in London.

This Geoffrey Lewes mayor this year was born in Wales and a tailor by art but using drapery did grow to good wealth. A wily wise man and very provident in all his doings. He was very good to the poor and much affected to the Lazar House of the Maudlyn without the south gate of this city over whom he was made warden and so continued warden many years even unto his dying days.

1520

John Broadmene

1521

John Nosworthy

In this year was the Monday called Mase Mondy or Cockwood Fool or rather Woodcock Fool for by reason that some certain Frenchmen were coasting upon the narrow seas and had made some spoils. Some men by the sea sides having seen a fleet of ships at the seas noised & gave advertisement that it were enemies which would come aland & spoil the country. At which news being upon a sudden all the people of this city & country werer so amazed that they knew not what to do. But it was who that could run out of the city, some to Cockwood, some to Haldon, some to Dawlish and some elsewhere. The mayor in this hurley burley seeing the people thus disorderly to run out of the city commanded the gates to be shut & made fast, but in the end the fleet which was seen was of merchants who having been at Rochelle for salt & else where passed hence into Flanders.

This year the Duke of Buckingham was beheaded.

Cardinal Wolsey passed this year over to Calais & carried the broad seal of England with him.

This John Nosewortheye the mayor was a very wise and a learned man, professing the laws of this realm, who governed so well this city that none or few before him did better. For the least all his private business and did wholly attend the causes of the commonwealth which he reformed many abuses and established many good orders. First, heretofore the great disorders of the courts of the Guildhall and of the provosts and caused to be made a great press with leaves, locks and keys for the safe keeping of the records which tofore lay abroad without any key and by that means all the records of the from the Conquest until the end of King Henry the third were kept and the writer hereof by chance found one court roll of the said King Henry's reign in a tailor's shop without East Gate of this city. He prescribed and did set out the duties of every particular officer and restrained them to the keeping of them. The attorneys of the courts he caused to be sworn for their just dealings in their clients' causes. In this year there was a dearth and a scarcity of corn and for the ease of the poor commoners he caused to be made a general provision of corn which thing having not been done and the common people finding the benefit thereof did the more like and love him. He reduced the corn market to be kept at certain hours and for the same did cause a bell to be set up which should be rung always at the beginning and at the ending of the market. But at the half market he caused the said [bell] to be tolled for until that time only the free citizens and inhabitants had the liberty to buy but after the bell was tolled then it was lawful for every foreigner to buy. He was very vareful to see the assize of bread & ale to be kept. He was very sharp and severe against notorious offenders but very friendly & loving to the good & honest. He was a great peacemaker especially among his neighbours for it he did understand of any dissatisfaction among them he would use all the good means he could for the ending thereof. He was a good housekeeper and kept good hospitality. Finally, he did so wisely and uprightly behave himself that he was honoured of the best reverence of the inferior and beloved of all being reputed the father of the commonwealth. In the end his brethren of the 24 considering that he had left at his own private business and had wholly dedicated himself to the service of the commonwealth which besides his travels was somewhat the more chargeable unto him, they did present and give unto him a piece of money above his ordinary allowance for charges.

In this man's time there was the Mazed [dazed or crazed] Monday called Cockewood or rather Woodcock Fool for news was brought to this city by one came from Cockwode that there was a great fleet or navy seen at the seas of the king's enemies and that they would seize and take land upon these coasts. The people being astounded at this sudden news as amazed at was who could first run out of the town and came towards the seaside they knew not where. The mayor seeing this Hurley Burley and saw that the most part of the people now run out of the town caused the town gates to be shut and would not suffer any more to go out of the gates but took order as was thought good for the safe keeping of the city. But in the end it was but a fleet of merchants bound eastwards.

1522

Richard Duke

This Richard Duke was a gentleman born but being a younger brother he gave himself to the study of the laws of the realm wherein he was well learned and practised and did much good to the commonwealth of this city and by whose advice as well all matters in law as of counsel were by him directed he was of great familiarity with Nosworthy the mayor the year past, they both being must and learned the city was the more to be governed under such men for they did not only continued and see to be kept the good & wholesome ordinances of this city tofore made but also did as occasion required amend and augment the same. And in these days the city was so well governed as it was not better in any way before. For the mayor and magistrates applied their offices, executed justice, punished vice and did govern in truth and diligence. The common council did daily assemble themselves and left nothing undone which might be for the good and benefit of the commonwealth. Every inferior was humble, obedient and dutiful to his superior, all controversies were appeased and all debates pacified. And by these means every man lived in his calling.

The mayor finding the many incommodities which did arise and grown by the common alehouses and tippling houses by reason of drunkenness, whoredom and other evils which in them were maintained he would not suffer any one to keep such houses but that he should be first bound for keeping of good rule in their houses.

This year was a controversy between the parishioners of St Mary the Moor and one John Bonefant concerning a messuage or tenement in the South Gate Street of the said city of which one Richard Russell, one of the 24, was a feoffee of trust to the use of the said parish. And when the matter was come to a trial and a jury returned the said Bonefant showed forth a release of the said Richard Russell, by which means the parishioners lost their lands. The mayor and common council not liking such untrusty dealing of any of their company called him before them and for the same his fact they dismissed him of their company and disenfranchised him of the liberties of the city.

In this year was a Parliament holden at the Black Friars in London for which John Nosworthie and John Bridgeman were burgesses for this city. Which Bridgeman was a wise man and of great experience having served in the wars in Spain under the Lord Brook of whose wardrobe he had the charge. In this Parliament there was demanded a subsidy of 4s the pound, whereat the most part of the lower or common house grudged and murmured, and no man spake more earnestly and effectively against the same than this Bridgeman which thing being made known onto the cardinal he sent for him and very sharply rebuked him for it but he maintained his sayings and at his next coming to the Lower House when the said bill was again read the spake against it. But he had so little thanks for his labour and being again most sharply rebuked that he never enjoyed himself but returned to the lodging where he fell sick and died and was buried in the Savoy in the Strand in London.

This year the Emperor Charles returning from out of Flanders towards Spain took England in his way and visited the king, his uncle, and during that time wars were proclaimed by them against the French king. Immediately whereupon the Earl of Surrey then Lord Admiral was sent to the seas who landed in Britain and won the town of Morlaix.

This year the Turk took the Rhodes.

1523

John Symonds,
Thomas Hunt

This John Symons died the 28th of Setepmber being Tuesday and the next day after the election of the new mayor one Thomas Hunt, baker, was chosen to occupy the place until William Hurst the new mayor chosen did return from London & took his oath. And albeit he were then absent yet all the residue of the officers then chosen were sworn according to the custom. This John Symons was a wise gentleman and servant to the king being his Customer for Devon

This year Christwernus King of Denmark who had married the Lady Elizabeth sister to the emperor was banished out of his kingdom and came to Dover to see the king, her uncle, and unto them Bishop Voysey of Exeter & the earl of Devon were sent with divers lords & knights to receive him and they conducted him from Dover to Greenwich to the king where he was received with great honour.

This year the city lent unto the king one thousand pounds which was repaid again.

1524

William Hurst

This year this mayor was much troubled about the punishment of one Joan Luter who being a well favoured woman and sweet fair and standing much in her own liking she slocked [to draw or lead away] many unto her and was become a very strumpet and a harlot. And for the same she was sundry times called before the mayor and council to take some course of life. Notwithstanding she continued in her accustomed manner and her misrule was such and so great that daily complaints were made thereof. But when no way could help nor counsel & admonitions prevail, the mayor fetched her from out of her house and carried her to ward to be carted, her lovers and companions taken this in grief used all the ways & means that they could to greet her to be delivered & could not, they quarrelled with the mayor as he going in the street and they were so hot that one Beamond, then the sword bearer and going before the mayor, was driven for the defence of his master to draw out his sword and to fight. Nevertheless, they had the worst side and she was carted and the most part of her champions, some were after killed, some hanged, some died in the pocks, and some went a begging and they all for the most part had a bad end. Upon occasion of this riot and rout an order was made by the mayor & 24 that what person soever were once banished and punished and carted in a ray hood for their evil and naughty life they from thenceforth should not be suffered to dwell and reside any more within the city and liberties of the same. And that every mayor suffering and permitting the contrary to pay the fine of 20 marks and the same to be defaulted by the receiver of the city for the time being out of his pension.

This year Cardinal Wolsey obtained a license of the king to suppress certain small monasteries to erect, build and endow his two colleges at Oxford & Ipswich which in the end was an introduction to suppress & dissolve all the monasteries of religious houses in England which after followed.

1525

William Benet

This year the farm for weapons forfeited for breaking of the peace was set to Richard Faux.

The Lord Henry Courtteney Earl of Devon was created Marquis of Exeter.

This year was doubted would be troublesome and that the commons would rebel about denying the subsidy as for by the Cardinal demanded but murmured at in the parliament house as is before said. The king therefore . . . & released the said demands casting the fault upon the cardinal. The writer hereof was born this year *next to the last day of October [?]*.

1526

Henry Hamlyn

This year the English angel was enhanced in Flanders and thereupon the merchants of England lost all the commodities of the realm to be trafficked. And did carry over only anglets and old gold. The king then understanding the same did enhance his gold from 40s the ounces to 45s and by that means the English gold with an overplus was in short time recovered home again.

1527

John Brytnall

This year the custom was extended concerning the child's portion and it was proved that if any died leaving wife and children his goods was to be divided into three parts whereof the wife was to have one third part and the children are to have one other third part and the executor or administrator to have the other third part. But if he had children and no wife then the goods are to be divided into two equal parts whereof the children are to have the one moiety [half] and the executor or administrator is to have the other moiety or halfendeale of the goods.

This year John Broadmore, sometimes mayor of this city and one of the aldermen of the same, did obstinately or rather forwardly refuse to give account and to pay such debts as he did owe to the chamber of the city and also being sundry times sent for to come to the common council did also refuse to come whereupon a fine of 10 marks was set upon his head and also ordered that he should come and submit himself to the chamber or otherwise to be disenfranchised and this being advertised unto him he came to the house at the next assently of the mayor and 24 and then and there did submit himself. A good precedent when the magistrates without respect of persons and without affections do minister justice uprightly as well to persons of higher callings as to the lower. This John Broadmore was a man of great wealth in these days and purchased very fair lands & possessions to his son Lawrence Broadmore but he sold it and what became of him it was never known.

This year an order was taken that every receiver of this city for the time being should yearly bestow upon the reperation of the city walls the sum of £10 and that the mayor for the time being should yearly appoint four men of the common council to be assistance to the mayor for the doing thereof.

The pope at these presents was in captivity and Cardinal Wolsey for the redeeming of him 16 barrels of gold. And the said cardinal also being with the emperor about the pope did cause the king to make breach of peace with him and also caused wars to be denounced & proclaimed by the king against the emperor.

This year the ambassadors came to the king from the French king and the Marquis of Exeter was sent to receive them who met them at Black Heath and from thence he conducted them to the king.

This year died the worthy and good citizen John Nosworthie.

1528

Robert Butler

This year the king was persuaded by Doctor Longsland Bishop of Lincoln and his successor that his marriage with the Lady Katherine, wife sometime to his brother Prince Arthur, was not lawful. Whereupon being grieved & unquieted in mind sendeth to the chiefest & most part of the universities in all Europe Doctor Cranmer, after Archbishop of Canterbury, and likewise to the two universities Oxford & Cambridge which did fully agree at the first in the matter and namely Doctor Moreman in Oxford but in the end by the conscience of the best the marriage was condemned.

1529

Robert Hoker

This year the Turks with a great army invadeth Hungary and cometh to Vienna in Austria and assaulted the same 11 several times but he had repulse and with the loss of many thousands he was driven with shame to raise his siege and to depart.

The king being upon the sundry advertisements from the best learned men in all Europe troubled in conscience and at length persuaded that his marriage with his brother's wife was unlawful and against the laws of God, did sue a divorce against the queen and Cardinal Wolsey being a judge delegate in the cause did so vainly trifle in the matter that the king was offended with him for the same.

A parliament was kept this year at the Black Friars in London where were many complaints and bills exhibited against the cardinal and also against the whole charge of England and they all condemned in a prenuncio and the cardinal then being out of favour was licensed to go & to depart to York. And then Thomas Cromwell, sometimes the cardinal's man, was called to the king's service and grew in great favour with the king.

This aforesaid Robert Hooker was the youngest son to John Hoker sometimes mayor of this city, a man very well learned in the civil law and being the youngest child of 20 he in his father's time was Registrar of Barnstaple and after his father's death in very short time was the sole heir to his father all his brethren and sisters being dead without any issue. In his mayoralty he bore himself so upright every way that none before him had run better. He was a great peace maker and in his year few old matters were followed in his court and as few were new begun before him.

1530

John Blackealler

Memorandum that by the custom of the city of Exeter every person condemned in any action in the courts of this city is to pay to the sergeants for living of the same one penny of every shilling if the condemnation be 40s and under but if it be above the party condemned shall pay 12d of every pound.

The Cardinal Wolsey was by the king's commandment arrested by the earl of Northumberland and by him delivered to the Earl of Shrewsbury to be brought to London and by the way at Leicester he died by his own procurement as it is thought.

The clergy agree and compound with the king for the preeminence & give him one hundred thousand pounds. They proclaim the king Supreme Head of the Church, *roi d supere*, unto the king do renounce the pope.

In this mayor's year in May 1531 John Ryse, Treasurer of the Cathedral Church of St Peter's, died. He was at that aged about 90 years, he was chaplain to Edward the 4th and a man very well disposed. He was a great housekeeper and of good hospitality, liberal to scholars and good to the poor. He builded the new Labrador House in the Church and had appointed to have given some portion of land to the Chantry priests called the Annuellers for keeping of hospitality. He was very frugal in his apparel, never wearing any other shoe than a single soled shoe. He never came to the fire to warm himself and being advised by a friend of this that considering his age he should use warmer apparel, wear lined shoes and to sit by the fire he said 'what shall I then do when I am old?', he was marvellously blinded in the popish religion and did take order that one thousand masses should be said for his soul upon he should be dead. The writer hereof was his godson and his father was his executor.

1531

Gilbert Kyrke

The foresaid Thomas Andrew, whose testament according to the custom of this city was proved this year, was a very famous and a good citizen. By art and profession he was a tailor and was twice mayor of this city and in those offices did very well and worshipfully acquit himself therein every way with good credit. And notwithstanding he had at his death sundry children in remembering his own first beginning he had as good a care for the poor people to be yearly relieved for ever after his death as he had of his own children. And therefore he provided lands wherewith 12 poor people are yearly to be relieved with gowns, hosen and shoes and with some money by such his heirs as who by his last will are charged therewith. And which hither to is truly kept.

The king this year upon the persuasions and resolutions of the best learned divines that the marriage with his brother's wife was unlawful and against the law of god he forsaketh her bed and in the end by judgement of the church he is divorced. And not long after he having good liking of the Lady Anne Boleyn he created her Marchioness of Pembroke and in the year following he married her.

This year one Thomas Benet, a master of art, was detected, arrested and condemned for heresy. He came from Oxford secretly to this city and here lived in private manner by teaching of children but in the end notwithstanding he lived most godly and virtuously yet the same being not liking the papists he was convented before the bishop and his clergy, they condemned him and delivered him to the secular power to be burned and the execution whereof was committed to Sir Thomas Denys then Sheriff of Devon and Recorder of this city. And he having received his writ *for the burning of heretics* commended his petty officers to set up the stake in Southernhay for burning of him. But the mayor and common council of the city would not suffer it and therefore he was carried to Livery Dole where he was burned. The manner of this whole history the writer hereof hath penned and set down at large and it is recorded in the book of the acts and monuments set forth by Mr John Foxe.

This year the chantry priests or annuellers of St Peters had erected and builded a pale before the new builded Calendarhay but it was pulled down by the citizens.

Memorandum that in this year by means of the Lord Cromwell the city obtained a grant of the king to be justices of the peace within their self by which means they avoidest great troubles which daily did grow unto them by the vexation of John Northebroke. Sir Thomas Denys, the Recorder of this city, did then attend at the court and he being made acquainted of the suit by Mr Blackaller did promise to further the same but in deed he was a secret hinderer thereof as the suitors for the same at their home did report.

1532

William Peryam

This year the mayor & common council & the whole commons were much troubled by one John Northbrooke but in the end he was so bounden that he remained quiet.

The king this year was divorced from Queen Katherine and married the Lady Anne Bulleyn, Marchioness of Pembroke, and in the same year the Lady Elizabeth, her daughter, now Queen of England, was born unto whom the Marchioness of Exeter was godmother.

This year died Sir William Courteney at Powderham.

This year one John Welshman, being given to too much blind prophelisising did interpret and apply them to the reproach of the king wherefore he was attainted of treason and hanged, drawn & quartered at the foches of Ringswell.

The foresaid William Peryam was a man born at Broad Clyst and of good parentage, his father being a franklin [a freeman or freeholder]. Having some care of him they brought him to this city and bound him apprentice to a Capper which was an occupation very good in those days and until the use of hats was received out of Spain and of himself being greedy to profit in the knowledge of his art did apply it so diligently that he did grow both in knowledge and in wealth and in the end, finding a better way to employ that which he had gotten to his better advantage, began to be a tin merchant and also an owner of sundry tin works and by that means he grew to good wealth and riches. He was but a plain dealing man but rough and soon offended if he was abused and which wrongs he would not lightly lay up. In his office of the mayoralty he behaved himself very upright and indifferent and wherein he would do nothing but by the advice of men of good knowledge and experience and by so much the better was his government. He left behind him two children, a son and a daughter, his son he caused to be brought up in knowledge and learning and at time convenient did put him to be an apprentice to a merchant of whom and of his issue how profitable member they were to the church of God and the commonwealth as shall be hereafter declared in his place. He died a very old man aged about 90 years.

About this time one Peter Carleighe, Doctor of Divinity and a canon of St Peter's, preached against purgatory where he said among other speeches that if the pope could deliver souls out of purgatory and would not do it without money nor of charity it were pity saying he were not in purgatory himself. This man waxed to be famous for his learning and preachings whereof when the king heard he sent for him to hear him preach who among other things he inveighed against adultery and fornication did for proof allege Terenz. The king, after sermon, finding the weakness of the man and the slenderness of his doctrine, willed [him] to go again to school to Oxford and be better learned before he did preach any more.

1533

Richard Martyn

Memorandum the pope and his usurped authority was utterly exiled and banished out of this land and in open [?] condemned. And the lords of the realm, and all governors and principal men were sworn to the king against the pope.

This year the Reverend and Godly Father Hugh Latymer was sent by the king with a commission to preach the gospel and came to this city in the month of June 1534. The first sermon which he made was in the churchyard of the grey friars without South Gate about the middle of which sermon it began somewhat to rain but yet he continued for the which his sermon and the people notwithstanding the rain, some for the good liking of the eloquence of the man, some for the novelty of the doctrine and some for malice to entrap him, they all abode and tarried out the sermon. And he himself being somewhat earnest his nose fell ableeding which caused him to end his sermon sooner then he thought to have done. The Friars not digesting nor brooking his sermon because it tended altogether against idolatory, superstition and popery which [was] one [of] the pillars & grounds of their religion they cursed and banned the man & interpreted his bleeding to be a sign of god's vengeance upon him for preaching of heresies. Nevertheless, the master and warden of the said Franciscans whose name was John Cardemaker had such liking of this doctrine that not long after he became a scholar and a preacher of the same and who for the testimony thereof was afterwards burned. This 2nd sermon he made in the parish of St Mary the more upon the feast day of the dedication of the said church which though it were a work day through the whole city yet in that parish the highest holy day in the year, When he came hither to preach the clergymen were very loath he should so do alleging the first to be so high and holy for a sermon day for they had in procession to be gone about the parish and many holy ceremonies and solemn mass to be sung and this time would not serve for that and for a sermon also. Nevertheless the commission took place and into the pulpit went Mr Latymer where the audience was so great and the church so full that the church glass windows were broken open for the people to hear the sermon, who the more he was he heard the more he was liked. At this sermon were sundry ladies and gentlemen attending and accompanying the Lady Margaret Dowglas the king's niece who at that time was in this country. All which ladies and their companies dined that day with Mr Hooker, father to the writer hereof, for he was the chief and principal of that parish. The master sermon which he made was in the charnel house which was then standing in the churchyard of the said city out of which house was a pulpit in the north wall towards the churchyard. At this sermon the auditory was marvellous great and attentive. About the middle of the sermon one Thomas Carew Esquire being advertised of this sermon came to the same and he not digesting the same approached and drew nearer to the pulpit and there breathed out his intemperate speeches against the preacher calling him heretic, knave and bade him come down or else he would (as he deeply swore) pull him by the ears and do to him I can not tell what. Nevertheless the good man proceeded and made an end of his sermon but the said Mr Carew receiving small thanks when the king was advertised thereof.

The foresaid Richard Martyn the now Mayor was a gentleman descended form a worshipful house being a second son to Sir William Martyn of Pydleton Pydlehampton in the county of Dorset and to Lady [blank] his wife, daughter to Sir Amys Pawlet knight and brother to Sir Hugh Powlet knight. His ancestors were sometimes barons and had their seats in the parliaments of this realm. They were lords of Tawstock which the Earl of Bath hath and of Torrington and in right of the wife Lords of Totnes and albeit the barony in success of time had his end yet the house was always of worship and possessed by knights even until this present time of Nicholas Martyn Esquire by whom the name lieth in peril for ever to be buried and extinguished unless he do raise up a younger house as he did with Joseph to recover the house to his old and Christinate state but to any purpose.

1534

John Brytnell

In this year at a parliament at Westminster in February all religious houses of three hundred marks and under were given to the king which stood with good reason to be as lawful for the king to have as it was for Cardinal Wolsey to suppress small religious houses for the erecting of his two new colleges the one in Oxford and the other in Ipswich.

1535

William Hurst

This year by a parliament holden at London all religious houses of the same of 300 marks and under were given to the king to be suppressed and Sir Peter Tregonnewell, Sir Thomas Arundell and others were appointed to be commissioners for the same in the west parts who came to this city in the summer time to execute their commission and beginning first with the priory of St Nicholas after that they viewed the same they went thence to dinner and commanded one in the time of their absence to pull down the rood loft in the church. In the meanwhile and before they did return certain women and wives in the city namely Joan Reve, Elizabeth Glendfold, Agnes Collaton, Alice Miller, Joan Reede and others minding to stop the suppressing of that house came in all haste to the said church, some with spikes, some with shovels, some with pikes, and some with such tools as they could get and the church door being fast they broke it open and finding there the man pulling down the rood loft they all sought all the means they could to take him and hurled stones unto him. In so much that for his safety he was driven to take the tower for his refuge and yet they pursued him so eagerly that he was enforced to leap out at a window and so to save himself and very hardly he escaped the breaking of his neck but yet break one of his ribs. John Blackealler, one of the aldermen of the city, being advertised hereof he with all speed got him to the said monastery, he thinking what with fair words and what with foul words to have stayed and pacified the women. But how so ever he talked with them they were plain with him and the foresaid Elizabeth Glanfold gave him a blow and sent him packing. The mayor, having understanding hereof and being very loathe [to have] the visitors advertised of any such disorders and troubles, he come down with his officers before whose coming they had made fast the church doors and had bestowed themselves in places meet as they thought to stand to their defence. Notwithstanding the mayor brake in upon them and with much ado he apprehended them and took them all and sent them to ward. The visitors being then made acquainted herewith gave thanks to the mayor for his care and diligence of their services and so they proceeded to the suppressing of the house and before their departure entreated the mayor for releasing of the women.

The monastery of Polsloe which lieth about a mile from out of the city was to be suppressed but the nuns had made by their friends such means that they had compounded with the king for the staying of that house but yet before two years ended the same house also was suppressed & dissolved. What the chaste life of these nuns so ever was before, it fell out that at the time when the house was suppressed so many of them had tasted so much of the fruit in the middle of the garden that the most part of them and as some said 12 of 14 of them were with child.

1536

John Blackealler
The whole records
of this year are lost

This year was a troublesome year and rebellions towards in most part of this realm northward some misliking the amendment of religion & taught to say their *pater nostre* in English because they had been over trained and brought up in a contrary doctrine. Some misliking the suppression of the religious houses. The two principal rebellions the one was in Lincolnshire which was soon appeased and the other was in Yorkshire. And for the Marquis of Exeter was sent into Devon and so well he was beloved that every man offered him his service and so many he had as were sufficient to have waged a great battle then for which they were now to go to serve which brought the marquis into such suspicion that not long after it turned to his confession. About two or three days before the said marquis came to this city. There was one William White, a skinner dwelling without the West Gate of this city, and one William Jordeyn, a brewer dwelling within West Gate, these two stood at the stall of one [blank] Ireland, a [?] maker dwelling within West Gate, talking of the present troublesome time and then the said Jourden asked his fellow Whyte what he would do and with whom he would take part, mary with him said he that hath the best right and weareth the crown of England. And I, said Jourden, will follow the greater part and will serve under my Lord of Devonshire and it were against the king himself. Upon which words the said Whyte arrested him and he was brought forthwith before the mayor and the matter being heard they both were committed to ward and prison. Where the said White died but Jourdene the year following was hanged, drawn and quartered.

A great broil also was in Somersetshire about taking up of corn for the king's service which one Plommer specially resisted for which and certain his traitorous speeches he was taken indicted and attainted of treason. He was a very tall man and of a stout stomach. He first brake the leather with which he was hanged and when his entrails were taken out, cast into the fire and the hangman taking out his heart he rose up and struck the hangman.

This year a collection was made throughout the country for the new building of Cowley Bridge which was then newly fallen down but the collectors when they were gave up their accounts were found to have spent more then they had gathered.

In this year there was a great plague of pestilence in this city in the summer 1537 in which died a great number of the common people and four of the 24 of which Robert Hooker, the father of the writer hereof, and Richard Martyn, late mayor, were two.

In the latter part of this man's mayoralty the king under his letters patents dated the 3rd of August the 29th year of his reign he made this city of Exeter a county of itself and divided & distinguished it from the county of Devon with all privileges and liberties belonging to a county and the first sheriff was William Burgan, sometimes townclerk, then made a steward and so consequently one of the 24 and so the sheriff.

1537

Thomas Hunt draper

In this man's year in the winter there fell great abundance of rains and the floods were very high and monstrous great and then one of the piers of Exe Bridge fell down. In the evening before John Cove, a tanner who had been at Doncaster under the Marquis of Exeter, was come home and to his house beyond Exe Bridge. And the same night about midnight as he lay in his bed the one end of his house next to the waterside of Exe fell down. His household servants who layin the loft over him, being asleep, then in bed and then in it fell all down into the water and were drowned. But he and his wife lying in the parlour were carried out into the river bed and all. Where she, by the order of her husband was willed to be quiet and not to stir. And he used sometimes his hands and sometimes his foot instead of an oar and by that means he kept himself in the west side of the river out of the violence of the stream and by god's goodness did recover to a little hillock where the waters were shallow and so they were both saved.

In this year in October upon St Edward's Eve Prince Edward was born.

Also William Jourden was arraigned and condemned of high treason before Sir Richard Pollard knight, a commissioner under the broad seal of England, for the same who sat then in the house of John Croston, Register, in St Mary Arches Lane.

Also William Lamprey in the end of this year was hanged for a felony he had been in the gaol about three years and could read and write and procured for himself paper and ink. And then for prolonging of his life he appealed and approached Mr Blackaller, mayor the year past, John Hindellor his sergeant, and sundry other men of good credit and honesty for misprison of treason whereof followed great troubles and the said Hindellor in great danger of his life, but in the end he had his reward and they were delivered.

In the end of this mayor's year upon the 12th of September 1538 the Gray Friars and the Black Friars of this city and the Priory of Polsloe were suppressed.

1538

Henry Hamlyn

This year Henry Marquis of Bath and the Lady Gertrude his wife were arraigned and condemned of high treason. He was executed for the same the 12th of December 1538 but she remained.

Also Sir John Russell Lord Russell and Comptroller of the king's house came in to these west parts as Lord President of the same. He had the whole abbey of Tavistock given unto him with the demesnes of the same where he lay for the most part and in this city hearing and determining of causes brought before him. He travelled all the coasts and seasides commanding bulwarks and blockhouses to be made in sundry places where he thought good and most meet for defence of the realm.

This year also by commandment from the king general musters were made through the realm which was taken in this city by Robert Tooker then weaver of the same who having tofore served in the wars under the Lord Brook in Spain was most skilful to dispose and order the same and did to the great pleasure of the beholders and to the commendation of himself. He rode in his armour and was attended with his hench men and with all things meet for a captain. To this muster the bishop and all the canons of the Close sent so many men as they had fit for the same. The whole company was about one thousand men but there were no more than was the most convenient.

The king this year sent out his commissions through out the realm for defacing and pulling down of all such idols and images as whereunto any offerings & pilgrimages had been made. And for this country Doctor Haynes of the Cathedral Church and chaplain to the king was a commissioner who not slowing his duty did execute his commission through out this diocese and among others he defaced & pulled down an image called St Saviour which was builded in the outside of the north wall of the chancel of the parish church of St Mre in the same for which he was marvellously hated and maligned at.

In the month of August 1539 John Boneffante of this city, gent., and one of the attorneys of the guildhall's courts was drawn, hanged and quartered in Southernhay for high treason. The matter and cause were this: there was great familiarity and acquaintance between this Boneffant and Adam Wilcocks, a proctor in the spiritual court, and John Northebrook, who professed none of these faculties but crafty and deceitful in both. These three supped on a night together at Northbrooke's house which was the lands of the said Bonefants and wherein the said Northbrooke could not give that increase as he would. After supper was done they having in talk the then present state of the world fell into the discoursing of prophecies of which one was that a mouldwarp [a mole] should come cursed of god's mouth and vengeance should befall him. The other was a Welsh prophecy that a dun cow should ride the bull and that then great changes should happen and when they had used many and sundry interpretations they in the end concluded that both were meant of the king and that he should come to destruction. And when they had ended they burned the paper wherein the said prophecies were written and so departed but they brought Boneffant home to his own house. The other two returned home again. But Northbrook having a further [?] then Adam Wilcocks could then [?conceive] Northbrook talked with him concerning their former communication and then said Northbrook, 'it is high treason against the king's person which we hath talked of this night at my house and therefore we must look to ourselves that we be not in danger for the same for you know,' sayeth he, 'that Mr Bonefant is a lawyer and a crafty man and knoweth what belongeth to the law and if he should secretly go to Mr Mayor and disclosed what we have talked and accuse us it will cost us our lives. Wherefore let us prevent him and play sure and go to Mr Mayor and first accuse him and so shall we save ourselves, whereby they both agreed and forthwith went to the mayor's house and knocked at his door for it was somewhat late and prayed to speak with Mr Mayor for matters touching the king and being come before him they told him that they had been in company with John Boneffant the attorney and he had spoken words of high treason against the king whereby they did accuse him, praying him in the king's name he might be sent for. Forasmuch as it was then very late in the night the mayor did by the advice of the said Northbrook command the city gates to be watched and warded until the morning and then to send for Boneffant which was done. In the morning very early Northbrook pretending good will unto Boneffant went unto his household, he being then in his bed, and distrusting nothing and being come to his bedside saluted him very courteously and told him that all the gates of the city were watched and warded for him and that very shortly search would be made for him. 'what,' sayeth Boneffant, 'for me?' 'Yea' said Northbrook, 'for you and therefore I do advise you to arise up quickly and shift for yourself and get you out of the way' and then by his advice he rose and went to a neighbour's house of his own where Northbrook had appointed. Immediately the search came and finding not Boneffant in his own house they by the appointment of Northbrook found him in the same house where he was gone unto. And carried him to the Guildhall. At this time it happened that Sir Richard Pollard was in the town whom the mayor made acquainted with the matter and prayed him to be at the examination of Boneffant which he was contented to do wherefore Boneffant was sent for and called before them. But Northbrook beforehand had secretly requested the mayor and Sir Richard Pollard to ask the said Boneffant whether he knew Northbrook and whether he were not an honest man or what evil he knew by him, who answered that he was a very honest man and knew no evil of him. And with these words so spoken the said Northbrook came in and as a man not knowing what matter was then in hand. He also asked of Boneffant the like question and then Boneffant made the like answer as he did before which thing Northbrook requested the said mayor and Sir Richard Pollard to witness and then he spake to Boneffant saying 'I cannot so say of thee, for thou art a very traitor and whore. I do arrest thee of treason.' And then he laid to his charge the speeches the night past which he had made and that he should say that the king was a mouldcarp and that he subvert the state of the realm and that he was cursed by God's mouth and that vengeance should come upon him. And for the proof hereof called forth Adam Willcocke to witness it. Boneffant forthwith denied not but that such speeches were past & spoken but he then laid them to Northbrook's charge and said that he it was that had so said but both Northbrook & Wilcock denied it and then Sir Richard Pollard told him that it was now too late. Not long after a commission was sent out for the inquiry of this treason which was directed to the mayor and to Sir Richard Pollard and others and then the matter being proved as was before Boneffant was condemned and upon the 10th of August he was executed to death as a traitor in Southernhay. Adam Wilcocks fell amazed and was distracted of his wits, his tongue rattled in his head and died most miserable. Northbrook had his house which he sought for but lived in great infamy all the days of his life and whose issue had but bad success.

Robert Tooker the Receiver built a piece of the town walls in Southernhay this year.

The aforesaid Henry Hamblyn now last mayor was descended of good parentage but lived by merchandise. His traffic was most in Britain. He was a very good man and careful for his commonwealth where he did much good generally to the whole city in the time of his office as also particularly to people of all estates unto whom he could do any good. He first was the deviser that the markets for wool, yarn and kersies were first set up in this city but great were his travels before he could compass it not only with his brothers whom he had much a do to persuade them but also with the Kirton [Crediton] men who impugned it nevertheless in the end the same took effect to the benefit of the commonwealth.

1539

Gilbert Kyrke

The foresaid Thomas Prestwoode the Receiver to continue that which his predecessor Robert Tooker be gone bought great store of the stones of the house of St Nicholas late dissolved and re-edified a great part of the decayed city's walls in Friernhay.

In the winter about the end of November one of the middle arches of Exe Bridge fell down and was new builded by Edward Bridgeman then Warden of Exe Bridge for which he bought great store of stones at St Nicholas late dissolved and then the prophecy was fulfilled which was, as it was then said, that the river of Exe should run under St Nicholas Church.

This year all the abbeys generally throughout all England were suppressed.

Also this year an act of Parliament was made for the new making of the haven of this city of Exeter.

Also the keeping of the receiver and stewards' dinners was this year laid down for the manner was that the receiver upon St George's Day should yearly keep a feast in the Guildhall and every steward upon the Monday of the election of the mayor should keep their several feasts in every of their houses upon a pain of £5 to be employed towards the reparation of the city's walls.

Also this year the yarn market with much ado and by the earnest suit and travels of Henry Hamlyn and other good citizens who gave towards the building thereof the roof of the cloister of St Nicholas and 40s in money but much a do there was before the same could be established for it had many enemies as well within as without the city.

In this year also Thomas Lord Cromwell put to death for which the king after did regret.

This year died in the end of September the Reverend Robert Weston sub dean and canon of St Peter's of Exeter. He was a very courteous and a friendly man unto all men, a great keeper of hospitality both to the rich and to the poor, and a great benefactor to scholars for many of them he relieved with continual exhibitions and especially of his kinsmen whose care and special device was to have them to be learned of which three of them being his nephews and sons to his brother John Weston of Litchfield profited very well & became to be good scholars whom at his charges he found and kept in Oxford the first was named Nicholas Weston who professed divinity and was bachelor of the same and after his uncle he was subdean of the cathedral church, he did read the divinity lecture in the charnel house to the great profit of his auditory and commendation to himself and of whom great good things were hoped if by death his days had not been shortened. The second was named Richard who when he had well profited in his logic and rhetoric and other good arts removed him from Oxford to London to the inns of the court and became very well learned in the laws of the realm. And was in the end the king's sergeant and also one of the judges of the realm and had his circuit in this country. The third son was named Robert and he professed the civil law and was fellow in All Souls' College. He was at the first of a more less disposition than his two other brethren but being threatened to be deprived of his college he was the more careful of himself and did so diligently follow his studies that he was the best and most singular learned civilian in the university and was reader of the king's law lecture. He was also doctor of the law and then leaving the university was dean of the arches and from thence by Queen Elizabeth he was sent into Ireland where he was made Lord Chancellor and there died. The said sub dean also had the like care of two others, his eldest brother's sons of which the older named John Weston by marriage he advanced him to a good living and the other he preferred to ecclesiastical livings who was a prebendary of St Stephens in Westminster and parson of Ashprington. Likewise also he had the like care of one Barbor son to his brother's daughter whom he kept at Oxford and being a fellow in All Souls' College did there proceed doctor in law and was after an Archdeacon in the diocese of Lincoln and had also other good livings. This sub dean also [was] a very pleasant familiar man with his servants and upon a time he being destituted of a good horseman spake to one of his men named Thomas Cotton (whom he afterwards preferred to the court and by good happiness was made knight) that he should provide him but yet such a one as was honest and wise. Which Cotton promised to do. Not long after his master called him and asked him what he had done. He answered him that he knew where were 3 or 4 very honest men but he doubted whether he could get any of them to serve him. 'Now then tell me who they are and if they be in this country, I doubt not but to get them'. 'Yea,' sayeth Cotton, 'they dwell in this country and you do know them well enough'. 'What are they I pray thee sayeth and tell me their names'. 'They are,' said Cotton, 'Sir Thomas Denys, Mr Hollersdene and Mr Roap who are taken to be very honest and wise men.' 'What?', said the subdean, 'I when thee are mad?' 'Nay,' said Cotton, 'it is you that are mad who will seek and look to have an honest and a wise man to be your horseman for it is the office of a varlet to curry a horse and to [?] his heels and not fit for a honest and a wise man for such are to be governors of the commonwealth and not to be a horseman.' Such talks many times he would have with his familiars and with his men had many times he received the like answers which he liked and accepted well.

This Gilbert Kirke now mayor the second and last time what he was it was not known a long time and therefore he was challenged many times that he was a stranger born and being no denizen a claim was pretended to confiscate his goods. But he acquitted himself very well and following the trade of merchandise he grew to great wealth, lived in very good credit and in the times of his mayoralty did so well as no man better notwithstanding some quarrels were between his wife and one Mrs Blackeall for superiority and who should go first in procession. The matter at length was ended and he having two daughters did bestow them well and his only son he left good living unto but by his death the son defaulted to his daughter. He was buried in St Mary Arches parish church.

1540

Thomas Spurreway

This year all the religious houses of St John's order called the knights of the robes were suppressed and then also was the hospital of St Johns in this city, by reason that there were 4 priests in it of that order, was also surpressed.

This year the king having been a widower almost one whole year married the Lady Anne of Cleves unto whom Sir Thomas Denys Recorder of this city was the Chancellor and one of her privy council. This marriage continued but a short time for she was married the first of January and sequestered the 6th of July following.

The yarn market which at the first was but thin and small was the resort thereunto now the house being builded and finished the same did very much increaseth whereat the Kyrton men did so much malign at it and were grieved with it that they supposed the same would be some hindrance to their market which was before that the only market for kersies' wool and yarn wherefore they did what in them lay to pull down this market again and brought the same in question before the lords of the council as also did entitle the bishop of this city with it but in the end they had the repulse and the market continued to be one of the greatest benefits of the commonwealth of this city.

In this mayor's year in June 1541 & the 33rd year of the king's reign there was a parliament holden at Dublin in Ireland in which was given to the king the title to be king of Ireland wheretofore both he and his predecessors. The cause thereof was this, the great O'Neil who dwelled in Ulster, the north part o Ireland, and who was a mighty prince over the Irish, was still at war with the king's subjects and many times invaded the English pale and did waste, burn and spoil the same. And did so much stand in his own conceit upon the good successes which many times did befall unto him that he would advance himself to be as good and as great a lord as was the king. And therefore when he was by his friends persuaded to submit himself to the king his answer was that the king in Ireland was but as lord as he was. But when the king was proclaimed king of Ireland he relieved himself and in the end he came into England and submitted himself unto the king whom the king accepted and created him Earl of Tyrone and his son Baron of Down Gamen.

This year died Thomas Parkehowse, one of the canons of St Peters of Exon. He was a man universally seen in all good letters but chiefly a philosopher and by profession a physician and did much good to many people and because he was a canon he would not seem to take any money of any man, but yet he used to practice that when so ever he sent for his bill unto his apothecary whose name was Nicholas Lynet he would subscribe under it *Accept it up on behalf of you and me* which when it was known it went for a by word through the whole country *Accept it up on behalf of you and me* which though it touched him somewhat in credit yet the gain was so sweet that he cared the less for the one so that he might have the other. He did use to preach very much and delivered his auditory with his pleasantness who were more created therewith than edified.

Thomas Spureway the mayor aforesaid was born at Tiverton and a gentleman of a good house but a second son. He first served under the earl of Devon and was in great credit under him and was his general receiver and also was his bailiff of Exe Island without the West Gate of this city. He married first the daughter of Geoffrey Lewes, sometimes mayor of this city, and after his death did dwell in his house and enjoyed the most part of his lands and goods. And partly by reason of the great credit he was in under the Earl and partly for the great wisdom, experience and subtletie he was very much esteemed and beloved in the city and being mayor did very well and with great commendation administer his office. He was a reasonable tall man of stature, well compact of body, wise, subtle and discrete, willing to please and loathe to offend any man. His long life wished and his death much lamented.

1541

William Buckenam

This year a young child called Thomas Hunt standing near to the wheel of the horse mill which Nicholas Reve, a brewer dwelling in the Butchers Row, had builded to the disliking of the millers was by some mishap come within the sweep or compass of the cog whole and therewith was torn in pieces and killed. And upon inquisition taken it was found that the wheel was the cause of the child's death whereupon the mill was forthwith defaced and pulled down.

This William Buckenam was nephew to John Buckenam who was mayor of the city the first year of the king's reign 1509. And they both came out of Suffolk and were gentlemen born and of a house of good worship. This man succeeded his uncle in all that he had and following his trade of retailing of silks & mercery wares did nothing but rather increase the stock left unto him. He was but a weak and a simple but very much self willed and being offended with any was not easily to be reconciled. He was very spare of his purse and too frugal or sparing in his diet. In his mayoralty he did neither good nor hurt and the year was quiet and out of troubles.

1542

John Buller

This year was quiet and the courts occupied nothing but in ordinary business.

In this year died Robert Tregonewell clerk and one of the canons resident of St Peter's, he professed divinity and was very well learned. He did read the divinity lecture in the Charnel House to his great commendation and did maintain Luther's doctrine in some points as also much disgraced the corrupt state and arrogance of the pope. Great good things were hoped at his hands but that vainly death took him away. He was born in Cornwall and brother to Sir John Tregonewell knight and doctor of law. He was a very pleasant and a very conceited man, courteous and gentle to every man, a liberal housekeeper and much delighted to keep 3 or 4 good geldings in his stable and had pleasure in hawking and in hunting with water spaniels.

1543

Robert Tooker

The court this year was as the last past.

In this year the Marquis of Nazarra in Spain, a noble, wise and a learned man, came out of Spain ambassador to the king from the Emperor and was lodged in the house of this mayor who gave him and all his company entertainment at free cost for 3 days and during his abode in this city he was in great liking with the writer hereof whom he would very fain later had with him and did promise to keep and entertain him at his return home in the university of Salamanca. At his coming to the court before the king the league between the Emperor and the king was nenewed and then forthwith wars were proclaimed by them both against the king of France and forthwith the king sent over an army to join with the emperor and besieged Landersoy where Sir George Carew knight was taken prisoner.

This year died Doctor William Horsey, a canon of this church & archdeacon of Cornwall. He was a great defender of the pope's church and being chancellor to the bishop of London was accused for the death of Hunne in Lollard's tower which bred him great displeasure and infamy and being found guilty by the coroners inquest of murder and for which he was arraigned but he found such friendship that he was acquitted but he thenceforth so evil liked his being at London that he left it and came to lie in this city. He descended of the worshipful house of the Horseys in Dorsetshire and gave the arms of that family . . .

In this year in the month of July 1544 the king passed over into France and besieged Bulloyne and towards which both men and furniture were send unto him out of all parts of realm. And out of this city the ship sent unto him 30 men at his own charges well appointed with furnitures. The city also sent [an]other 30 men in like order well appointed and furnished. Likewise out of the country of Devon there went Sir George Carew and Sir George Pollard knights and Roger Bluett and Roger Gifford which went out esquires and returned knights and besides many others. The king after one month that he had besieged Bulleyn he took it. He was attended there by Sir William Godolphin of Cornwall knight and Mr Roger Gifford and Roger Bluett of Devon whom he there dubbed knights.

This Robert Tooker now mayor was born in Moretonhampstead but of mean parentage. He was a tall man & a b[?]leigh of personage wanting not stoutness and courage of heart to the same. He was servant and a retainer to the Lord Brook under whom he served in Spain in the wars whereby he became skilful in warlike affairs. At his return home knowing the service was no heritage he fell acquainted with a widow named Joan Pole who dwelled in the Barton Place of the manor of Duryard under the mayor, bailiff and commonality where about a possession he was maimed by one of the sergeants of the city under William Crudge then mayor but he followed the suit so earnestly for the mayhem and was so well favoured that he received good damages and with that money he so employed it in his occupation for he was a baker that he became wealthy and did set a beer brewing house in Exeter and kept a lodging house by which means and by the good help of his brother Abbot of Buckland he built four houses within the city and also purchased lands for his posterity. He kept a very good and a liberal house and such was his good conditions that no one citizen was so well beloved among gentlemen. In the time of his office of the mayoralty he kept so bountiful a house as none before or since his time hath done the like. When he was chosen mayor he had sent unto him from sundry gentlemen and his servants 15 deer besides conies, capons, partridges, and other viands. At Christ-tide he had the like sent unto him. And in the summer there was lightly no hunting in forest or park within all Devon but he was remembered with some portion of it. He was besides of an unlearned man, wise and stout and for the same as also for his good acquaintance with gentlemen of all sorts he was put in trust to procure the particular for reducing and making this city to be a county which suit had many adversaries but that he by his wisdom and well handling of the matter did stop the same and he obtained his suit. And when he first exhibited his bill of petition unto the king who before was advertised of him and of his service the king gave him very good words and speeches and his suit the better considered. At this time he was enobled by the principal king at arms of the order of the garter . . .

1544

Thomas Prestwod

This year the haven or watercourse of Exe was begun to be new made towards the charges whereof the most part of the parish churches of this city gave some portion of their plate and jewels which in the whole amounted to 900 ounces of silver white parcel gilded and gilded.

In the end of this mayor's year in July 1545 and the 37 year of the king's reign the admiral of France with the whole navy of the French king came to the Isle of Wight, the king whose navy then lying at Portsmouth and the weather so calm that never a ship was able to go out. The king advertised hereof came in person to Portsmouth and with all speed that might he made ready his navy to encounter the Frenchmen. And among his ships there was one special one named the Mary Rose which was thoroughly appointed and furnished both of men and furniture and of this ship Sir George Carew was made Captain who had with him the flower of all the young gent in the West Country which ship in setting forth lie by too much [?]sails was drowned with all the company there being save of 400 men but 40 persons.

1545

William Hurst

This was a troublesome year to the king as well for his wars in France as in Scotland and at the seas or at land in which the fortune of every side was variable. After that the French fleet was returned homewards, Sir John Dudley, Lord Lysle and High Admiral of England having the whole fleet in readiness and furnished at all points with men and munitions and all other necessaries he hoisted his sails and went to the seas which when he found all clear and remembering the great bravados that the Frenchmen had made at the Isle of Wight he crew to the coasts of Normandy and landed there with 6,000 men at Treport where he burned the suburbs and the most part of the towns and villages there about. And then calling before him the sundry gentlemen to be dubbed knights he remembered above all others Sir Peter Carew whom he would have given the order of knighthood but he answered that he had in place one uncle which had served right well & worthy and therefore it to be too great an injury to take that order before him who was his elder and had better deserved it than himself. The Lord advertised that it was Gawen Carew whom he meant and of whom he spoke truly. He thanked him for his remembrance and so called them both and gave to them first the order of knighthood. In their company was one John Courteney of Ottery St Mary a younger son of Sir William Courtenay of Powderham, knight, who if he had had livings according he right well deserved the like order for he was the first that set foot on land and conducted an ensign of soldiers to the top of the hill and made a number of Frenchmen to flee and to give place.

1546

John Brytnall

In the first quarter of this mayor's office upon the 28th of January 1546 King Henry the 8th died and Prince Edward his son aged 9 years was proclaimed king and upon the 20th of February then next following being Shrews Tuesday he was crowned at Westminster. And forthwith the first thing that he took in hand was the reformation of religion. And for the better preparing of the people for receiving of the same he sent through out the realm godly and learned men to preach the gospel. And into this country he sent on Doctor Tong a very grave godly and learned man who had a commission for the same. He had a very sweet voice and an eloquent tongue and did marvellously persuade the people and went throughout this whole diocese. But after his return home he lived not very long, being supposed that some wicked papist had given him a dram which was the cause of his death.

The first year of King Edward the 6th

1547

John Mydwynter

This year was the battle of Mickleborough in Scotland where the Scots paid the price of their untruths and almost the whole flower of that land killed and taken.

Also a parliament was holden at Westminster in which were granted to the king all the chantries, free chapels and fraternities.

Also in the end of this year a commandment was sent out through the whole land for the setting forth of the religion set forth & established by statute and one William Body, Register of the Archdeacon of Cornwall being to put the same in execution he was killed by a priest and other his confederates in Cornwall which all for the most part were executed to death. About this matter Doctor Bruer, a canon of this church and chancellor to the bishop, was put in troubles who in the end was condemned in the pr[?]e and for [?]we not long after he died.

In the 2 of July 1548 & the 2 year of King Edward an order was made by the mayor & 24 that there should be set forth with all speed that might be for the cutting of the ground above Exe Bridge for the conducting of Exe in his right course to the middle of the bridge and that there be provided for the same tinners, weir makers, carpenters & timber for paleing against the waste side of the river at as convenient speed as may be.

1548

John Blackaller

In the beginning of this mayor's time the famous and learned man Peter Martyr Doctor of Divinity and Florentine born and under whom the writer hereof was a student in his house in Strawborough was sent and brought into England by the means of Archbishop Cranmer and was sent to be a reader in Oxford where he heard much to do with the papists who were bitter enemies unto him and to the doctrine of the gospel which he taught most sincerely. There were public deputations against removing the sacrament of the lord's supper and transubstantiation which he so opined and reasoned that his adversaries had the reproach.

In the last quarter of this mayor's mayoralty was the commotion in Devon and this [city] besieged by the commoners of the county of Devon and world. The siege began the last of June 1549 and continued until the 6th of August then following within the whole were 35 days. The whole discourse of which rebellion the writer hereof hath set and penned out at large as appeareth in the Chronicles of This Land at which he was present and at that time within the city where he was by the order of the magistrates rated towards the common charges at 10s the day.

1549

John Tuchfield

This year Bishop Voysie resigned his bishopric unto the good & godly man Miles Coverdale who the year last past did attend and follow the lord of Bedford in the service of the commotion.

The king remembering the good service done by them with great thanks confirmed the charter of the city and gave them the manor of Exe Island bearing date the 22nd of December & 4th year of his reign.

The manor of St Nicholas was purchased this year.

The receiver's & stewards' dinners by the advice of the Lord Russell were clean taken away and order taken that the fines appointed for the same should be yearly expended in reparation of the walls of the city.

1550

Thomas Prestwode

Memorandum that this year the great base money was decreed & made current. Also this year the bounds and limits of the county of the city of Exeter was by statute set down and confirmed.

Also the good bishop Coverdale finding himself very unable to attend his consistory and spiritual courts and not knowing where to be furnished of a meet man, for the same to be his Chancellor did by the advice of the writer hereof who then send him to Oxford who by means obtained Mr Robert Voysey Doctor of the law and reader of the king's law licence in that university to come into the country and him he did entertain and gave him yearly in money £40 and meat and drink and lodging to him, his wife and servants and the finding of his horses and a convenient lodging besides the avails of his office.

About this time died the worthy and godly man Simon Haynes, Doctor of Divinity, Dean of Windsor and of this church and chaplain to the king as he had before been to King Henry his father. And earnestly he inveighed against the pope and all his false doctrine. He had many adversaries as his brethren the canons of this church or namely William Larson Chancellor of the church, Thomas Southcom Treasurer, Adam Traverse Archdeacon of Exeter, John Holwell and Thomas Wyse, canons, Mr Cryspan and Gregory Basset, a revolted friar who so narrowly watched him that there were few [?sermons] but they would pick some quarrel against him but he in truth prevailed & they in their malice counfounded. This man after the attendance of Cardinal Poole sometimes dean of this church was made dean in his place. But forasmuch as the said Poole was not disgraced by ecclesiastical sentence all the leases that were made by the dean and his successors from the time of Pool's attendance to the times of King Henry until his restitution in Queen Mary's time were avoided and made of no effect.

1551

William Hurst

Memorandum that in July 1552 being the 6th year of the king's reign a commission was sent to Miles Bishop of Exeter, William Hurst mayor, Thomas Prestwood and others for taking of an inventory of all the plate, jewels, goods and ornaments whatsoever pertaining to any church within this city and country. And therewith the foresaid prayed there might be deducted out of their certificate the value of about 1,000 ounces of plate which some of the parishes had given before to the city towards the making of the new haven.

1552

William Tothill

Memorandum that this year there was a Cornishman taken and sent to the gaol at the castle of Exeter for prophesising or rather foretelling of the death of King Edward which then being advertised unto the lords of the council a commission was sent to Sir Peter Carew for the examination of the said fellow who being examined did confess the justify his words and moreover also did then set and prefix before which the said king should die and said also that the subsidy late granted should be never paid and declared also what troubles after his death should be for the having of the crown and who in the end should have it. And how that the bearer should stake his claim at London and that all England should be afraid of him and yet he should be taken at a bridge under which never ran water. All which his sayings came to pass and then he was released.

In the end of this year died the most godly, blessed & worthy King Edward the 6th upon the 6th of July 1553 & the 7th year of his reign being (as one writeth in an epitaph of his death) poisoned & invenomed both in his brain and his lungs with a perfumed handkerchief presented unto him. His first coming to the crown was not so joyful as his death was most lamentable and doleful. For which his death ended the preaching of gospel & the true religion. The godly government of Ezithias was turned to be tyrannical under a bloody menasses and after this Josias a passage made for Nebucamezar to take & possess Jerusalem, the holy city of God. For immediately entered troubles both to state of the church & realm, first Queen Jane was proclaimed, the people being at the sermon at St Peter's where Bishop Coverdale preached and the whole people left him alone saving a few godly men. And forthwith the religion was subverted, the pope [?]revived and persecutions with fire & faggot followed the same to the destruction of many souls as by the history thereof set out by Mr Fox it doth appear.

1st year of Queen Mary

1553

William Smythe

This year was a very troublesome and a subversion made both of the religion established in the time of King Edward and of a change of the state of the realm.

Among all the residue of the godly bishops dispersed and disgraced Miles Coverdale, bishop of this church, was one and the first of whom the enemies of the gospel made a most assured account that he should above all others be burned and so he had been by god's good providence Christian King of Denmark by his letters to Queen Mary had not gotten him to be sent into Denmark unto him. He was a very good a well-learned man in Latin, Hebrew and Greek tongues. And did not only translate the whole bible into English and sundry other treatises but also translated sundry books of which one is the Paraphrase of Erasmus upon Paul's Epistles. He was no better learned than he was also godly of life, as simple as the dove, as meek as a lamb and as gentle as is the fawn, a great keeper of hospitality and most beneficial to the poor and notwithstanding he had well deserved generally of the whole church and specially of his own church and diocese among [whom] he was never idle. Yet notwithstanding he was in danger of his life by unseasonable and corrupted if not venomal drinks given unto him both at Totnes in Devon and at Bodmin in Cornwall. And notwithstanding he was reputed and taken as he was indeed but simple in wordly matters yet in god's cause he was so stout that made Mr John Pollard, Archdeacon of Barnstaple, and Walter Hele, vicar of Ipplepen, to re[?]ent their corrupt doctrine in the cathedral church of Exeter. He was born in Yorkshire but his [mother] was named Elizabeth, a godly matron was a Scottish woman born and sister to Doctor Macade's wife who was preacher to the king of Denmark. He was in great favour with the Lord Cromwell and at whose hands he found great favour and in his time he published the bible in English but before he could sell them the Lord Cromwell was dead. And having no means how to sell and disperse them did send them out of Germany where he then dwelled to London and came secretly to sale and dispersed. The bishop of London named [John] Stokesley advertised hereof in all haste maketh search for all these books and caused them all to be brought for him thinking that when he had gotten them all in to his hands then should no more bibles be had but the monies was so grateful to Mr Coverdale that he did not only discharge what he owed with the same but also did print twice as many more and sent them over with him the bishop he was very much unquieted therewith and then asking some one of his friends what course were best to be taken herein it was answered and advised him that he should procure and bring the whole printing stock itself but the bishop not liking this counsel was content to let the matter pass. Immediately as soon as Mr Coverdale was there discharged he passed over into Denmark and after some stay made with the king we went in unto the Palvegrave where before he had dwelled and had a benefice bestowed upon him wherewith he lived all Queen Mary's time. And after her death he returned again into England and then he was sent for before her Majesty and Council to have taken again his old bishopric but by the advice of the writer hereof and other his good friends upon good considerations he left it & was then made parson of St Magnes in London where he continued preaching so long as health and ability would serve. For at length being driven to give over preaching he now followed the sermons of this and gave over unto them. It happened on a time that the whole parishioners being upon knelling the bell come to the sermon the preacher was not come and the people a long time awaiting for him and he not come some of them went to Mr Coverdale being in the church and requested him who made many excuses and resisted it. Nevertheless at length he was entreated and was led up into the pulpit who contrary to all men's expectations made so excellent a sermon as he did no better in all his life and this was his *Cignia contio* and the last that ever he made. He died in very old years being aged about 90 years and was honourably buried with the presence of the earl of Bedford, the Duchess of Suffolk and many honourable and worshipful persons.

Immediately upon the displacing of Bishop Coverdale the old Bishop Voysey was sent for out of Coleshill where he then dwelled and was restored to the bishopric again.

The Earl of Devon not long before released out of the Tower was now upon suspicion committed again to the same prison for suspicion of Wyet's rebellion but he was shortly delivered & travelled into Italy and there died in Padua.

This year there was a great mutiny about the Queen's marriage through the whole realm and which in the end it brake out into open rebellion. The chief of which was Sir Thomas Wyat whereupon p[?]ments were sent into Devon for the taking and apprehending of Sir Peter Carew, Sir Gawen Carew, Sir Arthur Champernowne knight and William Gibbes Esquire. Sir Peter Carew having some inkling thereof fled secretly to Lyme where by the means of one Payne of Chard he got a ship and was conveyed away. Immediately whereupon Sir James Basset had the gift of all his lands and goods & goods & entered upon the same. Sir Gawen Carew and William Gibbs were taken and committed to the gaol of the castle of Exeter, Sir Arthur Champernowne was committed to the custody of the city and lay in the chapel of the Guildhall and after a while they were sent for and carried to London where they were sent to the tower but in the end they were discharged.

In the first year of the Queen's reign the 18th of October 1553 a dispensation was by the commandment of the queen had in the convocation house at London concerning the sacrament where Doctor Moreman of whom was concieved a great opinion had the [?foil].

The foresaid William Smythe was mayor this year was by occupation a goldsmith, a very gross and corpulent man but a most inveterate Papist and an enemy to all such as were known or suspected to be true professors of the gospel and whom he sought by all the means he could to entrap but especially one John Bodley and John Peryam but they by the goodness of God escaped his devices. As was his religion so were his companions for daily he would be in company with the treasurer Southcom at bowling & with Blaxton & Friar Gregory whose conscience and unbulations tended to no other end then the troubling, waxing and persecuting of godly men.

In the end of this mayor's year upon the 25 of July Queen Mary was married to King Philip at Westminster.

1554

John Mydwynter

This year the company of the bakers of this city were incorporated under the city's seal first of April 1555.

This mayor built the little conduit in the Southgate Street in this city and [?]nded by enlarging of the foot path in Northernhay. He was in the [?] of King Edward a professor of the gospel and he being of great familiarity with William Herne, Parson of St Petrock's Parish in which this mayor then dwelled. They had sundry speeches between them concerning the religion then received and established, which whereof the said Parson Herne did so professeth and [?] that he said he would be rather torn with wild horses than ever to forsaketh the same and to say mass again. Nevertheless Queen Mary was not so soon entered but that he was clean changed & one of the first that said mass within this city. This John Mydwynter at that present came to his parish church and there seeing this parson in his massing garments and ready to say mass he pointed unto him with his finger remembering as it were his old protestations that he would never say mass again but Parson Herne openly in the church spake aloud unto him 'It is no remedy man, it is no remedy'. This John Mydwynter was born in Ottery St Mary and his father was a dyer but this man was a merchant. He was a man of high grain, proud and malicious. He could not bear with a better nor love an inferior, which brought him into great hatred of the people and the common council of this city mistrusting what he would do if he should be mayor did keep him back from the office of the mayoralty then accustomed and that he looked for. In the time of the commotion he was mis-liked and [?] believed that he durst not to come abroad and to show himself but kept himself close within doors and would suffer no access unto him. He was of good wealth and ability and had sundry children, namely four sons and one daughter. His heir consumed all and more and the others did not prosper so well as it were wished. He died of good years about 70. In the end of this man's mayoralty the writer hereof was chosen as the chamberlain of this city.

This year the 30th of May 1555 John Carrdemaker alias Taylor was burned in Smithfield at London. He was born in this city whose father was a cardmaker but he was brought up in learning and was a novice in the Gray Friars of the Fransiscan Order without the Southgate of this city and in the end warden of the same house and at that present time when Mr Latimer preached in the churchyard of the same house [in] 1529 and he tasted so much of his doctrine at that time that he daily increased therein till he confirmed it with his death.

1555

Morys Levermoore

This year the cordwainers were incorporated 1 April 1556.

This year at Michaelmas the writer hereof ended into the office of Chamberlain of this city having the fee of £4 by the year and his liveries.

This year died John Voysie bishop of this city of a pain going to his stool in the night time at his house by Sutton Cilsesia in Warwickshire. How well so ever he deserved of noblemen & gentlemen he deserved small commendations and thanks of his church and bishopric. For of 32 lordships and manors left unto him he left unto his successors not above 3 or 4 and of 12 houses but one and that ruinated and encumbered and of £1800 yearly rents he left about £320 and the same charged with sundry fees and annuities whereof ensued an utter spoil to this bishopric of the temporal lands or temporalities as Grandisson in some sort forasmuch the same did in his last & testament prophecy and hal[?]e. He was a very worldly wise man and in great credit with the king and council, by profession a doctor of law. He was chaplain to the king, dean of his chapel and of this church and by the death of Bishop Oldham was preferred to this bishopric. He was president of the principality in Wales and the Lady Mary, the king's daughter, being proclaimed Princess of Wales, he was her governor and did so well behave himself therein that she always during his life did honour and reverence him and would call him always by the name of her father. He was very much affected to his native country and to his kinsfolk. In the end he when he saw the great commodity which grew to the commoners in this country by the use of making [?] selling of kersies he . . . erected the art of weaving in his town of Colefield and procured sundry weavers of this country to go thither & to dwell there but which in the end came to small effect. To his kinsmen he was so much bent & affectionated that after his death they having not wherewith to maintain themselves in that prodigal manner as he used them they came many of them as [?thristles] men to a bad end. He was as courtlike a man as no man exceeded him in any courtlike behaviour which was the cause that he was so liberal to the noblemen which served unto him for his lands and livings. He died a very old man, being near about 100 years old and was buried in Colefield.

After the death of John Voysye the bishop succeeded James Troblefield to be bishop.

1556

Walter Staplehill

Memorandum that this year wheat was sold at 7s 6d and at 8s the bushel.

This year in June the queen sent over a great power of English men under the Earl of Pembroke to besiege St Quinteyns at the siege thereof which was taken the 15th of July 1557.

This year among sundry godly persons burned for religion Cranmer bishop of Canterbury, Doctor Rydlye bishop of London and Mr Latimer were burned at Oxford and Stephen Gardiner most miserably died at London.

This year also of the 8th of July William Buckingham one of the aldermen of this city was convented and called before the common council for abusing of himself against his brethren with varied unseemly speeches for which he was according to the former orders of the city condemned and adjudged to pay 40s for his fine and for which there was a distress taken being a piece of damask and then he paid it and after he was quiet.

This year the council chamber was sealed about with wainscot.

This mayor was a gentleman born at Trusham in Devon and by marriage of the widow of Thomas Spureway late mayor of this city he came from his own and dwelled in this city. He was a court keeper and had good understanding in the laws of the realm and therefore did the better govern the commonwealth of this city wherein he was so painful and did so well as few. He was diligent in the markets, for the good ordering of them he reformed the weights and measures as well among brewers and bakers as among the merchants and vintners. And all such as were defecteth he caused to be brought to the guildhall and caused number of them to be burned, melted and consumed in the open markets. All unlawful games he would not suffer to be kept within this city and all loose and disordered persons he would severely punish. And as in the execution of his office in public government so also he was careful of the state of the chamber of this city and for the revenues of the same. A great pity it was that he was not so zealous in god's cause, and the true religion as he was over much blinded in popery, for he was so much embrewed and seasoned therein that the many good virtues in him were blemished and spotted. And yet notwithstanding he knew that as well his officers which accompanied him as sundry honest men were contrary him in religion and when he might have grieved in those tyrannical days when fire and faggot carried the sway yet he would and did both friendly and lovingly bear with them and wink at them. It happened on a time that a poor man of this city was brought before him and accused for eating of bacon in Lent in his house contrary to the laws and that he was a Protestant. The poor man doubting what might become of him because the mayor was a severe man did so tremble and was afraid that he could scarce speak. The mayor perceiving it did give him good and gentle speeches and then he being examined did confess that his wife and children and for himself having no meat nor money he made some potage with a piece of bacon and a few herbs for them. The mayor perceiving the state of the man and his necessity did bid him afterwards to be better advised and to do no more so and so did dismiss him. He died the 28 of February 1557.

In April the earl of Bedford came to this city and he was very honourably received.

1557

John Peter

Memorandum an old order was renewed by the mayor and 24 for avoiding of unseemly and slanderous speeches of the 24 one to the other and also for the seemly and good order that every of the 24 should use in their speeches when they were assembled in council in the council chamber that every one should in direct and reverent manner speak his mind to the matter proposed without any preventing or interrupting one the other. And then Mr John Mydwynter was accused for that he had very slanderously and uncharitably given foul speeches both against his own brother Robert Mydwynter and Griffeth Ameredith then lying sick. For which he was condemned by the whole house to pay for the breech of the orders of the said house 40s.

This year upon the 5th of December died Griffeth Meredeth, a worthy and a good citizen, and who deserved well of the commonwealth of this city in sundry respects. He was born in Wales in the county of Radnor and descended from the noble family of Howell Vane, Lord of Weston who was slain at Agincourt Ford in France in the time of King Henry the fifth and was by him and others of his blood allied to the Pryses and the most part of the best gentlemen both in the county of Radnor and of the provinces and counties adjoining. His ancestor was named Elyson Eledred of Weston aforesaid a gentleman possessed with great and ample possessions and one that did bear in his time a great sway or rule in that country and [?] and his posterity continued for many years and in sundry descents. But as nothing is permanent under the sun and time devoureth and consumeth all things, so this house by little and little partly because the lands in that country is gavel kind land and partly among all the children alike and partly because many of his forefathers were not the best husbands, feel into declination and in a manner so consumed that it was out of all hope to be recovere. For this gentleman being bereft of all or most part of his ancestors' great possessions and inheritance was therewith forsaken of his many kinsmen and allies. For though he had many cousins yet but few friends or none at all that would pity his case or consider his estate. Wherefore being thus destitute and for the avoiding of such great extremities which necessity many times compelleth men unto. He left his native country and his small inheritance would needs seek fortune and so came into England and became to be a soldier under Sir Francis Bryan knight who then served in the wars in France but he wars being ended and his entertainment very slender he bethought himself of some better trade of life and then considering with himself that service was no heritage did after many devised resolve himself to learned the art and occupation of a tailor and professed the same. Wherein he prospered so well that in short time he was a very skilful and a perfect good workman and then he came to this city and after some acquaintance gotten with such as whom he like and liking well the place setteth here his rest and in short time made himself free of the city, setteth up his occupation and then to be to wife a very honest young woman born of good parentage and who in her older years was a very virtuous & a godly matron. He followeth his occupation very diligently and carefully wherein he made the more profit by reason of his honourable & gentlemanlike mind for albeit a small portion of his ancestors' possessions was left unto him, yet that abated no part of his stomach which was nothing inferior to any of his ancestors when they were in their best estate. For always he would single himself from the meaner & baser sort of people and would accompany and acquaint himself with such as were of the best credit, countenance and calling, and especially with gentlemen of the best sort. And by his modest behaviour and pleasant speeches he entered into such good liking and forthwith them that he gained all or the most part of their works into his hands and so in short time he grew to good wealth and ability. And by little and little he gave over his manual occupation and became to be a draper which was very profitable unto him, for having increased his wealth very much thereby he employed the same in buying and purchasing of lands and revenues by which in the end he lived as a gentleman and left the same unto his posterity and so his name and family being as it were extinguished in Wales, is now restored in England although not yet in so ample manner as it was in Wales. He had many good parts in him (though not without some imperfections for as the common adage is nothing is good all the way through). He was a great housekeeper and kept good hospitality among his neighbours and his doors were never shut against any honest gentleman, for they found always that entertainment as was to their good liking and to his commendation. He was trusty to his friend and ready to do good to all men, the oppressed he would help and the needy he would relieve. He was wise and of a very sharp will, ready to conceive and as witty to deliver his mind and of a man unlearned he would very pithily discourse any matter in question. To the commonwealth of this city he was a very good member and in the common causes of the same committed to his trust he showed himself very diligent, careful and trusty and which he followed and compassed to good effects, as in hereof are extent sundry testimonies. And among sundry his good actions this one thing is not to be forgotten, it was the manner in those days that such prisoners as for their offences were executed at the Forches at Ringswell, a place about some mile out of Exeter that the bodies of such as had no friends otherwise to bury them. They were very irreverently brought back to the city upon a staff between two men to be buried in the churchyard and therein their clothes for the most part were cast into the grave. This man pitying so inhumane and loathsome manner of their burial did for redress thereof vie and in-feoffee certain lands which he had at Sidford of the yearly [rent] of about 38s for the buying of shrouds for all such as had need & had no friends to provide shrouds for them. Which his godly care and provision hath ever since been duly kept and observed which his good example so moved a godly matron Joan Tuckefeld that she loathing the loathsome manner of the carraige of the dead prisoners coming to the city did purchase a piece of land near adjoining to the said Forches and did enclose the same with a stone wall for a burial place and hath given certain lands for the maintenance of the same. This man passed all the offices of the magistracy in this city saving only the mayoralty which he was to have occupied if the sickness whereof he died had not hindered & letted. He died in good years and left behind him 3 sons and one daughter and provided well for every of them. But his eldest son named Edward in whom he reposed a hope for the continuance of his name and house, now in some part restored, he caused to be instituted and brought up in good letters and learning first in the grammar schools then in Oxford and last in the Inns of the Court where he was a fellow in the Middle Temple and after for his learning a justice of peace in his country. His father gave him in marriage in his young years to Elizabeth, the daughter of Lewes Fortescue of Fallopit esquire & one of the barons of the Exchequerer . . .

This year the town of Calais was lost and as it was supposed by some device of Bishop Thrumbye of Ely and other of his consorts. For the queen being advertised from the Lord Wentworth then Deputy of Calais of their distrust & of the preparation which the French king had made and desired help. This bishop stopped & slowed the same and said he would keep Calais with a little [?] and by that means that town was unprepared and taken.

The queen of Scots is married to the Prince Dauphin of France.

The merchants of this city procured a charter of the queen to be incorporated and that no inhabitant within this city should traffic beyond the seas but he were of that company whereof ensued great troubles.

An order was taken that the widow of every one of the 24 should yearly at Easter and Christmastide have the half of such common bread as their husbands were want to have. The cause and occasion hereof was to encourage them by the example of Mrs Joan Tuckfeld to bestow their gods to such good uses as she did.

In August a poor [?seely] woman of Cornwall named Agnes Preest was burned in Southernhay for her religion.

The bushel of wheat in this market was this year at 6s 6d the bushel.

1st year of Queen Elizabeth

1558

John Buller

Memorandum that the 6th of October 1558 an order was taken by the mayor and 24 that whosoever of them did disclose any secret speeches or [?] had among them the same being commanded by the mayor not to be disclosed that the party so offending to be dismissed out of that house & company.

Memorandum that upon the 17th of November 1558 Queen Mary died at which time died also Cardinal Poole and sundry other bishops and forthwith the Lords and Commons being in Parliament assembled together and proclaimed Queen Elizabeth who immediately after her coronation took order for the suppressing of the false & popish religion and the setting up of the true service of god & preaching of the gospel.

Bishop Troblefeld of this city was deprived and committed with other deprived bishops to prison. He was a gentleman born and of a worshipful house in Dorsetshire, a man very mild, courtesy and gentle and not so forward in bloody matters as he had officers to follow it. He was desirous to have done some good in recovering some things of his decayed bishopric but what he did it is but to small effect.

This year an order was taken that every inhabitant when his course came to be a market man or a watchman he should do it in his own person or appoint such a one as should be sufficient & meet for the same.

Also this year upon the 30th of January began a parliament at Westminster and many were the suitors to be burgesses of the city for the same, in which order was taken for preaching of the gospel and meet for the same.

Also this year the wars were proclaimed between England and France.

Also this year upon an occasion that the house in this city named the Cornish Chough was afire. An order was taken that every man of ability, every corporation and the chamber of the city should have a certain number of leather buckets provided as also ladders and crooks for the same purpose but little was done.

The merchants this year of this city got of her Majesty a corporation under her letters patents dated the 28 of January 1558 whereof followed great troubles.

Also an order was taken by the mayor and common council that there should be a table made and hanged up in the guildhall wherein should be contained the several testaments of every such person as wherein any land was given to the city to any uses.

In September this year Mr Juell (bishop elected of Salisbury], Mr Cowlas Sergeant at law, Mr Pary and others Her Majesty's visitors came to this city and were lodged in the dean's house at which time they defaced, pulled down & burned all images and monuments of idolatry which were brought into the churchyard of St Peter's, and they within Queen Mary's days were accounted to be most forward in erecting them up and in maintaining of them were now made the instruments to make the fire and to burn them. Among many other good things which these visitors did they did deface all the altars & monuments of idolatry and forbid any more masses or popish services to be used and instead of barton's mass want to be said every morning they did set up the morning prayer. Yet hitherto used and great was the resort to the same and by so much they were it had the more enemies to impeach it. Sometimes they denied the bell appointed to be rung at it, sometimes they would not suffer the same to be used in the chancel, sometimes they would not suffer the singing of psalms and always some one thing or other was devised to hinder it but the chief doer was William Lason chancellor of the church but the matter being made known to the council it was established & still it doth it continue with great resort of the people unto it. The name of god being praised in reading, singing and preaching daily now without disturbance.

Item all the records & evidences of this city were examined & set in order by the travels and labours of Mr Walter Staplehill, Mr Robert Chaff, Mr Richard Hert & John Hooker the writer hereof.

1559

Robert Mydwynter

Memorandum this year began the troublesome suits between the merchants of this city and all the residue of the free citizens concerning the merchants' corporation.

Also the denial of the Chancellor Lason & others of St Peter's Church for singing of [?matins]mas at the morning, was by letters from the archbishop of Canterbury was inhibited by an order for the convenient using of singing from thenceforth.

Also this year there was a general watch at midsummer by way of mustering of 1200 soldiers well armed and appointed by commandment of the Earl of Bedford.

Also this year were sent down certain commissioners from out of the Exchequer concerning concealing of the queen's customs and conveyances of gold over the seas by merchants and upon sudden their compters were searched, their books taken away and carried to London and many of them bound for their appearance at the court of the exchequer where they were examined and set their fines and among others the mayor of this city then being was one.

Also this year was a proclamation devised by the council and proclaimed against the excesses of apparel of women.

Also Doctor Gammon in his sermons maintained certain articles of popery which upon Sunday the 10th of March by order he was commanded to [?remove] it and did it.

Also Peter Lake, one of the 24, for the unseemly terms and abusing of Richard Prestwood, one of the 24, was committed to ward until he paid for his offence 40s according to the order of the house.

Also this year Bishop Alley was installed bishop of Exeter and came to this city being accompanied with the Earl of Bedford whom the mayor and his brethren received at the Broadgate.

This Robert Mydwynter was brother to John Mydwynter, mayor in the 2 & first years of Philip and Mary and was his apprentice. They were both of one complexion but not of like conditions. For albeit this man were somewhat hasty & choleric yet without malice & forgetful of injuries and ready to do good to any man. He would be familiar with ever honest men and very affable to be spoken unto. He desired the love of all men and the good will of his neighbours and the more that he prospered and was beloved the more his brother was angry and disdained him. In his mayoralty he showed himself as he was – an upright justice and governed this city in very good order. His hospitality though it were in to much excess yet liberal and good. In nothing was he more stout than he was against bishop Alley when he brought a commission to be a justice of the peace within the city contrary to the liberties of the same.

1560

John Backall

A proclamation this year was made against the defacing of the monuments and tombs of all noble men, and that all images and places of idolatry should be destroyed and pulled down.

The queen, minding the restoring of her coin to a just value, decreed all the base money to the true value and the same to be stamped and then also crown was proclaimed to be current at 6s and the pistole at 5s 10d.

The pulpit next to the chancel was builded and set up this year and the old pulpit in the body of the church not used.

Bishop Alley procured a commission of the peace within the city and county of Exeter and was in the same nominated a justice of the queen and did require the mayor to accept the same and did also come himself to the hall to have sat there but it was denied him whereof he complained but in the end he was satisfied that it was nought.

This year one Danyell, a preacher, taught that none could be saved except he were baptised and did receive the communion but he received the same in the same place at St Peter's where he preached it.

Also this year there was a great dearth and scarcity of corn and at 6s 6d the bushel and by the goodness of God there arrived at Plymouth and at Topsham certain ships laden with rye and wheat which relieved the people both in price and plenty.

Also this year in June Pole's steeple was set on fire with lightning and both it and the church was burned.

Also John Peryam, one of the 24, for his unseemly speeches against Richard Prestwood did pay the broke and fine of 40s.

The company of the glovers and skinners and the company of smiths and cutlers were this year incorporated.

Sir Thomas Denys, Recorder of this city, died the 18th of February 1560. He was a gentleman, born of an ancient house but by times spent and greatly decayed but by this man restored again. He was well learned in the laws of this land, a man very wise and of great experience. He lived under and saw the days of seven kings and queens viz. Edward the 4th, Richard the 3rd, Henry the 7th, Henry the 8th, Edward the 5th, Mary and Elizabeth. He was servant to King Henry the 8th and of the Privy Council to King Henry the 8th. He married two ladies, the widows of two aldermen of London by whom he attained unto great wealth and by so much the better to keep [?] in court. He was Chancellor to the Lady Anne of Cleves and in great favour with the king and the best estates of the realm. He had been sheriff [blank] times whereof two times were together in the reign of King Henry the 7th having so soon ended one year but he was chosen so the next year also whereof when he understood he went to the king and told him that when his grace had chosen him sheriff the second time it was against his laws. Then the king demanded what was the penalty, he answered it was £100 whereof the one moiety went to his grace and the other moiety to him that would sue it. Whereupon the king sent to his attorney and required him to enter an action in his name against this Sir Thomas Denys and for the said forfeiture which he released forthwith unto him and bid him to serve the office.

1561

William Hurst

Memorandum that a boy dwelling in Woodbury was met by an unknown person who cut out his tongue of his head.

This year Doctor Argeaton of this city did set up sundry bills in diverse places of this city certain positions of his opinion requiring and challenged a disputation with whom so ever that would answer him. First, that it was lawful for every man with consent of his wife to accompany & have the carnal knowledge of any other woman, the second, that the pope was not to be called Antichrist, the third that it was no mis[?] that Christ lay three days buried in the grave, the fourth that the articles of transubstantiation was true, besides other affections for which he was bound to his good behaviour, they sent up to the high commission and lastly to [?]nt his opinions.

Also in this year there were many monsters born within realm as at Stony Stratford a calf was calved with ruffs about his neck, at Salisbury a child born having 4 eyes but no nose & in every hand 6 fingers. At London a child was born which had a round head and a round mouth, his hands like [?] for feet and his feet like a toad.

The high school in this city by a common contribution at the request of Mr Williams the schoolmaster and by the labour & industry of the writer hereof was new builded, sealed, seated & plastered.

This year William Herne, parson of St Petrock's in this city, gave to the mayor & 24 of the common council 240 of old angels amounting to £160 for the purchasing of Mr Horsey's lands then set to sale for the yearly relieving of the [blank] according to his devise, which thing is performed to this day.

This year in October the queen's majesty for preventing & stopping the sundry inconveniences which by the French king were meant & devised against her highness & the whole realm did send the earl of Warwick to Newhaven and towards that service she by her letters required 500 men to be sent thither out of this country toward which this city gave £40 besides 200 [?]ners sent out of this country.

1562

John Peter

This year there arrived at Plymouth five great hulks laden with rye by reason corn was scant and dear they were stayed and by order of the council the same was commanded to be sold at such reasonable prices as by certain justices then named should be set down.

The wars in France were very sharp & hot and a field was found between the Prince of Conde and the Duke of Guise the Prince was taken & the duke lost the field and a great slaughter of both sides.

This year there were commissions sent out through the whole realm for the enquiry and redress of the [?] of women's apparel.

The haberdashers of this city were this year reduced into one company or fellowship.

This year in the 28 of July the town of Newhaven being overlaid with the plague or pestilence and very hotly besieged and in great peril was yet upon honourable conditions surrendered unto the French king.

This year the Charter for the orphans of this city of Exeter was confirmed by act of parliament and exemplified under the broad seal of England the third of May *Regni quarto*.

The queen's majesty this year made her progress and came to Cambridge where she made a very eloquent oration in Latin to the whole university. The like she did at her like progress at Oxford in September 1566 when she was present at the public dispensations and at the end of the same at the request of the nobility and of the [?] ambassadors she made an oration but so pithy, so eloquent and so br[?] in the Latin tongue as it was marvelled at.

1563

John Peryam

This year John Trow came to this city & took the haven in hand to be brought to this city.

1564

Morys Levermore

Memorandum the company of the haberdashers were incorporated into one fellowship.

1565

John Woolcot

This mayor had passed all the officers towards the mayoralty for about 22 years past and by reason of his age and his small wealth it was not thought nor meant that ever the office of the mayoralty should have fallen unto his lot. Nevertheless, when the matter so fell out and no means found how the same might be avoided order was taken both that his house should be prepared and also he to be furnished with money for his diet which liberally the chamber did discover. He was in time past a great merchant and advanced very much whereby he had great wealth but in the end his losses were so great that he was very poor and lived in very mean estate. He was a zealous man in the Romish religion and too much addicted unto Papistry. And in the commotion time when the commoners of Devon and Cornwall were upon in rebellion for the same and he was within the city the time of the besieging of the same, yet his affection was such towards them that upon a day when he was captain of the ward in charge of the West Gate of this city he went out of the West Gate to the rebels without any commission and had conference with him which was not after forgotten but turned him to displeasure.

1566

Thomas Richardson

This year Sir Thomas Gresham knight begun to build the sumptuous [?] in London.

This year the 24th of October the exchequer of St Peter's was robbed but the thieves had such good consciences that when they had carried home the money and found it to be more than they needed, they carried back the overplus.

The coopers and the Heliers of this city were reduced and made one company under the city's grant and seal the 3rd of February 1556.

This Thomas Richardson now mayor was born in Cheshire and by means of one Michael Lynett of this city apothecary he was brought to this city and served under the said Lynett. When he came to ripe years and was married he kept a wine tavern and was a merchant adventurer for wines and following that trade in good order and diligently he attained to good wealth and ability and did not only serve this city by retail but also all the gentlemen in the shire of Devon by the tuns and hogsheads with whom for his good dealing he was in great credit and favour. He was of very good conditions and qualities given to all good exercises and a good company for any gentleman or honest man whether it were shooting, bowling or any other pastime and albeit he were very honest, friendly and courteous to all men so would he not receive wrong at any man's hands neither would he give his beard for the washing. He had passed and borne one of the offices of the city in every of which he used and behaved himself very well and to his great commendation especially in the time of his mayoralty wherein he neither in his hospitality nor in his government was inferior to any of his predecessors and for which he was well reported both in town and country.

1567

John Smythe

This year died the famous and worthy citizen of London Sir Thomas White knight, merchant tailor, late alderman and Lord Mayor of London, whose noble acts both for the increase of learning and for the maintaining of good [?] and in the most part of the cities and towns within this realm are recorded at large in the chronicles of this realm together with the great relief of the poor and sundry his good actions. Among other cities he remembered this city with one hundred pounds every tenth year to be delivered to this city unto 4 young merchants upon assurances to be paid at the times by his will and order li[?]ted.

In this year 1567 upon the 20th of May the writer hereof by the good will of the mayor and common council at the request of Sir Peter Carew passed over into Ireland for the recovery of certain lands appertaining to the inheritance of Sir Peter Carew where before the feast of the birth of the Lord he recovered the barony of Odrome for him which had been out of his ancestors' hands about 240 years and did put him in quiet possession of it.

1568

Robert Chaff

This year Collabear Weir by means of the great frosts was broken and after was new made in a timber frame.

This year Mary Queen of Scots fled out of Scotland and came into England at Workington and there she was stayed and after conveyed to safe custody and never returned home again but was the cause of many tragedies in this land, whereof would have been no end if she had not removed according to her deserts who for sundry treasons devised to the destruction of the queen's majesty she suffered death anno 1587.

This year there was a great lottery made at London which made a great show of great things but in the end it came to nothing.

1569

William Chaple

Memorandum that in the first of April 1570 William Alley bishop of this city died who was a good and a godly man and very well learned of whom you may read in the catalogue of the bishops of Exeter.

Memorandum also that in the summer of this year 1570 was a great plague of pestilence in this city and then the chiefest men of the same with their families departed thence into the country. And then John Wolton, a canon residentiary of St Peter's, remained in the city and then showing himself he was the man of god and a good shepherd preached every Sunday in the cathedral church, continued the exercises of the morning prayers and visited the sick people and most godly did preach unto them & gave them most godly exhortations to their great comfort & to his great commendation.

1570

Simon Knight

Memorandum that this year there was a great rebellion in the north parts of this realm made by the Earls of Northumberland and of Westmoreland concerning religion which both fled into Scotland, not long after Leonard Darnes began the like rebellion and being not able to make his part good fled into Scotland.

This year the yarn market was new builded and a composition was made with the C[?] and vicars of the Calendarhaye for fixing the beams in their walls.

Also William Bradbridge dean of Salisbury was consecrated bishop of Exeter in March 1574.

In June 1570 the cruel persecutor of god's people, Doctor Story, was for high treason executed to death.

1571

Thomas Brewerton

Memorandum that this year were great inundations through out all England whereof followed much harm.

Also one Agnes Jones of this city was burned in Southernhay for poisoning of her husband John Jones.

Pope Pious the fifth sent this bill of excommunication against the queen which was set upon the bishop b[?]'s gate for which one Felton the doer thereof was put to death.

1572

John Peryam,
John Blackeall

The famous and godly man John Jewell bishop of Salisbury died the 22 of September 1572. He was born in Devon, brought up in Oxford and a companion with Peter Martyr. He had great controversies with John Harding who was also born in Devon about his Apology. He was a notable ornament to the church of God both for his life and his doctrine.

There was a combat appointed to be fought in Trinity term between two champions the one named Mylor, a master of defense, and the other was named Thorne who was born in Devon, but it was taken up.

The Turk by the goodness of God had a great overthrow given him in the Levant Seas by Don John of Austria.

This year died John Peryam now mayor towards the end of his mayoralty and John Blackell was chosen mayor in his place to perform the rest of the year. This John Peryam was the son of William Peryam sometimes mayor of this city. He was a very worthy man in many respects and had many good parts in him. He was very zealous in the true religion of the gospel for the testimony whereof he was driven to forsake his native country and live as a sojourner in a strange land. He was dutiful to his prince for in the time of the commotion in King Edward the 6th his days he did not only serve in person against the rebels but also found the means to see and procure the Lord Russell then the general against them with money & other necessaries to his great comfort and the like furthering of the service. He was the chief governor of the company of the English merchants in Antwerp. He was twice mayor of this city in both which times his government was upright, a great favourer of the poor man's cause, an upright judge in all causes of law depending before him, severe against the wicked and lewd persons who received at his hands according to their deserts, and friendly and loving to the good and honest and them he defended against all injuries. He left behind him two sons worthy and notable good members of the commonwealth of which the one professed the laws of the realm and was one of the justices of the court of pleas and the other followed the trade of merchandise and was mayor of this city. As he lived so he died virtuously, godly and in prayer, whose memorial deserveth not to be forgotten.

Thomas Duke of Norfolk was arraigned in January of high treason, condemned and executed.

In this mayor's year in August 1573 the Earl of Essex passed over into Ireland and of affairs & good success there it is set down by the writer hereof in the Chronicle of Ireland.

1573

William Tryvet

This year died the good, godly and worthy widow Mrs Joan Tuckefold widow who left behind many good monuments as well for the perpetual relieving of the poor as by the leaving of a stock of money for the maintaining yearly for ever artificers and occupiers five citizens of the city, namely to the poor she hath [?]ed certain lands for the yearly giving to 12 poor women 12 fryse frocks or cassocks at Christ-time and 12 smocks at every Easter. And for the artificers to be distributed among them yearly according to an order by her set down £300 in money which every man receiving the same and putting in good securities to repay it shall occupy it for three whole years. Also she enclosed at the Forches at Ringswell with a stone wall a piece of ground for the burial of such prisoners as shall be there executed.

1574

Nicholas Martyn

In the month of December there fell such a sudden storm of hail, wind and thunder in Exeter as had not been seen before.

1575

John Peter

This year died the most notable and worthy knight Sir Thomas Devereaus, Earl of Essex, in Ireland whose life is recorded in the Chronicles of Ireland by John Hooker the writer hereof and [blank] Molyneaux in the Chronicles of England.

This year also died the worthy and honourable knight Sir Peter Carew at Roffe in Leynster and buried in the city of Waterford in Munster in Ireland in all such honourable order directed by the writer hereof as unto him appertainined. His life, birth, virtues & conditions are set down in the Chronicle of Ireland by this writer.

This year the butchers of the city were reduced into one fellowship and company by [?] in September 1575.

1576

Thomas Prestwood,
Robert Claff

This year in November Antwerp was spoiled by the Spaniards and in May following 1577 the Spaniards were avoided out of all the holts in the Low Countries and the same yielded to the States.

Also at the Assizes kept in Launceston the 16th of September 1577 one Trogeon & Thomas Harrys, schoolmaster, were condemned in a [?] for their Popish religion.

Also Cuthbert Mayne, a Popish priest, was attainted of high treason for having of one Agnes [?] & other like trash. After he was executed there was found in his bosom a book dedicated to the pope in which was his confession of his horrible [?] and of the pope's pardon for the same.

This year the highway between the city & Cowley Bridge was very well amended & repaired.

This Thomas Prestwood mayor for this year was son to Thomas Prestwood the elder who had been twice mayor and he was born in the city of Worcester, his father concieving a good hope of him by reason of his pregnant wit and forwardness sent him to London where he bound him apprentice unto a rich and a wealthy merchant under whom he prospered and did very well. And upon occasion being a traveller for his master and in affairs he came to this city and in course of time he became acquainted with the widow of one John Bodley of this city. She was the daughter of one John Gale of Kingswear gent. And having found favour in his sight he made his master therewith and with his good favour he followed his former suit to the widow, obtained and married her. And then leaving his master he remained and dwelled in this city and followed his trade of merchandise whereon he had been brought up and did prosper very well and increased unto good wealth and riches. He was very zealous in religion and greatly affected to the hearing of the preaching of the gospel and very friendly to all good preachers but specially unto Mr Coverdale unto whom he gave very liberal entertainment. In the service of his prince and of the commonwealth he was dutiful, diligent and careful as whereof he gave testimony in the time of the rebellion and commotion in King Edward the VI's days when he followed the Lord Russell in person and aided him with his purse and helped him to monies when he was distressed. In matters of the commonwealth he showed himself as he was politic and prudent time of his governments when he was mayor and in his good advices and counsels unto all as were mayors or officers in this city. He was in such favour with Lord Russell that somewhat for his sake and at his request the manor of Exe Island was the sooner obtained. He was also one of the purchasers of the manor and fee of St Nicholas and of such [?] rents which the king had in this city and towards which he defrayed a portion of money. He was to every man very courteous, friendly and affable and in his speeches very wise, pleasant and [?]merry conceited. Glad to do good to every body and loath to hurt one. He was a good housekeeper and kept good hospitality among his neighbours being desirous always to have good table according to the times to be well furnished with honest company among whom he would be very pleasant and merry. And so it happened that at dinner or supper times any man did come to speak with him if he were of his acquaintance or an honest man, he would invite and pray him to come to take part of his fare for sometimes sayeth he you may fare worse at home as I and other householders do. If at any time he met with any young man unto whom any wealth or livings did grow unto and did either prodigally waste his patrimony or did live [?] he would surely find some occasion or means to talk with him. And as a good father to his child he would give him the best advice and counsel that he could and which was done in such friendly and loving manner that he did very much good therein. In his later age by little and little he gave over his trade of merchandise and employed his wealth in purchasing of lands and in building of houses especially within the city which do yet remain as goodly ornaments to beautify the same. He died in good age and left his lands and possessions to this his only son Thomas Prestwood now mayor who beginning where his father left did not much follow the trade of merchandise in which also he was trained up but lived rather as a gentleman by his lands. He was nothing inferior unto his father in zeal of true religion towards God in due obedience to his prince and in beneficience to the commonwealth and in love towards his neighbours and more would he have been if too [?] a death had not prevented it. Among sundry his good doings he [?] up certain stones about the bounds and limits of the [?] of this city and reformed the office of the [?]worker. He was a very good housekeeper among his neighbours and would sundry times give good entertainment unto men of worship for which sometimes he was not so thankfully considered as he did deserve but he was so courteously dealed with all that he could not digest the unkindness showed unto him but in time he consumed and died in the first quarter of his mayoralty, the last of December 1577. And as his father and he were of like conditions, qualities & virtues in their lives so was one and the same grave their burial after their deaths. And no doubt in the day of the resurrection they both shall have the like seats and be crowned with the 24 elders of Israel with the like everlasting [?].

The foresaid Robert Claff after the death of Thomas Prestwood was chosen mayor to supply the room in his place. This being his second mayoralty. He was born at Wellington in the county of Somerset and descended of good parentage and kindred. He was first brought to this city be means of his aunt the wife of John Croston, Register to the bishop of Exeter. He was then put to the song school and was a chorister in the cathedral church and from thence he was taken and put to the grammar school and profited very well. Whereupon his uncle the Register seeing the forwardness of him did employ him to serve under him in his office and by the skill there learned and by his practice made a proctor in the ecclesiastical courts and afterwards Register of the peculiar courts under the dean and chapter. And partly by his own industry and partly by the liberality of his aunt who survived her husband and made him her executor he grew to great wealth and was twice mayor of this city which office he executed very well and uprightly with great wisdom and discretion. He was well learned in good letters and a man of very good conditions being of great modesty and gravity, very good friendly and loving unto all men, loathe to offend any but most willing and glad to do good to every body. He was somewhat timorous and did rather fear then fool any harm and if any unkindness were showed unto him he could not quickly nor quietly digest and forget the same. He died about the 70 years of age and left behind him every good report.

1577

George Peryman

Memorandum that the plague was very hot in London and therefore the term was twice adjourned to two times.

The pope, the king of Spain and the king of France concluded a peace with the Turks for five years because they would have the better leisure and time to persecute the professors of the gospel.

In the beginning of October 1577 Captain Frobisher returned home from out of Cataya laden with great store worth and gold metal of that county which fell not be nothing so rich as it was reported.

In the 11th of November there was seen in the South West a comet and blazing star.

In January Don John of Austria having the soldiers of Wallen who did serve under the Prince of Orange and the States of Flanders gave them an overthrow and slew 6,000 of them. But in August following, Anno 1558, the English men and Scots serving under the said prince gave Don John the like overthrow which Don John took in great grief and in September following he died.

Also one Thomas Spicer, upon a wager, did lade two hogsheads of wine upon one horse and carried them away from one celler to another by the space of one furlong long.

Also in August 1558 there was a cruel battle fought in Barbary between the king of Portugal and the King of Marmora and 2 other kings his confederates where all 4 kings were slain and about 40,000 men on both sides, among whom Thomas Stokely was also slain.

In this month also there were found hidden or buried in a dung hill in the fields behind St Clement's Church in London three images of wax of which one was said to be made for the destruction of the queen by way of enchantment. This was first found by a spirit in the likeness of a dog scraping up the dunghill and afterwards the party which practised this sorcery was found & taken.

Also this year in the 28th of June 1577 William Bradbridge bishop of Exeter died at his benefice of Newton Ferrers and buried in his own church at Exeter.

1578

Richard Prouze

Memorandum that upon the 23 of October 1578 there was a marvellous storm and tempest of lightning, thunder and rain and hail of 6 inches about which continued about 3 hours and wherewith great harms followed about Exeter. The like happened also upon the 15th of November then following.

This year in October Casimerus Duke of Bavaria and county Palatinate of Rheims came into England and as very honourably received and entertained, made Knight of the Garter and had the yearly of the queen of £1,000.

This year the Guildhall was new sealed and glazed, a new plump made in the high street at before the said hall door and a house of correction builded and the Watergate new re-edified. Towards the house of correction there was a liberal collection of the citizens given for which many of them did after repent.

Also an order was made by the mayor and 24 that who so ever should thenceforth be chosen and admitted to be one of the 24 should at his coming give to the chamber one spoon of silver gilded of an ounce at least.

Also, John Jones, goldsmith, to be discharged to be Receiver of the city gave to this city one basin and ewer of silver parcel gilded price £30 with which the spoons the mayor for this time being hath the use of it.

This year died Alice Mary alias Burgorosse the daughter of John Noseworthy and she gave to the city the sum of £50 to be used in the like order as is Mrs Tuckfell's money.

This year Mr John Woolton sometimes a canon in this church was consecrated bishop of the same at Lambeth in August and in September next following he came to this city using not the ceremonies the bishops so far used to have.

In July this year 1579 by the procurement of James Fitzmorrys of Desmond the pope sent certain Italians into Ireland to make conquest of that realm but the one and the other had evil success for Fitzmorys was slain and the Italians were driven out of their fort which they had builded at [?] and there Captain James de Valdres was taken and sent to London.

1579

William Chaple,
Simon Knight

Memorandum that Thomas Randall, parson of Lydford, and Stephen More were accused to hold the heresies of the family of Love for which Randall was deprived of his ministry and More [?[to recant & to do penance.

In April there was an earthquake in London and in most parts of this realm and in London two men were slain being at a sermon in Christ's Church at London.

Sir Francis Drake, after two years and 3 quarters that he had been in the Magdelan Seas and had compassed the world, returned in safety and with great wealth and riches.

The brewers of this city and suburbs were this year reduced into one company and fellowship.

This year William Chaple aforesaid died in the beginning of December and in his place Simon Knight was chosen mayor for the residue of the year. The said William Chaple was brought up in the trade of merchandise and by the same he grew to good wealth and giving himself to purchasing of lands he in a manner gave over his trade. He was a man wise and politic and who could reach so far in a common matter as much as the most part of men. He was well bent to the good of the common wealth but death so shortened his course that he had not the time to yield the fruits of his government nor to do that good which he was determined to have done.

The foresaid Simon Knight was born at Collys combe in Somersetshire and of good parentage. His father having many other children brought him to this city and found him apprentice unto a merchant named John Morgan after whose death he served under Mr William Hurst who having a good liking of the forwardness of the young man did employ him both at his side and beyond the seas and he did so well follow his business that he prospered very well and was of good wealth and ability and was at length twice mayor of this city and did very well in the first but in the latter he was so encumbered by litigious and troublesome matters that in following of them he was the more remiss in public matters. And among sundry virtues for which he was commended so for his too much well thinking of himself and standing in his own court to be wiser than others and also for too much gristing of other men he was much blamed and the less liked of.

1580

Thomas Brewerton

In the month of October 1581 by a commandment from her majesty there were a 11 horsemen with their whole furniture and well appointed sent into Ireland by the bishop, dean and chapter and the canons of St Peter's in this city at their own charges.

Also upon the 10th of October there was seen a great comet or blazing star and after that also was seen in the element many firey impression and also an earthquake in sundry parts of the realm.

Also the Lord Gray was sent over to be Lord Deputy of Ireland where in November he made a great conquest over the Romans and Italians which had fortified themselves at a place called [?] or St Mary Work and did put them all being 400 persons to the sword excepting 27 persons. In the fort he had and carried away 17 brass cast pieces [of cannon], great store [?] munitions and powder. Their captain, whose name was James de Valdra, he sent to London to her Majesty.

The sectaries of the family of Love were for the most part so hardly pursued that they [?]ted or were imprisoned and by that means that sect was in a manner extinguished.

This year in April 1571 Sir Francis Drake was dubbed knight aboard in his ship. This man was [born] in Tavistock in Devon.

1581

Thomas Martyn

Memorandum that the first of December Edmond Campion and sundry other Jesuits were indicted, arraigned & condemned to death for high treason and were executed for the same.

The Duke of [?], brother to the king of France, came to visit the queen's majesty and was most excelently entertained but many of the common people suspecting that they did not know did murmur much against him and also a book was printed against him for which one Mr Stubbes of Lincoln's Inn and one Mr Pery had their hands cut off. The Duke, after a few months, departed from hence to Antwerp where her majesty did accompany so far as to Canterbury but the Earl of Leicester and certain noblemen did accompany him to Antwerp where he was [?] to Marquis of Antwerp and Duke of Brabond.

The Prince of Orange was this year most treacherously slain.

King Philip dis-spoileth Don Anthony of the kingdom of Portugal.

This year there was a great plague in London.

This year certain men of the English pale in Ireland pretended in the absence of the Lord Gray then

Lord Deputy of Ireland to have taken the castle of Dublin, to have murdered the Lord Gray's wife and to have set at liberty the Earl of Kild[?]r then prisoner there but there were all taken and executed.

Memorandum that upon the 2 of July 1583 there was a meeting without Eastgate between the dean and chapter of St Peter's of the one part and the mayor and his brethren for the other part for an concerning the bounds of St Sidwell's fee set first down by an act of Parliament in King Henry the 6th's days but for lack of good looking unto the same was forgotten. For the church there were present Doctor Townsend, the dean of the church, Doctor Reynolds, Doctor Nycholls, John Rider and sundry the tenants of St Sidwell's and for the city were these Mr Thomas Martyn mayor, Mr Simon Knight, Mr Nicholas Martin, Mr Richard Prouz, Mr George Peryman, Mr John Peryam, Mr John Hooker and sundry other citizens where the true bounds were proved by the city and not denied by the dean and the rest.

1582

Michael Germyn

In January upon a Sunday a great number of people who delighted more in the vain pastime of bear baiting in Paris Garden than in serving of the lord and the due keeping of his holy Sabbath, many of them being upon a scaffold to behold the pastime the scaffold brake and with the fall thereof 7 persons were killed therewith and about [?40] persons were hurted.

The monster lying at Antwerp having not all things according to his will did under the colour of a muster determine to have ransacked the town and did kill upon a sudden a great number of the townsmen but yet he was disappointed of his purpose and driven to leave the town and country home into France.

In April 1583 there came two honourable ambassadors to the queen the one from the emperor of Muscovy and the other from the king of Pelnoia who were very honourably entertained.

The Lord William Earl of Bath upon Wednesday the 7th of August did marry in Exeter the Lady Elizabeth, daughter to the Earl of Bedford, unto whom the city gave a basin and an ewer of silver gilded and also made him a triumph in Southernhay in honour of his marriage.

1583

Geoffrey Thomas

The earl of Desmond who had continued in a long rebellion against the queen's majesty in Ireland was taken this year, slain and his head sent to London where it was set upon a pole upon London Bridge. Look more hereof in the chronicle of Ireland set out and penned by the writer hereof.

Great practices & devises were made and attempted by Francis Throgmorton Andrew and Somerfeld and sundry others for the destruction of the queen but the same were disclosed and they had their rewards.

The Lord Paulet Charles Arundel and others when they could [not] have their designs of the queen's death they fled into France & thence to Rome and as they fled traitorously so they died shamefully.

1584

John Davy

This year the lords of the council [in London] considering the daily devices and practices of the papists, Jesuits and rebellious people tending all to the destruction of the queen's majesty they devised certain instruments which was sent throughout the whole land unto which as they themselves had sworn to the due observation thereof so every subject should do the like and this was called an association. The effect whereof was whosoever should go about [?] or seek the destruction of her highness every man should seek to defend her and to be revenged upon every such practice.

Doctor Pary, by the persuasion of the pope who promised golden mountains unto him, did determine to have slain the queen and being in privy speech with her alone had a dagger about him of purpose to have done but the lord so daunted his heart that at that time his heart fainted and he could not do it.

Nevertheless afterward he attempting to perform the same at one other time or times he was betrayed and taken and then for his treason he was put to death & had the reward of a traitor.

Henry Earl of Northumberland being committed to the tower upon suspicion of treason fell into to that desperation that secretly he procured a dog [a firearm] which being charged with double shot did thereby kill himself.

Francis the good earl of Bedford died at London in July 1585 of the gangrene and the next following his [son] the eldest Lord Francis was slain in the marches of Scotland.

In September in this mayor's year Sir Francis Drake took shipping at Plymouth and sailed to Hispaniola where most valiantly took the towns of St Domingo and of Carteghena and the country there about and returned with great spoils and riches and honour.

In this month also Don Antonio named the king of Portugal being driven out of his country by King Philip arrived to Plymouth and upon St Michael's day he came to this city and was lodged at this mayor's house where he and all his [retinue] had their entertainment both horse and man gratis and without any penny charged.

In January sundry Jesuits were banished [from] the realm.

1585

Nicholas Martyn

The Earl of Leicester passed over this year into the Low Countries where he was received with great honour and made governor of the same.

In this year through long and continual rains and foul weather there was a great dearth and murrain of cattle and not long after a great dearth and scarcity of corn which continued three years together and notwithstanding order was taken by the lords of the council that the husbandmen should bring their corn to the markets and sell the same at reasonable prices yet it did not avail nor amend the matter.

The prince of Condit was driven to seek for refuge and succour in this realm and taking his ship he first came to Guernsey and then he came over to Weymouth and was looked for in this city but the wind so served him that he passed by to Plymouth and there he had by good means he was provided and furnished with 18 ships and 500 good soldiers and so upon the 21 of December he hoisted sails and passed over to Rochelle.

Memorandum that the assizes kept in the castle of Exeter in the lent, there were certain prisoners arraigned before Sergeant Flowerday and suddenly there came such a [?gloom] at the bar that a great number of people there being were infected and whereof there died in very short time the said Mr Flowerday, Sir John Chichester, Sir Arthur Bassett, Sir Bernard Drake, knights, Robert Carey and Thomas Risdon, esquires, justices of peace and of a jury which was to make then a trial upon one of the prisoners at the bar there died a 11 of them and only one man of the 12 escaped. The cause of the sickness was said to be this, Sir Benard Drake haven been at the seas took a Portugal ship who had been long at sea and the merchants and mariners were all worn out partly with sickness and partly for want of victuals and necessaries. These men with their ship he brought into Dartmouth haven and caused them all to be sent to the gaol at Exeter Castle where they infected the whole gaol with sickness and they all for the most part died thereof and infected also both city and country and which sickness continued a long time.

Sir Francis Drake returned from Hispaniola with great riches and honour which so inflamed the whole country with a desire to adventure unto the seas in hope of the like good success that a great number prepared ships, mariners and soldiers and travelled every place at the seas where any profit might be had. Some into Indians, some to Wyndgame de Coyi, some setting a way to China by the north pole and some to find that which was not lost whereby many were undone and themselves in the end never the better [?] as is the common saying *from bad to worst*.

This year one Peter Morys, a Dutch man, by an engine builded at London Bridge he conveyed the water out of the river of Thames that he brought it to the highest place in all London and served every honest [man] with fresh water who listed to have it which was very beneficial unto himself and a great number of the whole city.

In July a great conspiracy which was meant to the subversion of the whole state of the realm and the destruction of the queen was by the goodness of God discovered and the traitors namely Babington and his followers were apprehended and taken and in September 13 of them were executed to death.

1586

George Smythe

This year there was a parliament holden at Westminster where all the treacheries and practices of the Scottish queen were discovered and proved and she condemned. And notwithstanding great suits were made to the queen's majesty for the executing of her to death and had granted her warrant yet she could not consent thereunto. Nevertheless upon a sudden she was beheaded at Fortheringay in Northamptonshire which when she heard of was very sorrowful and much grieved. And Mr Davidson the secretary committed to the tower for delivery of the warrant.

An advertisement was given of the great preparation which was making by the pope, King Philip, the G[?] and the whole league against the queen and for the invading of this land which at the first was scarcely believed.

Sir William Stanley having the charge of a fort in the Low Countries most traitorously sold the same to the Prince of Parma and became to be King Philip's man whom the queen before that time did so like that she was minded to have made him a baron.

Sir Francis Drake took shipping at Plymouth and passeth into Spain where in the bay of Cadiz he burned a great fleet of ships there lying at anchor and from thence he passed unto the islands where about Terfora he took a great carrick of 1,200 [tons] and in June he returned again into Plymouth.

1587

John Peryam

In this year there was a great fight between the King of Navarra and the Duke of Guise in which the king had the victory and then the Duke and the leaguers trusting better to their devilish & secret practices and murders to destroy their adversaries found the means that the Prince of Condy was poisoned and for which his wife was had suspicion. The like thing was practiced against the king of Navarra but he escaped it.

Also a great preparation was made throughout the whole realm as well at land as seas for the withstanding of the king of Spain, his mighty (termed the invincible) navy provided and appointed for destroying of England and at the charges of this city (whereof her majesty afterwards made some payments) there were set forth two ships and one pinnace well appointed in all things namely the Bartholomew of Exmouth of 120 tons, the Elizabeth Rose of Topsham of 100 tons and the Gift of God of 20 tons. And upon the 21 of July then next following the said Spanish fleet being about 130 sails of great burden and whereof 4 of them were great galleasses came upon our west coasts and invaded upon a sudden to have surprised the Lord Admiral with all the English fleet which at that time was within the haven of Plymouth and distrusting no such matter. Nevertheless such shifting upon knowledge hereof was made that the Lord Admiral, Sir Francis Drake, Sir John Hawkins and Sir Martin Frobisher recovered to the seas and encountered the said invincible navy and by the goodness of god they were wonderfully dispersed and had the worst. For notwithstanding they were more in number and for force greater than any English ship and so s[?]l thoroughly appointed as to man's judgement it was impossible that they should have the foil yet in fight some were lost and two of the greatest galleasses in which stood their great strength was sunk and spoiled and the rest which escaped coasted along the seas about Scotland and thence into Ireland homewards and by the ways of God's mighty hand many of them, both ships and men, utterly perished and cast away. Of the manner of the fight at the seas and of their coastings and sundry other things incident unto this there are sundry pamphlets set out in print where at large the same be seen for which victory her majesty commanded the 18th of November to be kept holy and every man to resort to his church.

The earl of Leicester in the end of this year in his travelling between Bath and Billingsworth at his house of Langley where his first wife died, he solemnly died the first of December 1588. His fame was greater in his lifetime but he was not so soon dead but as a shadow which passeth away he was clean forgotten. His solemn funeral made some show of sorrow but generally his death more w[?]ed at than lamented.

In September Captain Cavendish, who had been back about two years at the Indians and had followed that course with Sir Francis Drake before him, returned home in safety at Plymouth and was richly laden. He gloried so much of his good success that he made the sails of his ships of silk and although his great wealth was thought to have satisfied for him for his whole life yet he saw the end thereof within very short time.

1588

Thomas Chaple

In the beginning of this year a great navy prepared with all things necessary under the guiding of Sir John Norrys and Sir Francis Drake passed over into Portugal and had with them Don Antonio the named King of Portugal and went to Lisbon and albeit their company in respect of King Philip's forces were not as it were a landfall yet they durst not to encounter with our men. And yet by reason of great sickness and other accidents these captains were driven to return without any victory which they hoped of and Don Antonio came to this city and here sojourned for a time.

The king of France by apparent arguments seeing and knowing that the Duke of Guise sought his destruction upon a sudden did send for him and having gotten him within his custody and [?]s caused him to be killed in his privy chamber wherein he was the more misliked that under colour as it were to deal in matters of counsel he should so tyrannise over the duke but such is the will of god to deal with his adversaries. And in July following the king himself was slain by a friar with a venomed knife who made a humble suit unto the king and he mistrusting nothing the friar taking his advantage suddenly as the king turned aside he thrust him into the body with his knife. And this king being the last of the house of the Vallois and none left of that house to succeed in the crown, the king of Navarra and the next of the blood being of the house of Bourbon was forthwith proclaimed King of France and notwithstanding he made and offered unto all his subjects and all good conditions of peace yet such was and is the malice of the pope and the leaguers that he could not prevail but driven to stand upon his forces.

The queen mother of France, the capital root of all the troubles in France, immediately upon the death of the Duke of Guise, died.

At Newton Ferrers in Devon there was a vision of a corpse or a dead body carried to the parish there to be buried and a great troop or company following the same. Sundry of that parish seeing afar of such a company and knowing none to be sick in the parish nor any bell to be rung they also followed after. But when they came to the church they found nothing but only a hole newly made in the churchyard. Immediately the same vision went thence unto a ferry fast by where the ferryman sat in his boat awaiting for passengers and at the sight of this vision some of that company in the boat fell sick and some one of them fell half amazed and went to his own home and died. The sickness brought out of Portugal so reigned in that parish and all that seacoast in South Hams that it continued long after.

Memorandum that this year there came into the most part of the havens of Devon and some in Cornwall many rich prices which were taken by the English men keeping the seas.

1589

Richard Prouz

Memorandum in the beginning of this year Sir Francis Vere knight, aged about 28 years and then serving in the Low Countries, did give an overthrow unto 17 ensigns of footmen of which he carried away 11 ensigns and overthrew two coronels of horsemen of which he carried with him one whole coronel both horse and men captives.

Geneva being besieged by the Duke of Savoy the siege was raised and they delivered.

In the winter there were sundry and many rich prizes brought into Plymouth and upon all the south havens in the counties of Devon and Dorset.

A great earthquake upon the 13 of December 1589 was a Waterford in Ireland.

The merchants of St Malo corrupted the gunner of the castle of St Malo who betrayed the town unto them and they forthwith entered and slew the captain.

In March the king of France encountering with the duke of May he gave him a great overthrow, the king having but 11,000, the duke 30,000 of which were slain 13,000 and the king of his 11,000 lost 4,000 and as many Spaniards, Walloons and Dutchmen and strangers as were under the Duke they were all put to the sword. He had at that instant three great victories in Lower Dolphony and at Marseilles.

In the month of September 1590 the plague began in this city.

In this year the conduit in the High Street in St Lawrence's parish, called the Little Conduit, was new builded.

Also, the house in the courtelege of the guildhall was new builded.

At the election of the mayor and officers Monday before St Michael's day 1590 Sir Robert Denys being the recorder because he could not come to the same by reason of the sickness he did send his letters to the mayor and common council for his excuses and referred unto them to make choice of some one man whom they thought good to supply his name and then they chose the chamberlain who took the secret voices of every of the 24 and presented the same before the commons.

1590

William Martyn

Richard Crossing noted: This year the plague was great in this city.

PART TWO

Richard Izacke 1591–1676

1591

Michael Germyn

John Tayler, a freeman of this city, for colouring of foreigners' goods was fined twenty nobles. The same person for suing another freeman at Westminster, out of the jurisdiction of this court was fined 20s. The cloth market removed from Northgate Street into Southgate Street, to be kept between the conduit there and the lane nigh the Bear. Racks in the Bonhay of late without authority erected to be again removed. The walls of the city ordered to be yearly cleansed and a yearly stipend appointed for the same. Charges paid for suing forth a commission of oyer and determiner. A suit depending between this city and the city of London touching the custom of certain goods, [?] scavage, whereof by ancient charters were discharged. Ordered that a bridewell or house of correction with certain ordinance for the good government thereof be speedily had, the charge whereof Mr Atwill's money is to be defrayed. Two hundred marks per annum allowed the mayor for his pension, which is to be continued by order of this house unto all future mayors. The same was by a subsequent order reduced to one hundred and twenty pounds per annum.

1592

Nicholas Spycer

Edward Drew, sergeant at law, elected recorder of this city and afterwards recorder of London. John Wood elected sword bearer of the said city. The Company of the Butchers within this city, disturbing the market, and taking away victuals of foreigners, were for this misdemeanour committed. Thomas Martyn, a member of this house, for absenting himself from the common council, being thereunto duly summoned, is dismissed hence. License in Lent to be given only to two butchers to sell flesh to them that have licence to eat the same, who are not to have licence again till the whole company of butchers have had their turns and the like privilege. The porters of the several gates of the city to have gowns every third year.

Richard Crossing noted: The front of the Guildhall pulled down & began to be built.

1593

Thomas Spicer

John Hele, sergeant at law, elected recorder of this city. Also Robert Northcott was chosen sword bearer of the said city. Goods seized on as foreign bought and foreign sold and compounded for. Persons appointed to measure and weigh all raw kerseys brought into the market to be sold and likewise to [?] all measures and weights. Wednesdays and Saturdays the foreign butchers are permitted to come here to market which is to begin at eight of the clock in the morning and to end at three in the afternoon. Crooks and ladders to be provided and hung up in some convenient place, for the better safeguard of this city, in case of any fire happening. The fore part of the Guildhall was new built. Our citizens paid their wages for this service in Parliament at 4s per diem. The receiver and stewards fined for not keeping their feasts this year. Two watchmen appointed and sworn by Mr Mayor from Michaelmas to Midsummer for the better prevention of the danger of fire and other annoyances. All accounts belonging to this city ought to be made up yearly.

Samuel Izacke added: Bishop Wolton having well governed this church 14 years space (being constantly an earnest effecter of conformity, against the opposers thereof) 13 March deceased and lies buried on the south side of the quire of his own church; in whose memory, on a fair stone fixed in the wall, are inscribed these ensuing verses:

Richard Crossing noted: The said front of the Guildhall new built.

1594

John Davye

John Samford, a member of this house, on his request is dismissed. Money advanced by the several members of this house to buy in corn for the public store, chiefly for the relief of the poor in this time of scarcity. The meal market, removed into Northgate Street, and from thence into the high street nigh St Olave's church. Freeman's goods privileged from all customs and elsewhere by our charters. Goods seized on as foreign bought and foreign sold, and compounded for.

Samuel Izacke added: John Coldwell, doctor of physic, and bishop of Sarum, about this time gave his see a strong purge, by consenting to the alienation of Sherborne Manor from his bishopric, he was assaulted in a dangerous juncture of time to give a denial; for after he was elected bishop, all his church preferments were disposed of, and before his election was confirmed, Sir Walter Raleigh, knight, importuned him to pass Sherborne to the crown, and effected the same, whereupon Sir Walter presently begged it of the queen, much after the same Sir William Killegrew, knight, got the manor of Crediton (a bough almost as big as the rest of the body) from this church of Exeter, by the consent of this Bishop Babington.

Gervys Babington was this year upon the second day of May installed bishop of this see, being translated hither from his bishopric of Llandaff in Wales, and having well governed this diocese two years and a half was removed and made bishop of Worcester.

1595

John Chappell

Goods seized and forfeited being landed the town custom not discharged. The bridges under Southgate and Eastgate are severally ordered to be amended. John Davye for speaking unseemly words to John Ellicott here in the chamber, they being both members of this house was fined and paid forty shillings. Goods seized on as foreign bought and foreign sold and compounded for. Post horse to be here always in readiness for the public safety of the city and for the special service of the queen's majesty. The several captains of this city, in respect of their great charges, are awarded £6 13s 4d and their lieutenants £3 6s 8d a piece by the chamber.

1596

John Levermore

A pension of £4 per annum, granted to John Hooker, in remuneration of sundry services performed by his father to this city. On the death of Richard Jurdayne, late receiver general of this city, Alexander Mayne was chosen in his place for the residue of the year. Every member of this house is to provide and have in readiness for the queen's service such a quantity of gunpowder as is imposed on him. Goods seized and forfeited, being landed, the town custom not discharged. The duty to be paid for land carriage of all goods imported or exported.

1597

George Smyth

The town of Tiverton being lately consumed by fire, £10 in money was sent them hence to relieve their poor. A particular rate imposed on merchandises brought in and landed at the port of Exeter. The duty to be paid for land carriage of all goods imported or exported. Ordered that no butcher do set his victuals to sale in any other place of the city than the old shambles or in the usual market place and on the market days appointed upon pain of forfeiture of five shillings. A hogshead of wine bestowed on Mr Mayor in regard of his extraordinary charges occasioned by entertaining the earl of bath and some other persons of honour.

Samuel Izacke added: Felons' goods forfeited to the city, and seized on accordingly by the Sheriff.

1598

John Peryam

Richard Crossing noted: He gave unto the mayor, bailiffs and commonality of this city one thousand pounds, also a fair basin and ewer of silver, the said £1,000 is to be leant by £200 to five merchants for three years & the profit thereof is by the mayor & justices to be given to poor sick, maimed & hurt people.

An order made that a fair book for the registering of all the benefactors of this city should be speedily provided. Also that the effigies or portraits of Mr Lawrence Atwill (a worthy benefactor of this city) at the city's charge be forthwith procured and hung up in the council chamber. Every inhabitant's dwelling house being on fire forfeits and by an act shall pay 20s for the better quenching of fired houses here, every alderman is to provide six buckets of leather, and every other member of this house four, on pain of five shillings a piece. Every inhabitant's chimney being on fire forfeits six shillings and eight pence. In all the city's mills there ought to be lawful beams, scales and weights. An ordinance made that all inhabitants within the city shall grind their corn at the city's mills on pain of 12d for every bushel. John Searle, appointed Porter of the Maudlin, who is to have the house there belonging to that office. Liberty given by the dean and chapter to enclose a place with ceiling in St Peter's church for the 24 and their wives and their seats to be covered with green baize by Mr Receiver. William Cotton (upon the translation of Bishop Babington to Winchester) was this year 16 May installed bishop of this diocese.

1599

John Howell

Mr Palmer's almshouse is appointed only for women and one Whittrowe's widow being therein placed and taking husband, contrary to the orders of the said house, was expelled. No more trees to be given out of Duryard Wood and every member of this house requesting any, forfeits forty shillings. A composition made with Mr Worth for damage done to the bridge and weirs by bringing wood and timber through the river of Exe. Recompense made to Mr Nicholas Spicer for a butt of sack lost by negligence coming up the new haven. Cowley Bridge and Exe Bridge, being in decay, to be repaired and also the quay to be cleansed of the mud therein. Mr Mayor and the stewards are to take care for the placing of the market and likewise to put rates on things there brought to be sold. The deep way between the Wynards and the Magdalene without the South Gate was this year filled up and paved. The benches in the council chamber to be covered or cushions there to be provided. Recognisances forfeited, and compounded for. A lodge to be builded for the porter of Westgate nigh St Mary Steps Church.

1600

William Martyn

Richard Crossing noted: He gave unto the mayor, bailiffs and commonality twenty pounds to be leant to 2 or 4 artificers for 3 years as Mrs Tuckfield's money.

Mr Peter Blundell by his last will and testament gave nine hundred pounds in money to this city and the town of Tiverton, the same to be disposed of by the mayor and common council of the said city according to the said will. A rate laid on every parish within this city to contribute towards the bringing home of the water in and through the pipes. The quarry in Northernhay to be set on work for the repairing of the pipes. Goods seized on as foreign bought and foreign sold and compounded for. Goods of a *Felo de se* forfeited to the city, and seized on accordingly. Every receiver on the passing of his account is to being in all acquittances touching his disbursements. William Tickell elected chamberlain of this city.

1601

Thomas Walker

The town of Tiverton being of late destroyed by fire, was relieved with a good sum of money collected of the inhabitants of this city as a voluntary contribution near £100. The porter of Northgate for sundry misdemeanours displaced. A committee appointed to make an inventory of all such goods as do belong unto the mayor, bailiffs and commonality of this city, and speedily to bring it in, to the end, the same may be here treasured up in safety, for the public good. A patent under the common seal of this city was granted to the society of the weavers, fullers and shearmen of the same. The like patent was granted to the joiners, painters, carpenters, masons and glaziers of the said city. Also a survey book of all the city's lands to be forthwith all made and provided. Also that the fore part of the guildhall (being in decay) be repaired and new flourished. My Lord Bishop refers the nomination of a school master for the High School within this city to the chamber who recommended Mr Perryman who was admitted accordingly.

1602

Richard Beavys, William Martyn

Goods seized and forfeited as foreign bought and sold and composition made for the same. Standards of measures received of my Lord Treasurer for the city's use. An order made for paving the street without the Southgate. Enacted that every alderman shall wear a scarlet gown and tippet, and every sheriff and receiver shall likewise wear a scarlet gown at the election of the new mayor. Five hides of leather seized on, being not well tanned according to the statute. Liberty granted to Mr Lawrence Bodley (one of the canons of this church) to erect a little room on his wall towards the high street, paying 1d per annum for the same. On the death of Richard Beavys, late mayor, William Martyn, one of the alderman, was chosen lieutenant for the residue of the year. £10 per annum appointed to the 4 waits of this city, with their liveries, and two boys to be trained up in music under them.

Richard Crossing noted: The said Richard Bevys gave £4 per annum for ever, for the marrying out of 4 poor maids, of the parish of St Mary Arches, St Olave, St John's Bow & Allhallows On The Walls, 20 shillings each.

Samuel Izacke added: Queen Elizabeth departed this life 24 March, and on the 29th of the same month was King James the first here solemnly proclaimed king.

King James I

1603

Nicholas Spycer

Richard Crossing noted: He devised all his lands in Halberton in Devon, called Slowe, to 12 trustees of the chamber for ever, for several uses, & especially to be leant out unto free men of this city, under the sum of £21, for 4 years upon good security.

The plague of pestilence being entered this city, a pest house (for the better relief of those sick persons infected with that disease) is provided nigh the said city, by the special care of the Magistrates here. Mr Chamberlain desired to transcribe the Black Roll into some book in the chamber. Goods landed at Topsham, and forfeited, the duty of the town custom being not discharged. The meal market placed before St Olave's church in the high street. Maudlin Fair and Lammas Fairs (in regard of the present sickness) not to be kept this year. An order made that the walls of the city shall be yearly cleansed. Also that the aldermen attending the mayor shall wear their tippets, of velvet, and the mayor visiting the markets of the said city to have the sword carried before him and to be attended by his officers. Also that no victualler shall kill his meat in his shop, street or shambles from the first day of May to Michaelmas then next following on pain of 3s 4d. Also that all innkeepers and others to remove their dung and cleanse their slaughter houses weekly on pain of 3s 4d. Also that no house or linhay within the city (for fear of fire) shall be covered with straw or thatch. Also that no inhabitant of this city shall presume to keep in his house a dog or bitch on pain of 3s 4d for every week. The aldermen in their respective wards are likewise ordered to appoint persons to ward and watch in time of sickness abroad.

1604

John Davye

A silver cup with a cover double-gilded presented to the earl of Bath from the city as a token of their love, whereon the city's arms were engraven. Two freeman for suing two other freemen out of the jurisdiction of this court, were fined £6 13s 4d a piece and in default of payment to be disenfranchised. A gelding seized on as a deodand, and sold by the Receiver for five pounds. William Horsham, dying in his Stewardship, Thomas Richardson was chosen in his place to supply the residue of the year. Sir Walter Rawley knight, being formerly at Winchester attainted of high treason, was this year [sic] on Tower Hill London beheaded, who was a person of such rare endowments of mind as this age did afford, whose worth and virtues to describe I leave to a more able pen, he being a native of this city. I held it not fit to pass him by altogether in silence. This mayor was a liberal benefactor to the city, who founded and built an almshouse in the parish of St Mary Arches within the said city for the succour and relief of two married couples and two single persons and endowed it with £16 per annum of the rectory of Morleigh in the county of Devon, the rectory and the presentment whereof he gave to the mayors and others of the chamber.

1605

Henry Hull

William Martyn (on the resignation of the said John Hele) elected Recorder of this city. A voluntary contribution made of money by the inhabitants of this city towards the erecting of St Sidwell's tower. Goods of an attainted person for felony, seized the city's use.

 Samuel Izacke added: On the 5th day of November, the Gunpowder Treason was discovered, and the Actors found and executed, whereof a great Scholar made this observation:

> *The Fifth of November, England, remember; what?*
> *The Pope's Conspiracy, God's great Delivery, that.*

1606

Richard Dorchester

Certain articles and orders to be devised and made for the good government of all the almshouses within the city and suburbs, whereof the mayor and his brethren are governors, according to the will of the founders, for the due observation whereof by the alms people, the same are to be placed in every of the said houses. A patent under the common seal of the city was granted to the company of the smiths, cutlers and saddlers of the same to be incorporated. A Committee appointed to view and repair Holloway without the Southgate. An exemplification of a decree in the Exchequer to be had touching the loading and unloading of goods at Topsham. If any inhabitant's chimney be on fire he forfeits 6s 8d. The rent and relief demanded of Mr Canon, hellier for the Archdeacon of Barnstaple's house, which being denied was recovered by a suit in law. Whosoever casteth out any filth in the street forfeits 3s 4d per an ordinance. New maces with the King's Arms engraven thereon made for the four sergeants. Northernhay Gates to be kept shut and locked by the tenant thereof, that is may not lie common for horses.

1607

Sir George Smyth, knight

The price of corn much increasing, a considerable quantity thereof is bought and put up in store for the good and necessary relief of the poor within this city. Twenty pounds in money given by the city towards the building of fitter seats for the judges of assizes that come this circuit in the castle, which was done upon the motion of Mr Recorder from the said Judges. St Nicholas Fair happening to be on a Sunday is deferred and kept on another day. A Patent under the Common Seal was granted to my Lord Treasurer, to be High Steward of this City. One Joan Clashe being troubled with the disease of the leprosy was sent down to the hospital of St Mary Magdalene without the South Gate. Some of Mr Atwill's money was lent to several parishes to keep their poor on work. Ordered that every member of the 24 upon his first admission into this house shall deposit £20 for one year. A keep of the gaol, sheaf's war and counter elected and his fees appertained.

1608

John Prowze

Mr Thomas Edwards, a physician and a member of this house, on his petition to be hence dismissed, and promise to give his best advice freely to the poor of this city, in their sickness, had his request granted. Mr Cleeveland bestowed on this city a silver cup gilded. Exe Bridge being very much in decay is ordered to be repaired.

Samuel Izacke added: Goods seized on as forfeited, being foreign bought and sold, and composition made for the same. A gelding, as a deodand, forfeited to the city, and seized on accordingly.

1609

Hugh Crossinge

The warden of the hospital of St Mary Magdalen is ordered to admit none therein but sick persons and such only as the chamber shall approve of. Sir John Acland, knight, gave fifty pounds in money towards the binding out poor children apprentices, vizt, for the binding out of twelve poor boys give marks to be lent with each of them, and six poor maids five nobles to be lent with each of them during their said apprenticeships upon sufficient security. A present of twenty nobles bestowed on Mr Recorder in remuneration of [?]. Gilbert Smyth and Samuel Alford two of the 24 having (without leave) for a long space absented themselves from the common council and being also thought unable to undergo such offices of charge as must shortly fall on them in regard of their places here, are therefore both of them dismissed hence. A hogshead of wine and a salmon pie ordered to be given to the Speaker of the Parliament by our citizens there, as a present from the city.

Samuel Izacke added: An Act of Parliament made for the continuance and repair of head weir on the river of Exe and the new leat.

1610

Walter Borough

John Pearse (one of Mr Hurst's almsmen) expelled of the said house, for disobeying the orders and constitutions of the same, vizt, by marrying a woman under the age of five and fifty years. Another present of five pounds bestowed on Mr Recorder for other services done for the city. An ordinance made that no person presume to draw water from any of the conduits within the city to brew withal on pain to forfeit 5s. The cloth market removed from Southgate Street to the high street and there appointed to be kept between St Martin's Lane and the Little Conduit. The plaintiffs of the two courts of the city farmed by the town clerk at £10 per annum. An exemplification to be had of the Act of Parliament lately made for Trew's Weir.

1611

John Lane

Richard Crossing noted: He gave £100 to the mayor, bailiffs & commonality of Exeter, the profits thereof is for Mr Hurst's almshouse.

Thomas Tooker elected sword bearer of this city, was arraigned before the Judges of Assizes at the

Castle of Exeter, found guilty and had sentence to die, and was accordingly executed at Heavitree for murdering his wife. £30 collected in this city, present to the poor of St Sidwell's, whose houses were there lately burnt. This mayor gave £100 to the city towards the better maintenance of the poor in Mr Hurst's almshouse without the Eastgate. Ordered that every person shall be elected a member of this house shall presently deposit 15s for a spoon and to lend £20 for a year. Several bridges over the new work or haven to be built. The river of Exe and the quay there being in decay to be repaired and cleansed. Goods seized as forfeited being foreign bought and sold, and composition made for the same. Edward Drew's sword, wherewith he slew William Peter, forfeited to the city, was bestowed on Mr Recorder. Several recognisances forfeited and composition made per them. A pension of twenty nobles per annum conferred on Mr Chamberlain's son, a scholar in Oxford. A deputation granted to Roger Mace to collect the duties and haulage of woollen cloths. Thomas Toker, dismissed of his office of sword bearer for his incontinency with the late wife of Stephen Toker deceased, and was afterwards executed for murdering his wife. For avoiding the danger of fire every alderman is to provide ten leather buckets and every one of the rest of the 24 of the common council six on pain of 20s. The Receiver and stewards are to bring each of them ten men well armed to watch on St Peter's Eve upon pain to every one of them five pounds.

1612

William Newcombe

John Clarke elected sword bearer of this city. £67 here collected was sent to Tiverton that town being lately burned. 3s 4d for ten years' tithe due for Duryard Wood was now paid to the parson or rector of Upton Pyne. £10 for aid money paid to the king's majesty, on the princess her marriage, from the city. A pump to be made in the place where the town well stood. Goods seized as forfeited being foreign bought and sold and compounded for. The goods of Thomas Tooker (late sword bearer of the city) on his attainder seized on and compounded for. Part of the city's walls being lately fallen down to be speedily repaired. Seats or benches with timber to be made in Northernhay over against Gallant's Bower – Northernhay levelled and a pleasant walk made thereon at the city's charge. A pension of £5 per annum granted to Valentine Tucker for his life. Another of £20 per annum to Mr Howell one of the aldermen of the city in remuneration [?]. John Martyn elected chamberlain of the said city. The coverage of leather demised for £12 per annum. The ground before the churches of St Stephens and Allhallows in Goldsmith Street granted to the parishioners. Mr Mayor's seat and the king's arms erected over the same in the guildhall. Ten pounds per annum settled on the Sword Bearer as his salary or pension.

1613

Jeffery Waltham

Leonard Cranbury elected Sword Bearer of the said city. The warden of the Mawdlyn ought to call the proctor thereof to an account monthly who is to do nothing in reference thereunto but by the warden's assent. Goods landed here ought to pay the duty of town custom and if they be transported and brought hither again, they shall then likewise pay the duty of town custom. Ordered that no water be drawn on at the great conduit to brew withal. Goods seized as forfeited being foreign bought and sold, and composition made for the same. The king's beam to be provided and hung up at the quay to weigh goods there brought. No freeman to be made by the mayor alone, without the chamber's consent. The butts in Northernhay, being in decay, to be repaired. The walk in Northernhay to be railed in with timber. A pension of 40s per annum granted to Thomas Martyn for service done and to be done. Twenty nobles allowed every mayor in lieu of his freeman and if any man pays a greater sum for his freedom the overplus thereof is to be paid Mr Receiver for the city's use. A patent granted to the Right Honourable the Earl of Northampton under the common seal of this city to be High Steward thereof with a fee of £10 per annum incident thereof.

1614

Thomas Walker

Elizabeth Seldon widow bestowed on this house a silver cup with a cover double-gilded weighing 50 ounces to be used by every mayor successively and also one hundred marks in money. A new feoffment to be made to others by the surviving feoffees of John Davy and Lawrence Seldon & Lawrence Bodley freely gave £400 towards the maintenance of a lecturer within this city. A minister appointed to say prayers at the Mawdlyn Chapel and a pension of 40s per annum allowed him. Thomas Pope from being exempted to be chosen a steward and a member of this house gives £10 in plate. Foreign butchers on market days to observe hours and the places of their standings appointed them. Goods seized as forfeited being foreign bought and sold, and compounded for. Lawful beams and weights to be provided for the public use and service of the city. An order made touching the yarn market, when the same shall begin and end. Also that the duty be paid for land carriage of such goods from Topsham to this city. The sergeants at mace of the city their yearly wages are increased to £10 per annum. A patent under the common seal of the city granted to the right honourable the Earl of Suffolk to be High Steward of the said city, with a fee of £10 per annum incident thereunto.

1615

John Marshall

The sheriff is to levy all amercements and recognisances [?]ed, and to account for the same. The bishop pretends a title to felons' goods, deodands &c within his fee but cannot make the same to appear. Goods seized as forfeited being foreign bought and sold, and composition made for the same. Twenty nobles per annum as a pension settled on Robert Sherwood to oversee the works of the city. No casks to be left in the open street or pain of 12d. Every wain, wagon or cart compassed with iron passing through the city its owner is to pay 4d towards the repairing of the streets. The goods of Alexander Hill (who was executed for felony) were seized on for the city's use. A gratuity of 20 nobles bestowed on Mr Recorder for his extraordinary pains in the city's affairs. The several members of this house in their respective order have agreed to boil the pot for the better relief of the poor prisoners in the Southgate. Mr Receiver ordered to lay out £6 in meat against the ensuing feast of Christmas to be distributed among the poor of this city. Also to amend the weir's banks and sluices upon the new haven. Several persons of honour entertained by Mr Mayor at his table at the city's charge.

1616

John Sheere

Ralph Hamner of London by his last will gave £100 to this city to be lent unto two young merchants for 7 years. John Beryman of London by his last will gave likewise £100. A legacy of £6 13s 4d given by Joan Hayman of Dartmouth to the poor of this city. John Peryam, a worthy member of this house and twice mayor of this city (who by his wisdom and discretion hath for many years together exceedingly furthered the peaceable government thereof), did this year by his deed under hand and seal present there the free gift of £1000 and brought in the money accordingly to be lent to 5 merchants for 3 years each to have £200 and to pay yearly 20 nobles for the interest thereof, which is to be disposed by 2 justices of the peace to poor people maimed and he also gave a basin and ewer of silver weighing 73 ounces. Stephen Robyns appointed to collect the duties and customs of the cloth hall. Felons' goods forfeited to the city and seized on accordingly.

1617

Ignatius Jurdayne

Richard Crossing noted: He was eminent for acts of piety, justice & charity.

Nicholas Ducke elected recorder of this city. Six pounds paid to the receiver in lieu of a heriot on the death of a tenant of the said city. A collection of money to be made by and from the inhabitants of the city and suburbs towards the filling up of Holloway without the Southgate. Mr Receiver Ducke being chosen Reader of Lincoln's Inn, two hogsheads of claret wine were presented to him from this city, as a testimony of their love. A copy of a decree had out of the Exchequer touching the fishing in the river of Exe. The profits of the plaintiffs of the courts granted to the town clerk for £12 per annum. The new work or haven and sluices being in decay to be amended.

1618

Thomas Martyn

This mayor gave the sum of thirty pounds in money to the mayor and justices of this city to be given and distributed amongst poor householders oppressed with children and no part thereof to common beggars. William Birdall elected sword bearer of the said city. Licence given by the chamber to Joan Wilcoxe which placed in Mr Hurste's almshouse to marry. Felons' goods forfeited to the city and seized on. A rent in Sydford of 26s 8d per annum decreed in chancery to the city. The sum of £3 6s 8d bestowed on Roger Fishmore, coroner of this county, for several services done in reference to his said office, and could not recover those fees by law due to him. Every receiver is ordered for the future to pay Mr Mayor £3 6s 8d (as Mr Haydon's gift) towards the boiling of the pot for the prisoners in Southgate. A sluice to be made in the new haven, Trew's Weir to be repaired and also the key for the better passage of boats and lighters there to be cleansed. 40s paid the city in lieu of a heriot on the death of a tenant in the manor of Duryard.

Samuel Izacke added: Sir Walter Raleigh knight, in the first year of this King's reign, at Winchester, before Commissioners of Oyer and Terminer, was attainted of High Treason; which said sentence did lie dormant almost 16 years, during which time he continued a prisoner in the Tower, until about three years last past, when he was permitted to go at large, and had a commission for a voyage to Guinea, and after his return, was remanded to the tower; the record of the Attainder being brought and certified into the King's Bench, he was, by *habeas corpus* directed to the Lieutenant of the Tower, brought to the bar, where being demanded what he could say, why the court should not proceed, and grant execution against him, replied that king had employed him as General of a voyage and gave him power of the lives of others, and whether this did amount to a pardon or not he knew not. To whom the court replied, that the King pardons no treasons by any implications, but by express words, and so execution was awarded against him, and he committed to the sheriffs of London and Middlesex, and by them was brought to the gate house, and the next day, being the 29th of October the same year, was beheaded in the great court at Westminster. He was a person of rare endowments of mind as this age did afford him in any capacity, take him as a statesman, soldier, sailor or learned writer: *Tam marti, quam Mercurio* his own motto, in every respect he well deserved, whose real worth and virtues to describe is a sufficient task for an abler pen; well remembering that old sentence *Præstat nulla quam pauca dicere de Carthgine*, I cease. Some say that he was born at Budleigh in Devon; others, that he was a native hereof, and born in the house adjoining to the Palace Gate: on either account as our country-man, I held it unfit to pass him by altogether in silence.

1619

John Prowse

Joan Garnesey, widow, placed in Mr Hurst's alms-house marrying (contrary to the orders of the said house) she and her husband were both removed and expelled thence. Thomas Mogeridge gave £200 towards the maintenance of Dr Bodley's lecture. Lodgings provided for the judges here at the city's charge. Ordered that a silver salt cellar double-gilded of £16 price with the chamber's money be bought, whereon the city's arms are to be engraven and to be used by every mayor. Edward Hert, Town Clerk of this city, surrendered to the chamber his said office, whereof John Martyn, Chamberlain of the said city, was elected into the said office of town clerk. Every wain, wagon or cart compassed with iron passing through the streets its owner is to pay 4d towards the repairing of the streets.

1620

Hugh Crossinge

This mayor gave the city the land of St John's Hospital within the Eastgate for the use of a hospital. No cook within the city to dress any victuals on Fridays or Saturdays. Our citizens serving in Parliament paid their duty. A commission issued out of the Chancery and brought down on the state of charitable uses.

1621

Walter Borough

This year on the 26th day of August Bishop Cotton died and upon the 20th day of November then next following Valentine Carye was consecrated Bishop hereof. This mayor was a liberal benefactor to the city who gave £20 per annum for ever for the support of St John's Hospital within this city out of his lands in St Paul's parish, which are now of a greater yearly value. When more than one person at any time shall be elected into this house as members thereof, they are to be placed and take precedence according to their seniority of being stewards. Goods seized as forfeited as being foreign bought and sold and composition made for the same. Three pounds paid the city for a heriot on the death of a tenant. Mr Receiver ordered to amend and rectify the bounds in the perambulation walk. A night watch appointed to be kept from Allhallowtide to Candlemas to be set every night by the receiver and stewards of the said city.

Samuel Izacke added: A patent under the Common Seal of the city granted to the Right Honourable the Earl of Suffolk, to be Lord High Steward thereof.

1622

John Modyford

An heriot paid the receiver on the death of a tenant in the name of Awliscombe. Mr Mayor ordered to keep no more breakfast Sundays for his officers. Ordered that no more canon bread or money shall be given to the mayor or officers at Xmas or Easter, saving the constables within the gates, porters and scavengers. A committee appointed to take an inventory of all the city's goods at the quay. Mr Receiver is desired to lay out in beef for the poor of this city against the ensuing feast of Christmas £6 or £6 13s 4d in his discretion. The cloth hall to be fitted up and the ancient duties thereof to be paid. George Passemore instructed to collect the duties of the town custom. The barton of Sloe in the parish of Halberton on the death of Mrs Honour Spicer fallen in hand. License given to Mrs Grace Sheere, widow, by the chamber, to send her son Joseph Snowe, an orphan, beyond the seas. Mr Thomas Wakeman is ordered to fill up a pool of water with earth in Exe Island there lately made by him to the great annoyance of the inhabitants. Goods seized as forfeited being foreign bought and sold within the said city according to the custom. The 3 next persons to the receiver are yearly to view the defects of the city's works and to report them hence.

Samuel Izacke added: The Chamber, in procuring the charter for establishing the hospital of St John's within the East Gate of the said City, and in repairing and new building of the edifices thereunto belonging, did expend above £400.

1623

John Gupwill

The conduit water for this year to be conveyed through a pipe of lead to Mr Mayor's house. Upon the death of John Martyn, late town clerk of this city, Samuel Izacke was chosen therein. No constable or others shall from henceforth have any more canon bread. The Commission of Deputy Lieutenants of this city to be renewed. 8 placed within the city appointed for the placing of Mr Spicer's candle lights in the winter season. £5 paid for renewing of the commission of the deputy lieutenants of this city. Mr Receiver desired to lay out the sum of £6 or £6 13s 4d at his discretion in beef for the poor of the city against the ensuing feast of Christmas. £3 paid the city in lieu of a heriot due on the death of a tenant. £10 paid Mr Mayor by order of this house in recompense of the great charge he hath lately been at in entertaining my Lord Russell at his table. Gaver and stakes to be speedily provided for the amendment of Trew's Weir.

Mr Mayor is desired to keep Mr Blundel's feast on St Peter's Day next coming according to the intention of the donor, and the usual allowance to be paid Mr Mayor for the same. This mayor gave the sum of thirty pounds in money towards the building of St John's Hospital.

1624

Thomas Crossinge

William Prouze elected chamberlain of this city on the death of John Martyn. The cloth hall appointed to be kept at St John's within the Eastgate of the said city. Overseers of the bridewell or house of correction appointed to see the law duly executed on such persons as shall be there committed. A license for alienation under the great seal of England sent to London to discharge a [?]. A patent under the city's Common Seal granted to the Right Honourable William Earl of Pembroke and Montgomery to be High Steward of the said city, with a fee of £10 per annum incident thereunto. Mr Receiver ordered to remove certain young trees out of the nursery within St David's parish and to replant them in Duryard Wood. A present of £300 bestowed on the king's majesty from this city as a token of their duty. The plague of pestilence was this year very hot in the city, which began in the month of July and therein so continued about the space of one whole year, whereof died some thousands of persons.

Charles I

1625

Thomas Walker

A petition sent to the king about the mayor elect refusing to accept of the said office.

Samuel Izacke added: This mayor being elected, refused to accept of the Office (in regard of the contagious sickness here still reigning) but withdrew himself into the country, whereupon a petition was sent hence to the king, who commanded this mayor to undertake the office, on his allegiance, whereunto he readily yielded obedience, and performed it very worthily.

Richard Crossing noted: This year was a great plague in this city.

This mayor was a worthy benefactor to the city who gave £400 to the city, the interest of £200 whereof is to go to poor persons maimed the residue to St John's Hospital. Elizabeth Dowrich widow (his daughter) gave £100 for the same purposes. The postern doors in the castle and the city's walls to be stopped up. Our citizens paid their wages for their attendance and service done in Parliament. The muster rolls of this city to be made up and 4 marks per annum to be settled on a muster master to be speedily procured. A pest house was now purchased of Gregory Soper for the benefit of this city. The pipes and cisterns whereby the water is brought home to the conduits being in decay to be repaired. Mr Mayor is devised to keep Mr Peter Blundell's feast this year according to his will. John Biddle, widow, of the parish of Holy Trinity, being leprous, is admitted into the Mawdlyn Hospital. No idle persons were now permitted to beg openly in the streets or at doors.

Samuel Izacke added: No common beggars in the open streets of the city were permitted, but presently sent to the Work House, or House of Correction, to get their bread by the sweat of their brows, idleness being the root of all evil, it being no less true than a witty saying, *That the Devil tempts all Men but the Idle Man, who tempts the Devil, but Idle Man's Brain being a Shop for the Devil to work in.*

1626

John Tayler

John Levermore, a member of this house, for sundry misdemeanours dismissed hence. The beadles of this city are allowed 50s per annum for their wages. The Earl of Suffolk sues the city for his yearly pension of £10 as high steward thereof. No estates in the city's lands to be granted longer than for three lives. Ten pounds paid Anthony Batt on the surrender of his muster master's office. Mr Receiver is desired to lay out £6 13s 4d in victuals against the ensuing feast of Christmas for the necessary relief of the poor of this city. Also to take gave and windeat out of Duryard Wood to repair Trew's Weir and the haven. Monies collected given by several benefactors towards the foundation and maintenance of St John's Hospital within the Eastgate of the said city. Mr Mayor is desired to keep Mr Peter Blundell's feast this year according to his will. A present sent from this house and bestowed on Mr Justice Doderidge.

1627

John Acland

Upon the death of Bishop Carye, Joseph Halle was elected the 23rd December this year was consecrated bishop of this church and diocese.

    Samuel Izacke added: Bishop Cary having well-governed this church about 6 years, 10 June died, and lies buried on the north side of the quire of St Paul's Church, London, but hath a stately monument of marble, with his effigy portrayed in alabaster, erected to his memory in an aisle at the upper end of his own church. Upon whose decease –

    Joseph Hall, Doctor of Divinity, was elected and 23 December consecrated Bishop of this diocese.

    The plague being in Salisbury money was here collected and sent unto them. George Passemore, a member of this house, on his petition is hence dismissed. The 3 keys of the orphan's chest are to be kept, 1 by the mayor, 2 by the youngest alderman and 3 by the chamberlain. A pump to be erected nigh St Paul's church. £70 paid the earl of Suffolk for composure of differences between him and this city. Six dozen of wood given to the chamberlain and 4 dozen to the town clerk out of Duryard Wood. Citizens to be here elected to serve in Parliament, wherein the sheriff is charged to maintain the ancient custom of the said city. John Hayne, for giving the reproachful word of the lie to Thomas Tooker here in the council chamber (both members of this house), was fined and paid 20s. This year our charter was renewed under the great seal of England.

1628

John Lynne

Richard Waltham elected recorder of this city. In the Lady Chapel of St Peter's Church is a fair monument erected and made to the memory of Sir John Doderidge knight, first sergeant at law to Prince Henry then solicitor general to King James of famous memory, after that principal sergeant at law to the said King James and lastly called by him to be one of the Judges of the honourable court of king's bench, whereof he remained a judge the rest of his life, whose epitaph is thus inscribed

        Learning adieu, for Doderidge is gone
        To fix his earthly, to an Heavenly Throne,
        Rich Urn of Learned Dust, scarce can be found
        More Worth enshrined in six foot of ground.

    He gave a legacy of £5 to the poor here. At his request of the Lord Bishop licence is granted that water be brought in his palace through the city's pipes for his necessary use only at the will of the chamber.

    Ordered that the serge market be again kept in the Southgate street. Felons' goods forfeited to the city and seized on. 40s paid the receiver in lieu of a heriot on the death of a tenant in the manor of Duryard. Richard Tickell elected chamberlain of the said city.

1629

Nicholas Spicer

A gelding as a deodand forfeited to the city and seized on, without the Northgate. Money here collected and sent to Cambridge that town being infected with the plague. A new feoffment made to the corporation of Nicholas Spicer's land by the surviving feoffees. All contracts here made to be perfected within three months or the bargains to be void. Eight days' notice to be given before any new member or officers be elected. No act here made to be altered but by 13 affirmative voices. The farmer of the quay is to keep Racks Lane sufficiently repaired. Ordered that the serge market be removed into High Street above Allhallows' Church. Also that the butts in Northernhaye be repaired by Mr Receiver. £10 per annum appointed to Mr Roger Mallocke for the judges' lodging in their circuit. Stocks and cages without the Westgate and the Northgate to be forthwith provided for the punishing disordered persons. All officers and their wives are to attend on Mr Mayor and Mr Merry's Sundays unto St Peter's Church and from thence home again. A patent under the city's Common Seal was granted to the Right Honourable Richard Lord Weston, Lord High Treasurer of England to be High Steward of the city, with a fee of £10 per annum. The sickness increasing in London ordered that the pest house here be put in good repair and that no Londoners be entertained without their certificates. A storehouse to be provided at St John's for safe keeping of powder.

1630

Thomas Flaye

Ordered that the old shambles be made fit for a market place for corn. Mr Mayor, sued in the exchequer for the wastes of the city, Northernhay and Southenhay, at the suit of the king's Attorney General. A pension of £20 per annum granted to Ignatius Jurdayne, of the aldermen, for his life. Four pounds extraordinary paid Mr Mayor towards the passing of banisters. The cloth hall and town custom demised to George Passemore for 3 years at £50 per annum. Nuisances in the river near Topsham by laying stones there complained of to be redressed. Beds, bolstered sheets with other necessaries for the boys in St John's Hospital to be provided. Corn brought into the storehouse for the necessary supply of the poor of the city. Mr Receiver is desired to bestow £10 in bread in this time of scarcity and to distribute the same amongst the poor of this city, as benevolence on them from this house. A piece of plate of £20 to be presented hence to the Earl of Dorset and another of £10 to the Earl of Manchester in token of the city's thankfulness for their respects towards them. The Earl of Arundel coming to this city was welcomed by Mr Mayor and his Brethren and a present of £5 value in sweet meats bestowed on him by the chamber.

Samuel Izacke added: Prince Charles was born 29 May at St James near Charing Cross, and baptised on Sunday 27 June then next following, at whose birth heaven itself seemed to open one eye more than ordinary, a star appearing all that day, and two days thereafter the sun was eclipsed.

1631

Nicholas Martin

Peter Ball esquire elected recorder of this city on the death of Richard Waltham esquire. St John's Chapel within the Eastgate is to be fitted up for a free grammar school. The constables of the county of this city were all paid several sums of money by them formerly disbursed towards that passing of banisters. A present of £8 value sent to Mr Noye as a gratuity for his pains taken in the city's affairs. A commission upon the statute of charitable uses to be speedily taken out and persecuted. £8 in bread Mr Receiver is desired to get, and to bestow the same on the poor of this city against the feast of Easter now ensuing, as the gift of the chamber. Six pounds per annum settled as a benevolence on the muster master of this city. Goods taken on two felons (since executed) restored to the right owners. A recognisance broken and compounded for with the chamber. The sum of £6 13s 6d allowed Mr Mayor by this house in lieu of his freeman. Several other recognisances forfeited and composition made with the chamber for the same. Several weirs being in decay are forthwith ordered to be amended. A conveyance touching the intended free school was now sealed by Mr Francis Crossinge. This mayor gave the sum of £200 in money for the support and enlargement of the hospital of St John's within this city, whereunto was added £130 more by his wife Dame Susanna Ladry (so named by her second marriage) which money was bestowed in purchasing the inheritance of two houses in Northgate Street, now the several possession of George Tuthill, merchant, and Peter West, glasier.

Samuel Izacke added: The Lady Mary, the King's eldest daughter, was born on 4 November at St James aforesaid.

1632

John Hakewill

Peter Balle recorder of this city and a patent under the common seal of the office granted him. The free school within the Eastgate of this city was this year built, founded by the mayor, bailiffs and commonality of the said city for the education of youth in good literature who allow the master thereof £30 per annum stipend and £10 per annum to an usher. All accounts belonging to the city are to be made up and audited within 6 months of every year. The 3 keys of the box wherein lies the common seal are to be kept 1 by the mayor, 2 by the eldest alderman and 3 by the youngest. Felons' goods forfeited to the city and seized on. The quarry pit in Northernhay to be filled up. A special commission brought down for the trial of a suspected traitor. A hospital constituted at St John's for boys, for whom beds are to be provided, gowns, caps and all other necessaries.

1633

Gilbert Sweete

The city (on the behalf of the poor of the same) by a decree in Chancery, recovered of the Dean and Chapter of the Church the sum of £420 which was now paid in accordingly. None of the city's lands to be estated for a longer term than for three lives. Thirteen years arrearages of rent at 40s per annum due from the house of the archdeacon of Totnes in St Peter's Churchyard was now paid to the city. Every housekeeper within this city in the winter season between Allhallowtide and Candlemas ordered to set forth lights in the evening before their doors. Nicholas Vaughan elected Muster Master of the city and a stipend of £4 per annum settled on him. Ordered that a register be here made of all the city's charters. John Crocker, a member of this house, on his petition and reasons alleged was hence dismissed. An estate of a *Felo de se* forfeited to the city and composition made for the same. Part of Northernhay fitted for the private recreation of the mayor, aldermen and common council. The city's titles to their wastes, Northernhay and Southernhay, questioned by his highness the Prince and well defended by the city in a suit concerned for the same in the court of the exchequer. Mr Mayor is desired to keep Mr Blundell's feast this year according to his will on St Peter's Day. Paid Mr Mayor in lieu of his freeman £6 13s 4d thought no person in this year paid so much. The new work or haven for the passage of lighters to and from the quay to Topsham was now cleansed and repaired. Samuel Izacke added: James, Duke of York, was born 13 October.

1634

Francis Crossinge

Richard Crossing noted: He was a special benefactor to the hospital of St John's and an advancer of it.

Philip Earl of Pembroke and Montgomery, elected Lord High Steward of this city and a patent under the Common Seal thereof with a pension of £10 given him for the same. An answer made under the common seal to Thomas Chaffe's bill of complaint in the court of requests. The worsted combers of this city to be incorporated into one fellowship. Every member admitted into this house is to lend £20 for one year and to give a silver spoon of 15s value when two persons or more shall be elected into this house at any one time they must take place here according to their seniority of being stewards of the said city. Marmaduke Waggott for keeping the guildhall pump in good repair is allotted to have 6s 8d. Ordered that a lime kiln be forthwith erected on the quay. Jasper Ratcliffe appointed deputy to the clerks of the markets to fure and seize all such weights and measures. A felon's goods forfeited to this city. A footpath in Southernhay to be made and gravelled and a stile there to be erected to preserve the said path. George

Follett chosen proctor of the Mawdlyn and 40s per annum stipend allowed him for his pains therein. Mr Mayor is desired to keep Mr Peter Blundell's feast this year according to his will. A new cap of maintenance with a suitable scabbard for the sword to be bought for the sword bearer's use.

Samuel Izacke added: A fair cap of maintenance, of velvet, richly wrought with gold, with a suitable scabbard for the sword of justice usually carried before the Mayor, was procured and made use of accordingly by the Sword Bearer, in honour of the city.

The key of Duryard Woodgate to be kept only by the receiver for the time being. Sir Nathaniel Brent (the Archbishop of Canterbury's deputy) visited this diocese. A Latin Sermon preached before him in the Chapter House and welcomed by city and clergy.

1635

Adam Bennett

Upon the death of John Clarke, one of the stewards, Stephen Olivean was elected in his place, to supply the residue of the year. Elizabeth Jurdayne, widow, by her last will gave £500 to charitable uses to be employed within this city, which by an order of the privy council was applied for the maintenance of a free English school (within St John's Hospital). Every inhabitant between Allhallowtide and Candlemas shall set forth a light to his fore door, which is so to continue till 9 of the clock at night on pain of 6d. Alice Hele, widow, gave £300 in gold to make fit and beautify St John's Chapel within the Eastgate. All acts here made are first to be drawn out in a waste paper book before they are entered. Several attempts made to bring in the river through the city. Goods seized as forfeited being foreign bought and sold. For every pack of wool brought into the city 4d is to be paid. The wool hall settled at St John's, and the articles touching the same plainly set down. Retailers keeping shops within the city, being not free thereof, punished. No foreigner is to be here admitted a freeman without the chamber's consent. A pension of £4 per annum settled on Thomas Robinson, the mayor's cook, being weak and aged on the surrender of his place in whose stead William Pearse is elected. John Hayne, sheriff, fined £20 for not keeping two of his feasts in the sessions week according to the ancient and laudable custom of the said city. The carts belonging to the quay are not to go through the streets shod with iron wheels. The receiver to be paid the balance of his accounts three months after the perfecting thereof.

1636

Roger Mallocke

John Crewkerne elected chamberlain of the said city. The sum of two and thirty pounds in money and a garden recovered by virtue of a decree obtained in the High Court of Chancery of Dr Michell for the poor people of St Katharine's Almshouse. A new church-yard consecrated by Bishop Hall in Friernhay. The duty of the grave maker there explained and his fees ascertained. For haulage of every pack of worsted combed wool 4d is to be paid and 6d for weighing the same. A felon's goods forfeited and seized on accordingly to the city's use.

1637

Thomas Crossinge

Richard Crossing noted: He gave £60 towards the building of the hospital of St John's & £8 per annum during his life for the maintenance of one boy in the said hospital.

The several accounts of all the benefactors bonds to be kept by Mr Town Clerk and a yearly pension allowed him for his pains therein. Peter Hellyar elected School Master of the English Free School in St John's Hospital. A wine bush set up on the outer side of the Eastgate, being disgraceful to the city, is ordered to be taken down. An enclosure of late made by my Lord Bishop in St Peter's Churchyard to be likewise taken down. The town custom of the city demised to John Browne at £32 per annum. Ordered that no more gravel or stones be taken out of the shillhay for whose defence and better preservation a buttey is there to be [?]ed. Mr Receiver is ordered to plant some young trees in Duryard Wood.

1638

James Tucker

This mayor gave £100 to the city to be employed in the same manner vizt and end that Mr Peryam's and Mr Walker's monies are. In regard to the multitude of prisoners at present in the Southgate 13s 4d weekly for their better maintenance is allowed them by and from this house. The chapel at St John's Hospital to be by my Lord Bishop again consecrated. A heriot seized on for the city's use on the death of a tenant in Duryard & redeemed for £5. Sundry elms were this year planted in Northernhay and Southernhay. Ordered that Southernhay be forthwith nailed in and a pit there to be filled up with earth, chiefly to keep the poor on work. Licence granted to Richard Saunders to sue Nicholas Bolte at the Common Law, they both being Freemen hereof. Bailiffs executing tin presses within the liberty of this city to be punished. Pales erected by Dr Burnell Chancellor of the church between his garden and the city walls to be taken down. The butchers' slaughter houses within the walls of the city to be removed. Richard Ducke, one of the city's learned council, voluntarily relinquisheth his place. A piece of plate of £20 value presented to the earl of Bedford for his respects to the city.

1639

Robert Walker

A voluntary collection here made for the poor of the town of Taunton in Somerset visited with the plague and a sum of £185 17s 4d sent them as a present hence. [?] here propounded for the public good shall be put to the vote, albeit the mayor consents not thereunto. Any person marrying an alderman's daughter may freely claim his Freedom of the City. When the number of the aldermen be full, the mayor of the next presiding year shall be an alderman the year following his year of mayoralty and the youngest alderman to be omitted, until it comes to his turn by seniority. A present of sweet meats bestowed on the Spanish Ambassador at his lodging without the Southgate. The ordering of the markets is left to the discretion of the mayor and bailiffs. Lammas Fair not to be kept this year for fear of infection of the plague. Mr Mayor is desired to keep Mr Blundell's feast this year according to his will. The common sewer or passage of water near St Martin's Gate in St Peter's Churchyard to be cleansed. Mr Mayor and Mr Simon Snowe elected our citizens to serve in the ensuing Parliament. No person to be named for a steward that hath not first born the office of a constable. A piece of plate of £20 value bestowed on my Lord Keeper Coventry as a token of this city's love and due respect towards him. The tower on the city's walls to be fitted for a common storehouse for powder.

1640

John Penny

A cart to be forthwith provided for the punishing of whores. 20s forfeited to the city by means of a house in Southgate Street being on fire. 4 ladders and 2 dozen of leather buckets to be provided in case of fire happening here. A writ of *coronatore eliqeudo* to be procured for the election of a new coroner. John Bickley and Gilbert Till, two of the musical waits of this city, are dismissed of their places for several misdemeanours committed by them. George Passemore chosen overseer of the city's works and a stipend of £20 per annum allowed him. No serges to be hung on the city's walls on pain of 6d for every cloth. Watch and ward night and day appointed at the gates of the city for fear of the plague.

1641

Richard Saunders

All inhabitants are to have clubs in readiness for the city's safeguard by the ancient orders thereof. Bishop Hall, having well-governed this church for the space of 14 years, was translated and installed Bishop of Norwich whereupon Ralph Browning was elected and 3 May this year consecrated bishop of this diocese, who albeit he lived almost 19 years after his said consecration, yet by reason of the intestine wars and rebellion in this realm he never came hither to this city. Thomas Bridgeman gent did by his last will give £500 to this city for the relief of the poor therein. Sir George Chudley's request of having a water pipe to come into Bedford House from the Little Conduit denied. All innkeepers are forbidden to entertain any person or to lodge goods, coming from places infected with the plague without licence first had of the mayor in that behalf. Ordered that Bedford Postern Gate leading into Southernhay be shut up and closed. A letter sent at London to Mr Recorder to perform his duty here or to leave his office. An indictment was here preferred against Samuel Clarke and Thomas Forde for refusing the offices of constables which by [?] was removed up to the king's bench, and brought down at the assizes by a writ of *nisi prius* and tried here and a verdict found against them. Robert Bletchindon elected sword bearer of the said city, whose pension of £10 per annum was continued to him on William Birdall's resignation. Mr Mayor is desired to keep Mr Blundell's feast this year according to the tenor of his will. The old cap of maintenance and the scabbard of the sword were privately disposed of by the late sword bearer and the profit thereof convected to his own use.

1642

Christopher Clark

Walls erected in a lane by St Katharine's almshouse are to be again pulled down. No sea coal ashes are to be cast into the streets on pain of 4d for the first offence, the 2nd 12d. Mr Mayor is appointed to keep the only key of the powder house. 10s paid the messenger for bringing a writ for the election of new Parliament men here. The porters to be allowed candle light at their several gates. A watch to be kept every night winter and summer. All the trees in Northernhay and Southernhay taken down towards the making of carriages for the city's defence and other public uses in reference to war. 500 weight of match to be provided and brought into the common storehouse. An engineer sent for and here entertained, to whom for his welcome a gratuity of £10 is given, and also a stipend of £30 per annum settled on him for his attendance and service here. Ordinances or great guns to be mounted on their carriages and powder allotted to try them. The gates of the said city in these times of danger to be constantly shut at six of the clock at night, and iron chains to be provided for them for their better fortification. Edmond Prideaux esquire elected recorder of the said city. A present of £100 bestowed on the earl of Stamford general of the rebels in these western parts. Another present of £300 bestowed on Sir John Berkeley governor of the said city for his Majesty.

Samuel Izacke added: The city was twice this year besieged by the King's Forces; first by my Lord Hopton about Christmas, who having only viewed the same, presently drew off his army and marched into Cornwall. Secondly, by Prince Maurice, who laid close siege thereunto and 3 September following got possession thereof, being surrendered to him on Articles.

Richard Crossing noted: In this year the city (being besieged) surrendered unto the king's army. A sad time, occasioned by the differences between the king & his parliament.

1643

Sir Hugh Crocker, knight

Sir Richard Lawdy knight by his last will gave £100 to be employed in the same manner [as] Mr Peryam's monies. Edward Portbury (for his long and good service done the city under Mr Town Clerk his master) is admitted to be one of the attorneys of the said city to practice in the king majesty's court at the guildhall. Adam Bennett and James Gould, two members of this house, for neglecting their attendance here on frequent summons were both dismissed of the said society. Ordered that the city's plate be sold to supply their present extraordinary occasions. Also that no estate be made in the city's lands for any longer term than 31 years or 3 lives. John Canne chosen the city's plumber to bring home the water to the conduits through pipes & £10 annual fee to him. The king coming to this city (being in pursuit of the rebels who were marched into Cornwall) bestowed the dignity of knighthood on the mayor, the city presented his majesty with £500 and bestowed £20 on his servants. The queen afterwards coming hither for residence, £200 was likewise presented to her majesty, and £12 on her servants, who lodged at

Bedford House, where during her abode she was delivered of child, baptised in the cathedral church, named Henrietta Maria, a very beautiful and hopeful princess. Prince Charles being likewise here the city presented him with £100 of good money.

Twelve Doctors of several professions born within this city, who lately lived divers years at once, if not all present, one whereof is the author these ensuing verses, namely Dr Robert Vivian, who saith thus:

There were twelve Doctors born in Exeter,
Within the walls, who lived long together,
Of these were five Divines, and four physicians,
Which lived together, but three sole Civilians.

The names of the said 12 doctors are 1, John Bridgman, Lord Bishop of Chester; 2, George Barrcofte; 3, George Hakewill, Chaplain to Prince Henry and Archdeacon of Surrey; 4, Michael Germyn, Chaplain to the Queen of Bohemia, and, 5, Anthony Shorte. These are the 5 Divines. 6, Sir Simon Baskervile, knight; 7, Robert Vilvayne; 8, Richard Spicer; 9, Anthony Salter. These are the 4 Physicians. 10, William Spicer; 11, Joseph Martyn and 12, Robert Mitchell. These are the 3 civilians.

1644

Nicholas Spicer

Richard Saunders and Walter White, two members of this house, neglecting their attending here on frequent summons were both dismissed hence. Ordered that all the members of this society shall attend their places here on all occasions or else other persons shall be chosen in their stead and room. The king's general pardon obtained for the city, the charges whereof are £80. An ordinance made for the removal of all dung and other public nuisances out of the city. William Pearse elected the city's cook on the death of Samuel Fish. A deputation under the common seal made to William Chichester to collect the town custom duties. Several persons of honour entertained by Mr Mayor at the city's charge. The cloth hall granted to Gilbert Madocke for one year at £20. Ordered that the leather market from henceforth shall be kept at the New Inn in the high street of the said city, as it hath formerly been.

1645

John Cupper

The Receiver General was displaced & another was chosen in his room etc, James Gould. All shreeves [sheriffs] to be elected in the council chamber by a private scrutiny. Henry Miller, on the recommendation of the committee of rebels, was admitted a freeman of the said city and also an attorney of the courts belonging to the same. Robert Walker, one of the aldermen of this city, by colour of an ordinance of Parliament, was dismissed of this society. John Lynne, another aldermen of the said city, and John Colleton, Receiver General of the same, for absenting themselves hence were both dismissed of this house. Richard Saunders, Adam Bennett, Walter White, James Gould, Richard Crossinge, John Loveringe, James Marshall and Philip Crossinge were all again restored to be members of this house by colour and pretence of an ordinance of Parliament.

Samuel Izacke added: This city was besieged by Sir Thomas Fairfax (General of the Parliament's forces) and on articles surrendered to him.

Richard Crossing noted: This year the city (being again besieged) surrendered unto the parliament's army.

1646

Walter White

A rate imposed for the carriage of all goods from the quay into the city. John Dore elected Chamberlain of the said city on the death of John Crewkerne. Also John Cogan was chosen sword bearer of the same city. Goods seized as forfeited being foreign bought and sold. None but country butchers are to sell victual in the yarn shambles on market days. A felon's goods forfeited and seized upon accordingly for the city's use. When the judges came hither at the assizes, it is ordered that a present of 20 nobles be presented them and are no more to be invited at the mayor's table here. An indictment exhibited against the city about a highway near Exe Bridge at the assizes which was traversed and a verdict found for the city. Lewes Greenslade chosen overseer of the works on the haven & £10 per annum pension allowed him. William Symes admitted to be one of the attorneys of his majesty's courts within this city on the recommendation of Mr Edmond Davye, one of the city's council.

1647

Adam Bennett

John Lovering being chosen receiver and one of the bailiffs of this city for this year, refused to be sworn and was therefore fined £100 and three months thereafter another person was chosen in his place, Nicholas Brokinge. The walls of the city being in decay are ordered to be speedily repaired. Ordered that no lease be granted by this house but the lessee is to covenant to make his estate appear to be in being within a year after notice, on pain of forfeiture. The sum of £6 13 4d is appointed to every mayor in lieu of his freeman, as formerly. The sum of £8 is allotted to every mayor to bestow on poor wayfaring people in distress. A new town clerk is elected in the place of Mr Samuel Izacke who was sequestered from the said office in the height of the rebellion for his loyalty to the king's majesty. John Farthinge chosen into the said office who (for conscience sake) refused the same. Thomas Westlake was afterwards elected town clerk, who enjoyed the said office twelve years even till such time as King Charles 2nd (after 14 years exile) was restored to his crown & kingdoms & then the said Samuel Izacke (by virtue of the king's writ and laws) was again restored into the said office, which at present he well enjoys and long may he so do.

1648

James Gould

Ordered that Exe Bridge, the sluices, weirs and banks on the new haven be repaired. Also that the cisterns and pipes which convey the water to the conduits of this city be likewise repaired. Weights and measures provided and delivered out for the public use of this city. Forty young elms were this year planted in the Bonhay. 50 shillings given to the mayor's cook to buy him a livery. Our citizens serving in Parliament paid their wages after the rate of 4s *per diem*. This mayor by his last will and testament gave £100 in money to the poor of this city and £100 more towards the maintenance of the poor boys in St John's Hospital within the said city. 30 January the King was barbarously murdered by his own sworn subjects in the height of their rebellion, pretending (as the Jews did to our Saviour) they had a law by which he must die, a sin so horrid as that justice knew not well how to punish nor mercy to forgive. Samuel Izacke added: The scene of his tragical exit on the scaffold, was that after His Majesty had made a sedate pause, stretching forth his hands, the disguised executioner severed his royal head from his body at one blow. The blood of the royal martyr was dipped up with handkerchiefs by several of the crowding spectators, to different purposes. By some out of respect to the memory of so pious and virtuous prince; by others, as insulting trophies of such their barbarous villainy. His corpse, wrapped up in lead, was privately interred, February 9th 1648, in the Chapel Royal at Windsor.

 Richard Crossing noted: A most sad time, the king this year was cruelly put to death. The said James Gould gave by his will £100 to the hospital of St John's.

1649

Richard Crossing

Richard Crossing notes: These (Richard Saunders, Adam Bennet) were deputy mayors, appointed by the chamber for this year, in regard that Richard Crossinge (who was elected mayor) refused to serve in the said office, because the kingly government was then by armed violence obstructed.

 This year Richard Crossing was chosen Mayor, which office he refusing, no fine was imposed on him nor any other mayor chosen for that year, but supplied by deputies. Richard Crossing being also chosen one of the bailiffs for this year refusing also to be sworn was therefore fined 100 marks and William

Cowell chosen and sworn in his place, which was the year next ensuing. One thing not to be forgotten, is, that in this year there happened an accident in an inn commonly called the White Hart in the Southgate Street. An old well, long neglected, which the owner had a purpose to cleanse, and caused one Paul Penrose to go down for the scouring thereof, who therein suddenly fell dead. Whereupon a second person named William Johnson (which persons were both of them by profession carpenters) was employed to go down after him, who presently in the said pit likewise died. A third man adventuring himself to preserve his friend had there likewise perished, if with all celerity he had not been drawn up again, who, almost dead, was by rolling, and pouring oil and aqua-vitae into him with much ado preserved, who, when he came to himself, affirmed that there came such a strange stench out of the caverns of the earth that deprived him of breath; hereof divers men censured diversely. Some that there was a Cockatrice in the pit, some one thing, some another, but the general received opinion, that it was by a damp.

1650

Richard Evans

This mayor gave £500 to the city to be employed in the same manner as Mr Walker's and Mr Peryam's monies are, tis meant the interest thereof which is to go only to the parish of St Sidwell's, its poor. All persons refusing to pay the duty of town custom to be forthwith put in suit of law. A copy of a decree taken out of the exchequer touching the duty of the town custom. Ordered that six ladders be made, the crooks of the city to be made serviceable, and the wells and pumps within the said city to be repaired and all (in case any fire should happen) to prevent the same. The fees and duties of the town custom granted to Mr Richard Saunders for five years. Richard Cullinge, being elected one of the Bailiffs of this city, for this year and refusing the said office, was fined one hundred marks & William Cowell was chosen in his room. Sixteen men are appointed for the night watch who are to have 8d a piece for their labour, one of the stewards is constantly to set and swear the said watch & the constables of the several quarters within the said city by turns are to attend the said service.

1651

Richard Sweete

Edward Foxwill elected to be one of the stewards this year refusing to be sworn, was fined thirty pounds so there were but three bailiffs who freely bringing hither £13 6s 8d with a submission was remitted the residue. A decree out of the exchequer for our right of the watercourse belonging to Duryard Mills in a suit there depending between the city and Mr Coplestone. This mayor had £200 allowed him for his yearly pension. Sundry trees taken out of Duryard Wood and given freely towards the reparation of St David's church. Ordered that 500 trees in Duryard Wood with the coppice thereunto adjoining be sold to pay the city's debts. Also that the Receiver do disburse the sum of £6 13s 4d in some necessaries & present the same to the judges of the assize at their next coming hither as a gift from the chamber. Also that a noisome place near the custom house in St Peter's churchyard be cleansed and that iron grates be set thereon to prevent the like nuisance for the future. A gratuity of £10 bestowed on Zachary Trescott in London for his pains taken about this city's affairs. Trew's Weir being in decay the receiver is to get Gaver and Windeatt to repair the same. £10 paid Mr Roger Mallocke for the judges' lodging at 2 several assizes here. A gratuity of £13 6s 8d given Henry Milles for his labour in the city's affairs.

1652

Ralph Herman

A new receiver chosen (upon the resignation of the old) to put himself in a capacity of being elected into the office of the mayoralty of the said city. This mayor gave £400 by his last will to pious uses and benefit of this city and an annuity of £8 per annum to the hospital of St Johns and his dwelling house charged therewith. Ordered that no tombstone be laid on any grave in the new churchyard without the chamber's licence. A lawful beam and scales to be erected and placed in the yarn market. An engine for the speedier quenching of fire to be procured, and also 4 dozen of leather buckets to be in readiness in case of any sudden fire happening for the public use of the city. All contracts made with the chamber to be perfected within 2 months by having their deeds sealed or the bargains to be void. On the death of George Passemore, John Sprague was chosen overseer of the city's work. Francis Fryer elected master of the workhouse or house of correction. The sum of £6 13s 4d laid out in a present for the judges and accordingly bestowed on them. The banks of the new works or haven being in decay to be amended. Another present bestowed on the judges of the value of £6 13s 4d. The ceiling and benches under the guildhall and the pump before the same to be amended.

1653

Simon Snowe

Richard Crossing noted: In this year no common beggar was permitted to beg openly in the city. He [the mayor] hath given £148 towards the school master's house and the education of a boy in the hospital of St John's and since hath settled the lands of 2 houses & a stable in St Kerrian's parish of about £16 value per annum for ever on the said hospital. He was a great instrument in the setting up of the public brewhouse and maid's hospital and in repairing the cathedral church of St Peter and library there, & gave £50 towards the seats in St Stephen's church.

Richard Izacke elected chamberlain of the said city. Ordered that a common brewhouse be elected for the benefit of the poor of this city. Two silver flagons with the city's arms engraved thereon of £25 value presented and bestowed on Mr Manton from this chamber for his pains taken in purchasing the Irish lands for this city. An iron chain to be set up at the lower end of the yarn market to keep of horses on market days. William Stephens elected marshal of this city and a coat for that office to be given him, with a badge of the city's arms thereon. A commission to be sued out of Chancery for charitable uses on the statute 45 Reg. Elizabeth. Ordered that £110 per annum be paid Mr Mayor for his pension out of the New Inn. Also that the 4 sergeants at mace have new gowns every fifth year. A gratuity of £3 conferred on Richard Hingston, coroner of this country, for service down in his said office. Ordered that no carts or wagons do pass through the city on market days. Thomas Bampfield elected recorder of the said city. The fees and duties of wheelage within this city to be collected by Ambrose Paige. A new receiver chosen for the residue of the year on the resignation of the old. The members of this house (on due summons) to meet at the council chamber by a certain hour on pain of 12d & also there to appear in their gowns on pain of 12d more & all for the use of the poor. Francis Lippingcott on his request dismissed hence being a member of this house.

1654

Richard Crossing

Richard Crossing noted: In this year a hospital for maids was began to be builded. He [the mayor] paid £8 per annum to St John's Hospital for certain years. And in his life time gave a term in certain houses & £300 in money (in all to the value of £500) towards the erecting of a decent corn market & with respect to a rent charge of £30 per annum granted by the chamber by their deed indented out of the said corn market &c, unto the hospital of St John's, towards the maintenance of five poor boys for ever.

A beam, weights and scales for the weighing of wool to be forthwith gotten and placed in the wool hall and the said hall to be planched. The cloth hall to be removed unto St John's Hospital. Constables reimbursed their money laid out for passing of banisters. One hundred and fifteen pounds in money paid Mr Thomas Gibbons at several times for his service done in Parliament attending there as a citizen elected and sent up from hence. Ordered that a bill in the name of the mayor & bailiffs be forthwith exhibited in the high court of chancery against George Speke esq. for the new building of Wynards' Hospital (burned in the late troubles) and for the increase of the Poor's Maintenance there. A deputation under the common seal made to Richard Saunders to collect the town customs duties. Ordered that the interest of Mr Bridgeman's £500 shall go towards the binding out of poor boys in the hospital. This year there happened a strange accident in Paris Street, without the East Gate of this city, being parcel of the suburbs thereof. One John Bettison, minister of the parish of St Mary Clyst, about three miles distant hence on the 11th day of January, about 6 of the clock in the evening of that day, returning homewards from this city, being mounted on a good gelding, & having his wife behind him (the well in the said street being decayed & the mouth thereof covered over only with a few thorns or frith) the gelding with his riders still sitting him, fell down therein. The neighbours, hearing a noise presently brought forth lights, and perceiving the disaster, soon procured means to help the said parson & his wife out of the said well, who were taken up safe and sound, without any harm, then the gelding was likewise taken up but so much bruised that he suddenly died.

1655

Nicholas Brokinge

Mr Gilbert Keyte of London freely gave £400 to this city for the maintenance of 4 children in the hospital. The duties of wheelage within the city granted to John Sprague for £4 per annum. The receiver and stewards for this year in lieu and recompense of their several prospective feasts to be kept according to the ancient and laudable custom of this city do undertake and promise to bring home the water to the conduit in Southgate Street. Ordered that all accounts belonging to this city be speedily brought in and audited. Four scavengers elected within this city to see the streets and lanes thereof kept clean and withal at every court to present all public nuisances arising within their several quarters. Several recognisances forfeited and composition made for the same.

Samual Izacke added: Several persons of quality, for their loyalty in proclaiming Charles II, King of England etc at South Molton in the county of Devon, were taken prisoners, brought hither and so confined in the High Gaol, where they were often visited, their wants supplied and plentiful provision daily made for them by the honest inhabitants of this city, and county adjacent. Commissioners of Oyer and Terminer shortly thereafter coming hither for the trial of the said prisoners, who being found guilty of high treason, John Penruddock and Hugh Grove, both of the county of Wiltshire, Esquires, were beheaded in the castle, other of them were executed at the Gallows in Heavitree, two or three reprieved, and the rest banished [from] the Kingdom and sold for slaves.

Richard Crossing noted: At his [the mayor's] death by his will he gave £100 to the poor and £400 more the profits to be disposed of to the poor, as Mr Peryam's and Mr Walter's money was disposed.

1656

Thomas Forde

This mayor by his last will and testament gave £250 to the city for pious uses. Richard Ducke esquire did likewise by his last will and testament devise £50 to be employed for the use and benefit of the maid's hospital within the said city. John Mayne bestowed £100 towards the maintenance of a child in the said hospital. John Loveringe bestowed £120 for the use and benefit of St John's Hospital in the said city. This house advanced £100 towards the repairing of the highway from the lower end of Paris Street to the bound stone leading to Livery Dole. Goods seized as foreign bought and sold and composition made for the same. None but freemen are to exercise their trades, open their shop windows or sell their goods within the said city. The irons about the carts' wheels belonging to the quay are to be taken off. The sum of £120 19s paid Mr Thomas Bampfield at several times for several services done in Parliament attending there are one of our citizens. Constables reimbursed their money laid out for passing of banisters. The pipes to be amended for the better conveyance of the water home to the conduits. £15 paid George Pitts for entertaining the judges these two last assizes.

1657

James Pearse

Ordered that the serge market be removed from Southgate Street into the cloisters and the fish market into Southgate Street. An officer appointed for trying and furing the weights and measures within the city. Goods seized as foreign bought & sold & composition made for the same. A pair of scales & weights to be had for weighing the bakers' bread, and other public uses. Also that boxes be set up at all the gates of the city & almshouses for the use of the poor. Also that 100 trees in Duryard Wood shall be taken down to enclose St Peter's Churchyard. £100 paid Mr Mayor towards the railing in of the said churchyard. A deputation under the common seal granted to Thomas Moore to collect the duties of the petty custom belonging hereunto & sundry persons to be put in suit of law for refusing to pay the same.

1658

James Marshall

Ordered that the corn market be forthwith removed from the high street into the old shambles, where a decent place with all necessaries thereunto purposely provided and several orders made for the good government of the said market. Goods seized as foreign bought & sold & compounded for. Also, that all carts for the future shall go in the city unshod of iron, on pain of 6s 8d on the owner thereof. Also that Mr Peter Blundell's feast (according to the will of the donor) be hereafter yearly kept by Mr Receiver General of the said city. Goods seized on for neglecting to pay the duty of the town custom. Also that several dangerous pits in Southernhay be filled up with all speed.

1659

Christopher Clarke

Ordered that St Peter's Churchyard be paved in the public way leading towards the Broadgate. Also that £110 per annum be paid Mr Mayor for his pension out of the New Inn. Also that £22 a piece be paid to the 4 captains of the trained bands of this city for & towards their disbursements & charges in providing drums, colours & other necessary accommodations incident to their said offices. Also that the said drummer's colours & other arms belonging to the militia of this city be delivered up to the new captains thereof lately chosen. £30 per annum must be paid out of the profits of the corn market for the maintenance of 5 boys in St John's Hospital as the gifts of Richard Crossing, late one of the aldermen of the said city & [?] for performance whereof the chamber hath covenanted by deed under their common seal. This year, 11 May, King Charles 2nd was in several places of this city solemnly proclaimed king of England &c & in London 2 May. The rebellion in this kingdom began in the mayoralty of one Christopher Clarke & ended in the time of the mayoralty of another Christopher Clarke, it began in the year of our Lord 1642 & ended this present year 1659. Ordered that £700 be bestowed in plate presented to the king's majesty from this house.

Samuel Izacke added: Many of the Commons of this city arose and put themselves in arms, declaring for a Free Parliament, the tumult appeared so great, as that most of the shop windows were not opened for two or three days space. At which time here being several gentlemen of quality, of the county of Devon, 'twas by them agreed, that a Remonstrance should be forthwith drawn up and sent to the Parliament, which was as followeth:

To the Right Honourable William Lenthall, Esquire, Speaker of the Parliament

We the Gentry of the County, finding ourselves without a regular government (after your last interruption) designed a public meeting to consult remedies, which we could not so conveniently effect till this week at our General Quarter Session at Exon, where we found divers of the inhabitants groaning under high Oppressions, and a general defect of trade, to the utter ruin of many, and fear of the like to others, which is as visible to the whole country, that occasioned such disorders, as were no small trouble and disturbance to us, which, by God's blessing upon our endeavours, were soon suppressed and quiet without blood; and though we find since our first purposes and alteration in the State of Affairs, by your reestablishment at the helm of government, yet conceive that we are but in part redressed of our Grievances, and that the chief expedient will be the recalling of all those members that were secluded in 1648, and sat before the first force upon the Parliament, and also by filling up vacant places, and all to be admitted without any oath or engagement previous to their entrance; for which things, if you please to take a speedy course, we shall defend you against all Opposers, and future Interruption, with our lives and fortunes; for the accomplishment whereof, we shall use all lawful means, which we humbly conceive may best conduce to the peace and safety of this nation.

Which was without delay accordingly sent up, and presented by Thomas Bamfield Esquire, and became a precedent to many other cities and towns in England, even to do the like, whereby the Army in and about London, consisting of 14,000 old foot soldiers, were dispersed throughout the kingdom, whereof 1,500 were sent hither, and all to prevent the like insurrections that happened in Exeter; whence ensued an Ordinance of Parliament, that no soldier should presume to depart five miles from his quarters on pain of losing his arrears and death. Then marched General Monk into the City of London with his army consisting of 7,000 old soldiers, whom God in his wonderful mercy was pleased to make instrumental of restoring our Sovereign Lord King Charles the Second to his undoubted Dominions, after a long and tedious exile, without the effusion of one man's blood, who landed at Dover 26th May 1660, and came into London the 29th day of the same month, and was crowned king at Westminster the 23 day of April then next following to the great joy of his three kingdoms.

On Friday 11 May 1650 Charles the Second was proclaimed King of England, Scotland, France and Ireland at several public places within this city, viz. at the Guildhall, the little conduit in St Peter's Churchyard, at the Bear corner in South Gate Street, at the great conduit, and at St John's Bow, with great solemnity, during all which time the said conduits ran with wine. The mayor, aldermen, common council men, officers and liverymen being in their scarlet and other gowns, robes and liveries, respectively, attended on by a troop of horse, commanded by Major Hagedott, and the several companies of the trained bands herein, with many thousand inhabitants on foot, shouting loudly for joy, the bells ringing, cannons playing from the castle, whilst the soldiers gave many a volley of shot, and at night tar barrels, and bonfires capered aloft, all of which was thus done with the greatest expression of gladness that possibly could be imagine.

1660

Christopher
Lethbridge

The king was crowned with great pomp and solemnity at Westminster 23 April being St George's day, 1661. This was the first elected mayor of this city after the king's return from 14 years banishment. Sir Peter Balle knight restored to his office of recordership of this city, having been many years thence sequestered for his loyalty. Ordered that £200 be bestowed in a piece of plate & presented to the Princess Henrietta from this chamber. John Gauden, Doctor in Divinity, was this year 2nd December consecrated bishop of this diocese, who coming from London hither was by the way met withal & saluted by sundry gentlemen both of the city and country & with great joy and solemnity being guarded and attended on by several coaches, and the best part of 1000 horsemen (most whereof the inhabitants of the said city) brought herein.

An order made by the mayor & bailiffs in court that if any person should be imprisoned upon any plaint and the plaintiff not bring his declaration into the court in writing, within three weeks after the arrest, the defendant shall be discharged. A collection be here made for the relief of the poor against the feast of Christmas. Goods seized as foreign bought & sold & composition made for the same. The serge market removed from the cloisters to St John's Hospital, & from thence again into Southgate Street where under a good covering are standings erected. £500 raised out of the estate late Ellys Heles esquire deceased and given to the city for the purchasing a workhouse. A gratuity of £10 conferred on Robert Blechindon late sword bearer hereof, so as he releaseth his right & interest in the said office.

Samuel Izacke added: Granvill Weeks, gentleman, elected Muster Master of this city and county, and a pension of £6 per annum allotted him for the same. Sir James Smith, knight, and Robert Walker, Esquire, were elected our citizens to serve in Parliament appointed to be held at Westminster on the 8th day of May next ensuing.

Richard Crossing noted: [the mayor] he built several alms[houses] near South Gate in the city of Exeter for poor people.

1661

Henry Gandye

The Lady Katherine sister to Adolphus the 6th, King of Portugal, in the month of May 1662 arrived at Portsmouth & on the 21st day of the same month was married to our King Charles the 2nd by Dr Sheldon, then bishop of London. A gift of £300 value presented to the Queen Mother as a testimony of the joy of this city for her safe return hither. Two members of this house departing hence without licence given by Mr Mayor, were fined. Provision of corn made chiefly for the relief of the poor of the city, for and amongst whom Bishop Gauden sent Mr Mayor £50 to be distributed. This year 2 June a decree was obtained in the High Court of Chancery in the name of the late mayor Richard Crossinge and the then bailiffs of the said city against George Speke Esquire for repairing of the Wynerd's almshouses without the Southgate of the said city & increase of the maintenance of the poor there part by the prosecution & at the sole charge of the said city. The musical waits of the city were now again restored to their places and pensions. Bishop Gauden was this year 15 June translated hence and made bishop of Worcester; on whose removal Seth Ward, Doctor in Divinity 20 July then next following was consecrated bishop of this church and diocese. Ordered that a crimson velvet cushion be brought and placed on the desk before Mr Mayor's seat in the church. Twenty nobles paid Mr Mayor in lieu of his freeman for this year as formerly. The king (in pursuit of an Act of Parliament) grants commissions, under his Great Seal, to several gentlemen in every county of England, for regulating all corporations therein, by whom were ejected sundry members of this house & in their stead were placed John Butler, Alan Penny, Anthony Salter, doctor in physic, and George Potter, and made aldermen Isaac Mawditt, Stephen Olivean, Thomas Walker, George Tuthill, Peter Hagedot junior, James Slade, Benjamin Oliver, William Sanford & Isaac Mawditt junior, & all made common council men.

Richard Crossing noted: He [the mayor] hath given £16 per annum for ever for the maintenance of two poor boys, of the parish of St Paul's, in the hospital of St John's. In this year almost the whole chamber to 4 persons left their places, with most of the constables of the city & county, refusing to make the Declaration which was required by a new Act of Parliament which Declaration with other oaths certain commissioners appointed (who were most of the county of Devon) tended to them.

1662

John Martyn

This mayor being chosen & refusing to accept of the office, the king's majesty was presently advertised thereof by way of a petition hence, who commanded him to undertake the same; whereunto he did readily yield obedience, and performed his trust with much credit and reputation. Christopher Brodridge merchant elected a member of the common council. A patent, under the common seal, granted to my Lord Duke of Albemarle to be High Steward of the said city. No citizen is to suffer any person to keep wares under his stall or bulk upon pain of twelve pence for every day. Robert Vilvayle, doctor in physic, sent Mr Mayor £20 to be bestowed on the poor here. A present of £10 in plate bestowed on Sir William Morrys knight one of his majesty's secretaries of estate for his respects lately shown this city. James Bronnsford, a freeman, for colouring of foreigners' goods was disenfranchised. A fair brass candlestick to be bought and hung up in the guildhall. Thomas Bampfield esquire for having for some years past officiated in the recorder's office by way of sequestration, freely makes restitution of those profits he thereby received to the poor of the city, being informed that Sir Peter Balle had received satisfaction from this chamber for his sustained loss. Two new receivers were this year chosen & sworn successively, the former of them still first relinquishing, even to complete the number of being made capable to be elected into the office of mayoralty of the said city. £6 13s 4d bestowed on Richard Hingston, coroner of this county, in recompense of service done relating to his said office. The surviving feoffees of Mr Walter Borough's lands are to make a new feoffment thereof to this corporation The new stone weir of late erected nigh Bonhay Bridge is ordered to be again taken down and sluices there to be placed as formerly. Four guardhouses to be erected & made within the four gates for the better shelter and repose of the soldiers to watch therein for the safeguard of the city. John Heskett admitted an attorney to practice in his majesty's courts within this city.

Richard Crossing noted: He [the mayor] gave 400 pounds to the chamber of Exeter by his will for the binding out of poor boys apprentices to good masters which were to be taken out from the public workhouse & so to be continued as the mayor & justices shall think fit for ever.

1663

John Butler

This year also were two others chosen receivers successively for the same purposes which are mentioned in the year next precedent. John Parr, being elected one of the bailiffs of the city for this year and refusing to be sworn was fined £100 & disenfranchised, who upon his submission & those reasons offered by him, laying down £15 was discharged the rest & restored to his freedom. Isaac Mawditt died this year in the time of his shrievalty, 3 August, and within four days thereafter Stephen Olivean the present Receiver was elected Sheriff for the residue of the said year. Paris Street without the East Gate of this city was this year paved throughout at the city's charge as necessary and as commendable a work as hath been done in our age. A stipend of 20 marks per annum conferred on John Force to be assistant unto Mr Receiver for the collecting in of the city's rents. Several sums of money paid the constables by them disbursed for the passing of banisters. The petty or town custom duties granted to Anthony Delton for £20 per annum. The duties of the cloth hall granted to Nicholas Yeo for £16 per annum. Several recognisances of sessions forfeited and composition made for the same. John Birdall, marrying an orphan without the chamber's licence, was fined and paid £30. A gratuity of £10 bestowed on my Lord Duke of Albermarle's secretary for service done. A collection here made of money against the ensuing feast of Christmas for the poor. Several goods seized on as forfeited, being foreign bought & sold & compounded for. A cart to be provided for the removal of the dung & other nuisances out of the streets & land of the city. £100 brought in by George Speke knight by virtue of a decree issued out of the high court of Chancery touching the Wynards Hospital & £36 arrears for the poor therein. Nicholas Mussell (a person maimed in his majesty's late service) chosen grave maker in Friernhay churchyard). Mr Mayor is desired to keep Mr Blundell's feast this year according to the donor's will. Ordered that two butteys be forthwith erected and made in the west side of the river of Exe, to the end the water may be again recovered into its ancient course. Edward Foxwill elected a common council man, who refusing to accept of the said place, was fined £100 who on his submission was abated £60 thereof & only paid £40. John Gibbons elected a member of the common council of this city.

This Mayor died, 21 March, on Tuesday night and the Monday following Easter Anthony Salter, doctor in physic (and brother-in-law to the said Mr Penny), was elected mayor and the Monday thereafter sworn for the remaining part of the year. In the interval, viz. 23 March, the King Majesty's Declaration for war against the States of the United Provinces, was here in this city with great solemnity proclaimed, the Lieutenant & Aldermen going in scarlet, the rest of the Company, together with the several corporations in their gowns & formalities, by the Deputy Herald at Arms, with a troop of horse, trumpets, drums, etc. John Parr, merchant, elected a member of the common council of the said city. Northernhay was this year levelled & a pleasant walk made thereon & above 200 young elms there planted. Articles touching the new churchyard in Southernhay sealed, made between the city & the dean & chapter & the said burying place enclosed with a brick wall and also consecrated with all solemnity by Bishop Ward 28 October, being St Simon & Jude's Day

Samuel Izacke added: And called by the name of Trinity Church Yard, lying within the parish of the Holy Trinity, whereon was made this ensuing copy of verses:

What bold-faced Sadducee dare now mistrust
That long'd for Resurrection of the Just?
Whose Martyr'd Temples, which before our Eyes
Were once dis-tomb'd, more beautiful arise:
And that the Saints have Elbow-room to rest,
This day a Plot profane, is truly blest.
Thou Angel of our Church, may'st thou ne'er be
Translated, 'till to Immortality;
That all our Foes who do us disregard,
May be kept out by this our well-fenc'd Ward.

Stephen Toller for opposing the orders touching the good government of the wool hall was disenfranchised. Bartholomew Anthony chosen one of the common council, who, refusing, was fined £40. Edmund Starre elected one of the common council and refusing the same was likewise fined and paid £50. James Clutterbuck, admitted to the liberties of the city by way of redemption on the fine of £50. John Birdall likewise so admitted to the same on the fine of £30. A pension of £6 per annum allowed to William Hoop muster master of this city. A pest house purchased & improved by building for the good of the poor of the city in case of sickness. Robert Wadge admitted master of the bridewell or house of correction. The king's arms to be forthwith erected nigh the head of the new haven. The street or way between Quaygate & Westgate & also from the high street into Friernhay churchyard to be speedily paved. And the way between the Wynards & the Mawdlyn hill head to be well gravelled & repaired. The sickness being very hot in London watch & ward to the gates of this city & suburbs thereof are appointed & strictly to be observed. Several fairs put off in respect of the said sickness. A collection here made for the poor of the said city of London & [blank] sent to them in this their necessity.

Samuel Izacke added: A comet for many days together appeared within our horizon, whence ensued a war between us and the Dutch.

1665

Nicholas Izacke

At the Snayle Tower houses of offices for the ease of the citizens are again to be erected. John Elwill elected a common council man, who refusing to subscribe the declaration against the covenant of late enjoined by Act of Parliament was therefore fined £60. Next above Exe Bridge on the west side of the said river a new weir was now erected at the city's charge. Ordered that no persons or goods be received into this city from infected places without Mr Mayor's licence. The petty or town custom duties granted to Anthony Delton at £22 10s per annum. Nicholas Yeo elected proctor of the Mawdlyn Hospital & a deputation granted to him thereof. Ladders & crooks to be provided in readiness in case of any fire happening for the prevention thereof. This year on the last day of February the king's majesty's declaration for war against the French king was here in this city with great solemnity proclaimed, the mayor & aldermen arrayed in scarlet, the rest of the common council men attended by their several officers together with the sundry corporations in their gowns & formalities, by John Hornbrook, Deputy Herald at Arms, with a troop of horse, four silver trumpets, with joyful acclamations of the people was this service performed. Money paid James Rogers & John Tucker, constables of this county, for passing of banisters. Katherine Thomas widow admitted into one of the almshouses without the Southgate founded by John Palmer baker. St Nicholas Fair was this year put off for fear of our citizens should be infected with the sickness, which now reigns in many places of this kingdom. Paid Mr Chamberlain £30 for abridging several Act Books of this chamber. Paid Mr Heskett £5 more for his pains taken in & about the militia of this city. Two houses in the high street over against the new inn there by a sudden fire happening in the night time were suddenly burned to the ground. £100 in money was now lent to the city by Mr George Leach of this city, brewer, for one year gratis, even to keep the poor on work. Mr Richard Halle was by this chamber presented to the rectory of St Edmonds on the Bridge. William King of this city, weaver, was admitted into one of the almshouses in Racks Lane. Some part of the walls without the Eastgate being of late demolished were now again repaired. Richard Moore elected hallier and keeper of the wool hall & a deputation hence granted him thereof. John Collyns & Andrew Quash elected & sworn members of this society. A relief here paid by Dr Fulwood, archdeacon of Totnes, for the tenement he now dwells in, due on the death of his predecessor. £5 in money bestowed on Mr Recorder for his pains taken about the city's charters. A . . . Paris Street a gelding seized on as deodand & sold by Mr Receiver General for £5. A new gown & beaver bought & bestowed on the sword bearer. A piece of plate of £12 value bestowed on Sir Thomas Clifford, knight, for his great regard of the present affairs of this city. Northernhay granted to John Baker for 5 years at the rate of £6 per annum. The city's charters were now sent up to London by Mr Chamberlain to be there advised on by council learned in law to present them and the liberties of this city. Upon the death of Richard Kelland, late keeper of the prison at Southgate, John Vicary was elected in his rooms & place, even to succeed him in that charge. A present of £5 value conferred on the right honourable John Earl of Bath in his passage through this city as a testimony of our respects towards him. £40 more conferred on Mr Recorder for his pains taken about the said charters & his care of the city's business committed to him. A piece of plate of £20 value presented to Mr Secretary Morrys his lady, for his great care in preserving the rights & liberties of this city, & £5 given his secretary. John Force admitted an attorney in his majesty's courts within this city. William Hoop elected a member of this society, who refusing it, was therefore fined £50. A fire broke out in London this year on the second day of September, which for many days together could not (by all the use of art) be quenched, insomuch that from the tower there to temple stairs all buildings were destroyed, of which calamity above fourscore churches were consumed, & by computation five & fifty thousand houses. It proved so dismal that the whole city was almost laid in ashes & by the spectators thereof twas deemed that since the destruction of Jerusalem there never was & until the end of the world there never will be such another conflagration. Within the walls were two hundred seventy & three acres of ground whereon buildings stood by computation, destroyed & 73 without, five parts of six within the walls consumed & burnt down & without the walls more demolished, then left standing within. The fire did eat into stones & devoured iron bars, the ashes were blown above 20 miles, never was the hand of god more visible, the loss was inestimable & incomprehensible.

Richard Crossing noted: The second of September 1666 near the expiration of Nicholas Isaac's mayoralty, 5 parts of the city of London within the walls were destroyed by a most dreadful fire and more was burned without the walls of London than was left standing within. Of 97 churches, only 11 stood unburnt, the fire did eat into stones and devoured iron bars. The ashes were blown above 20 miles. Never was the hand of God more visible. The loss was inestimable and incomprehensible.

Samuel Izacke added: The King's Arms near the head of the new Haven, were erected at the City's Charge, as formerly. Two hundred pounds in money and necessaries were sent hence to the Town of Bradninch, being of late almost consumed by fire, by a voluntary contribution of the inhabitants here made. The great organ erected in the Cathedral Church, being the fairest and by many sounds the deepest of any organ in the kingdom. Part of the City's Wall near the East Gate fell down, and repaired.

A new pulpit in the choir erected, much more beautiful than the former.

1666

John Acland

An English bill in the court of Exchequer is to be forthwith exhibited against George Browninge for erecting a new mill near Trew's Weir to the prejudice of the city. A commission on the statute of charitable uses issued out of the Chancery & here executed chiefly about Sir John Acland's benevolence to the poor. A new pump erected where the town well anciently stood. The town custom for this year granted to Anthony Delton for £42. A committee appointed to meet weekly for the settling of the wool hall at St John's Hospital & a deputation under the common seal granted to John Comyns to collect the duties thereof. Upon the death of John Cogan, late sword bearer of this city Thomas Willinge was now elected to succeed him in that office. Auditors appointed to state the city's accounts for the year last past. Several sums of money paid the constables of this county for passing of banisters. The inhabitants of this city are ordered to hang out candle lights every night at their fore doors between Allhallowtide & Candlemas for the benefit of passengers travelling up and down the streets about their affairs. A deputation under the common seal granted to Lawrence Ward for this year of the cloth hall at the rate of £20. The city's walls towards Northernhay of late fallen down were now repaired. A collection of £270 & 10s in money being here made for those poor persons who suffered by the late fire in London, was accordingly sent unto them. Mr Thomas Carew, having of late performed many offices of love towards this city, a piece of plate was presented to his lady of £12 value from the house by way of acknowledgement of the foresaid respects & kindness. A deputation under the common seal granted to William Stevens & others to seize on goods foreign bought & sold. Robert Sparke elected one of the beadles in the room of William Downe deceased. Mr Walter Borough's lands by his surviving feoffees made over to the chamber. Mr Philip Shapcott elected one of the city's learned counsel. A stipend of forty shillings per annum conferred on Mark Potter, one of the beadles of this city for the punishment of vagrants. Thomas Woodyets admitted into Mr Hurst's almshouse without the Eastgate on Jane Braye's death. New gowns bestowed on the sergeants at mace & coats on the beadles. Ordered that no inhabitant of this city do set forth any tables or things in the streets beyond the bulks of their shops. The way leading into the new churchyard in Southernhay to be paved. Ladders to be provided by every parish within this city for public service, in case of fire here happening. A ditch to be made in Southernhay to prevent the passage of wagons there. Sir John Acland's trust made over to 12 feoffees of this house. Mr Blundell's feast according to his appointment was this year kept by Mr Mayor. Mr James Slade surrendering his office of receivership, Mr Thomas Walker was elected receiver for the residue of the year. The king's proclamations for peace between us & France, Denmark and Holland, 4 September, this year were in this city at several places solemnly published. Bishop Ward, having well-governed this church for the space of five years & upwards, was translated hence to the see of Salisbury 5 September in whose stead Anthony Sparrow, doctor in divinity, was 14 October then next following elected bishop of this diocese & 3 November following at London by Gilbert archbishop of Canterbury was thereunto consecrated & 23 of the same month of November here by proxy installed. In five week's space died three dignitaries of this church, namely, 1. Robert Hall, doctor in divinity, a canon-residentiary and treasurer of the said church departed this life 29 March; he was the eldest son of that worthy Prelate Doctor Joseph Hall, late bishop of this diocese, who imitated his father's virtues in sundry particulars, chiefly in learning, constant preaching, and hospitality, wherein he exceeded. In his time he was accounted a Nathaniel, indeed, an upright honest gentleman in whom was no guile. 2. James Smyth, doctor in divinity, another canon-residentiary of this church & chanter of the same, deceased 20 June. The next following 3rdly & lastly died Mr John Bury, 5 July next thereafter canon-residentiary of the said church.

1667

Thomas Walker

Southernhay was now levelled & pleasant walks made therein & about two hundred young elms in several rows there planted. Mr John Spark, Mr William Glyde were elected & sworn common council men of this city. Gowns were now bestowed upon the four porters of the gates of this city. The town or petit customs of this city were for this year granted unto Anthony Delton for £42 to be paid quarterly by equal portions. The cloth hall likewise granted to Lawrence Wood for this year at £20. John Loosmore elected overseer of the city's works. Goods seized as forfeited being foreign bought & sold & composition made for the same. Money repaid constables of this county discoursed by them for the passing of banisters. New coats & breeches conferred on the beadles. The bank in Longbrook Street & the water piped there, thoroughly repaired. The justices seated in the upper end of the guildhall new covered with green cloth. William Jones esquire elected & sworn one of the city's learned counsel. Joan Carter, widow, admitted an almswoman into one of the houses belonging to the Ten Cells. Several sums of money estreated as sessions fines brought in. The mayor's pension increased from £110 per annum to £160. Anthony Salter, doctor in physic, late one of the aldermen of this city, departed this life 25 April being St Mark's Day & was decently interred in the cathedral. Stephen Olivean another member of this society likewise died 25 May. Bernard Sparke, merchant, deceased this year 15 August & 17 of the same month Agnes his wife died & were both buried together in one day and in one grave, in the body of the cathedral church. John Sparke, clerk, & Elianor, his wife, about 8 years since likewise died in one day & were likewise buried in one grave.

Samuel Izacke added: Because we liv'd and lov'd so long together,
Let's not behold the Funerals of either:
May one hour end us both; may I not see
This my Wife buried, nor Wife bury me.

This mayor being intimately acquainted & powerful with the dean & chapter of this church prevailed with them to grant as an estate freely of & in a tenement commonly called the New Inn lying in St

Stephens parish in the high street of the said city for one & thirty years absolutely on the surrender of the old lease therein having about two years yet to come.

Samuel Izacke added: Anthony Sparrow, doctor in divinity, was 14 October elected bishop of this diocese, and 3 November next following at London by Gilbert, Archbishop of Canterbury, consecrated thereunto, and 23rd of the same month of November here by proxy installed.

Richard Crossing noted: He [the mayor] was knighted by the King upon the presenting an address.

1668

George Tuthill

The great conduit in the high street of this city was now new beautified. An ordinance was made by the mayor & common council of this city that no person not being a freeman hereof should presume to sell or put to sale any wares or merchandise within the said city or liberties of the same by retail (except victuals & that upon the usual market days used in the said city only) or keep any open or inward shop or other inward or outward room for show, sale or putting to sale of any wares or merchandises not to use any art, occupation, mystery or handicraft within the same city on pain of forfeiting of £4 for very such offence to be recovered by action of debt, bill or plaint. The town or petit customs of this city for this year were granted unto Anthony Delton for £59. Roger Broadmead elected porter of the Eastgate on the death of Roger Gale. Southernhay demised to Edward Blackmore for 21 years at £10 per annum. A new gown, beaver & satin doublet bestowed by the chamber on the sword bearer. Humphrey Green elected one of the four pensioners belonging unto St John's Hospital upon the death of William Brend. George Ivye on his humble petition was admitted into the liberties of this city as a freeman thereof by way of redemption paying £50 fine. New gowns bestowed on all the sergeants at mace of this city. Rebecca Hoskins, spinster, being infected with the disease of the leprosy was admitted into the hospital of St Mary Magdalene without the Southgate of the said city. The prince of Tuscany making a voyage hither purposely to visit our king, landed at Plymouth & taking this city in his way towards London, was here nobly entertained, who lodged at the New Inn.

1669

Peter Hagedot

John Martin esquire, late one of the aldermen of this city, died 24 day of October & 28 of the same month was decently interred in St Peter's church. John Tucker elected proctor of St Mary Magdalene's hospital without the Southgate. The town or petit customs of this city granted to Anthony Delton for £59 per year. George Bullyn elected one of the four beadles upon the death of Richard Luscombe. Hugh Jenkyns clerk elected rector of the parish church of St Edmonds upon the bridge and a presentation thereof made unto him under the common seal of this city. Mr Henry Smith, Mr Thomas Bale elected & sworn common council men of the said city. This mayor procured three couple of swans & placed them in the river of Exe. The little conduit in the high street of this city new beautified and sundry benefactors' coats of armoury blazoned in several shields surrounding the top thereof. Christopher Lethbridge, esquire, late one of the aldermen of this city died 27 July & 10 August next following was decently interred in St Mary Arches church. The Right Honourable John Earl of Bath Lord Lieutenant of this city & county came hither upon Friday in the evening being the second day of September who was received by all the trained bands hereof. And went hence the Tuesday following, during his short abode in this city, Mr Mayor one day at dinner very honourably treated him at his table. In Trinity Term a decree was had in the Exchequer chamber against George Browning defendant, to an English bill there preferred against him by the mayor, bailiffs & commonality of this city, for erecting a fulling mill near Trew's Weir & diverting the watercourse from the new haven, whereby the boats & barges were hindered of their free passage upon the river to the decay of trade here & consequently of the king's majesty's customs, the scope of which decree was that the said defendant should before the end of August next following so repair & fortify the banks again, as that no more water should through the river come unto the said mills which if the defendant should neglect to perform at his sole charge the plaintiffs were sufficiently to do the same.

There happened on Midsummer Eve about Midnight, a grievous fire in the stable belonging to the house commonly called the Blue Anchor in the High Street of the said city, near St Luce's Lane there, which consumed several stables with their appurtenances, one horse and divers swine & endangered the dwellings of the neighbourhood, nay the whole city, but by God's blessing, on the ready means then used, the same was mercifully prevented for which great deliverance God give us thankful hearts & evermore ascribe the praise to his name.

The foresaid Mr Lethbridge founded & in his lifetime finished his almshouse within the Southgate of the said city for six poor people. In the month of June a sturgeon in length 9 foot, in compass 6 foot, was taken in the river near the Red Rock, or Goodman's well, on this side of Topsham, by an inhabitant of this city.

1670

Sir Benjamin Oliver

Ordered that the guildhall bell be tolled by the space of a quarter of an hour upon every public meeting at the council chamber to give notice to the members thereof for an orderly appearance therein. Fifty & six young elms planted on one of the banks of the new haven between the two bridges there. In Rockes Lane a well was digged of 30 & 5 foot deep, & commonly bore water 20 & 5 foot. On the 23rd day of July, being Sunday, between 7 and 8 of the clock in the evening, the king's majesty coming down by sea to view the new citadel at Plymouth, & taking this city in his way homeward by land, lodged here that night in the dean's house within the Close, where his majesty was bountifully entertained & at the sole charge of the city, who presented him with £500 in gold, which was thankfully received by his majesty, who expressed much favour towards the said city, and knighted their mayor: the next morning early about 3 of the clock, his Majesty went hence, & lodged that night at the Earl of Pembroke's house at Wilton near Salisbury, & the day following came to Whitehall. His majesty's short abode in this city hindered the great conduit in the high street from emptying a hogshead of claret, which the city had provided for that purpose, & afterwards made a free disposition of the same to p. for his said Majesty's his service. A [?] order was obtained before the king & council on a petition there preferred by the mayor, bailiffs & commonality of this city against George Browninge for drawing the water from the new haven for the setting on work certain fulling mills lately erected near Trew's Weir, the same being adjudged a public nuisance.

Richard Crossing noted: He was knighted by the king who came to this city the 23rd of July from Dartmouth and parted very early the next morning.

1671

William Sanford

Several young trees planted in St Bartholomew's churchyard on the south side thereof & west. Upon the 7th day of February, about the middle of the night, a fire happened which burned 4 houses to the ground, & in one of them, all the persons, namely, Thomas Hayne, his wife, and their niece, a little maid about 17 years of age, without the Westgate. The King's declaration for war against the States of the United Provinces was on the 16th day of April this year in several places within this city with great solemnity proclaimed. The mayor & aldermen walking in their scarlet gowns attended on by the rest of the common council & officers of the said city, together with the several corporations in their gowns & formalities, by Mr John Hornbrook, Deputy Herald at Arms in his coat brandishing or flourishing a naked sword, & six trumpets sounding. The day following, being by his sacred majesty's command, was here accordingly so kept a public fast day, for God's Blessing on our naval forces in the intended war. Mr Endymion Walker, Mr Robert Dabynot & Mr George Saffyn elected & sworn common council men of the said city. The fore part of the Guildhall was new beautified & the leads thoroughly repaired. The common bridewell in Exe Island (hitherto given by Dr Vilvaynes to pious uses chiefly for the maintenance of the children in Hele's Hospital within this city) was demised to Edward Hill, brewer, for 14 years at £110 per annum. According to an ancient & laudable custom of this city, the members of this society (not only for the increase of mutual love amongst themselves but also reverence to magistracy) have agreed & tis accordingly so ordered that every Sunday morning they here at the Guildhall meet arrayed in their gowns & attend the mayor unto St Peter's church & return with him again to his dwelling house. The king's majesty (in order to his promise made the last year when he visited this city in person and as a signal testimony of his love towards the same) was pleased to send hither the effigies, or portraiture at length, & richly framed, of his dear sister, the Duchess of Orleans (lately deceased), a Princess born within this city, and for beauty was esteemed one of the fairest in Christendom; which said picture being placed in a fair case of timber, richly adorned with gold, is erected in the open Guild-hall of the said city, and there to remain as a perpetual monument of His Majesty's high favour towards this his truly ancient, loyal and honourable city of Exeter. Hele's Hospital, founded by Sir John Maynard knight, His Majesty's Sergeant at Law, and others, for the maintenance and education of female children born within this city and county thereof, was now decently constituted & well settled & fifteen poor maids therein admitted, a governess or mistress over them appointed, and likewise a President, Steward, and other officers elected, for the better government of the said house. Also, at the lower end of Paris Street, without the East Gate of this city and within the parish of St Sidwell, a new Workhouse was now erected & built from the ground & encompassed with a fair wall, intended for the keeping to work therein the poor of the said parish and city; & 'tis hoped that that the same will succeed well, & prove as necessary a work, as this age hath devised; towards the raising of which foundation, the citizens & inhabitants hereof liberally contributed by way of a collection.

1672

Henry Gandy

An ordinance made by the mayor & common council of this city for the preservation of the liberties of the freemen thereof, & punishment of foreigners that shall [?] to keep open shops or expose their goods to sale within the same. Several young trees planted on the banks of the new haven. John Gyles elected porter of the West Gate on the death of Samuel Pitts. Joseph Cheek, brewer, for marrying an orphan of this city without the consent of the chamber was therefore fined the sum of ten pounds & paid the same accordingly. Thomas Fook on the death of Thomas Ball, late porter of the North Gate, was chosen into the said office. George Browning's petition to the king & council for rehearing the cause about the foresaid mills, for reasons offered by our cross petition thereunto, was thence dismissed. Robert Walker esquire (late mayor of this city) having served in sundry parliaments as a citizen hereof departed this life on the fourteenth day of August & was decently buried among his ancestors in St Mary Arches Church. St Sidwell's Street paved to St Ann's chapel from the East Gate by the Dean & Chapter of this church, being lords of the said manor.

1673

Isaac Mawditt

Samuel Izacke added: Part of the City Wall at the lower end of Southern-hay, towards Trinity Churchyard, in the night time suddenly fell down, and was forthwith newly erected, being ninety foot in length and thirty foot in height.

Richard Symons, executor of the last will & testament of Elizabeth Flay, widow, deceased, brought into the chamber a silver basin and ewer, parcel guilt, by her given to the mayor, bailiffs & commonality of this city to be used by the mayors thereof from time to time successively as the proper goods of the said city. And also five pounds in gold & fifty pounds more of lawful money to lie in stock & to be employed for the best benefit for the better repairing of the almshouses erected within this city by her husband & herself as occasion shall require, and also several writings in a box concerning the lands belonging thereunto, for all which a receipt under the common seal of this city was given to the said executor. Peter Hagedot esquire (late mayor of this city) upon the sixteenth day of April died & was decently buried in St Peter's church. Mr John Snell, Mr John Carwithean, Mr John Cholwell were elected & sworn common council men of the said city. The peace between us & the Dutch was here proclaimed. Mr John Skinner was elected the city's chaplain appointed to supply Dr Bodley's lecture. This mayor procured a considerable stock of money, £300 freely advanced and given by several members of the chamber & other inhabitants of the said city towards the providing of corn for a public store in this time of scarcity; and the price still increasing, only for the relief of the poor herein, to whom it was delivered out 2d or 3d a peck cheaper than 'twas bought in the market. Thomas Walker, Esquire, one of the Aldermen of this city (on the death of his late father) was elected as citizen to serve in Parliament. John Acland esquire (late mayor of this city) upon the fifth day of August died & was decently buried in St Olave's church the eighth day of the same month. Edward Seymour esquire speaker of the House of Commons in parliament and one of his majesty's most honourable privy council having obliged this city in many public affairs, thereof being now in the country, was invited & honourably entertained at the mayor's table 22 August at dinner. Also, the right honourable John Earl of Bath, Lord Lieutenant of this city & country, having likewise expressed his great favour towards the welfare of the said city on many occasions, & coming hither, had the like invitation, & 2 August was as honourably entertained at dinner by the mayor, & both of them at the sole charge of the said city.

1674

Christopher
Brodridge

On Tuesday the nine and twentieth day of December, the house of one Richard Jewell within the parish of St Sidwell in the suburbs of this city, casually fell down, about seven of the clock in the morning of that day, grievously bruised the said Jewell, and destroyed his wife & a grandchild therein. Richard Lane, Esquire, gave the sum of £100 towards the re-edifying of Grendon's almshouse, commonly called the Ten Cells, situate in Preston Street within the said city. And for the better maintenance & relief of the poor people therein, and likewise of those in Bonvill's almshouse in Rack Lane within the said city, he freely gave the Fee of a tenement called New House in Dorsetshire, of the yearly value of £50, only charged with twenty pounds per annum during the life of Elizabeth Yeo his sister, which he bestowed on her. The city's coat armoury of honour with its supported mantle, crest & motto properly blazoned erected in the guildhall towards the upper end thereof where the sword is usually placed while the mayor is there sitting in the court of judicature. John Butler esquire (late mayor of this city) upon the tenth day of August departed this life & was decently interred in the body of St Peter's church on the twelfth day of the same month. Four & thirty [?staves] painted & towards the higher part of them the king's & the city's arms blazoned in their proper colours were provided for the constables of this city & county, & delivered to them accordingly as badges of their respective offices, & that they might be the better known & encouraged in the due execution thereof, as is commonly used in the city of London. Thomas Shute, clerk, elected rector or parson of the rectory or parsonage of St Edmond's parish upon Exe Bridge upon the resignation of Hugh Jenkins, clerk, late incumbent thereof, & a presentation of the same under the city's common seal granted to him. Christopher Bale, Francis Worth, Edward Crosse were elected & sworn common council men of the said city.

1675

John Parr

Sir William Courtenay of Powderham in the county of Devon, baronet, made a Free and Franchised Man of this city. Edward Cotton, Doctor in Divinity, and Treasurer of this Church, died 12th November, & was buried the 16th of the same month, near unto his grandfather Bishop Cotton's grave, in the south side of the quire of the cathedral church, behind the Bishop's Chair; in his lifetime he was beloved, and his death bewailed by all ranks, sorts & conditions of men that knew him, for he was a right honest and worthy gentleman, a constant and excellent preacher, a great lover of hospitality, a daily liberal benefactor to the poor, and a universal scholar, insomuch that the old Hexameter may justly be attributed to him: *a master in the seven arts.*

Nicholas Redwood, clerk, elected to preach Dr Bodlye's lecture within this city, & to continue the same during the will & pleasure of this chamber. Francis Worth, one of the Common Council of this city, and one of the bailiffs for this year of the same, died 20 January & was decently interred in St Petrock's Church; in his place of a bailiff John Lee was elected to supply the same for the residue of the year. William Smalridge & Nicholas Still are admitted two of Dr Vilvayn's pensioners for part of his benevolence bestowed on scholars in Exeter College in Oxford. Three small bells in St Martin's tower taken down & all new cast into one. The great bell in St Peter's North Tower, called Peter Bell, being cracked, was taken down & new cast, & three other bells in the South Tower there, Grandison, Stafford and Cobthorn, being likewise crazed, were all taken down & new cast.

The Right Honourable Christopher Duke of Albemarle, Lord High Steward of this City, and Lord Lieutenant of the same city & county, & also of the County of Devon, coming hither to settle the militia in both counties, made his abode here about the space of three weeks, lodged in the Deanery, where he kept Open House for all Comers and Goers during the said time, his Grace twice honoured the Mayor's Table twice with his presence, where he was sumptuously entertained. He was also made a freeman of the said city in the forechamber belonging to the Guildhall, where his Grace being attended on by Sir Edward Seymour, Sir Copleston Bampfield, Sir Arthur Northcott and Sir Hugh Acland, baronets; Sir John Roll and Sir Simon Leach, Knights of the Bath; Sir Thomas Daniel, Sir William Walrond, and Sir Henry Ford, Knights Bachelors; with divers other gentlemen of quality, were then likewise sworn Freemen of the said City. For which said service, fees belonging to sundry officers, the duke left forty pounds in money to be divided among them. The Farm of the quay at Christmas, falling into the Chamber's hands, they bethought themselves how to improve the same for the best advantage of the city and county adjacent; in order whereunto they cleansed the quay and river, levelled the island thereunto belonging, and encompassed the same with a firm stone wall, whereby the merchants' goods may be the better landed and secured: at the lower end of the New Haven they likewise did cut out a new leat through the marsh ground; about half a mile in length and also a pool, wherein near a hundred sail of ships may with safety at all times ride; and from thence to the said quay boats and barges may daily pass up and down through the river, to load and discharge the merchants' goods (which formerly could hardly be so done in a week's time) for which good end sundry new and other lighters are here provided in readiness, and the rate for conveyance of all goods and merchandises abated almost a third part; which worthy undertaking being thus projected, was this summer vigorously carried on, and completed by the daily indefatigable endeavours of Mr Henry Smith, Receiver General of the said city, whereby he hath very much obliged us all. In which said work, the Chamber having expended about the sum of three thousand pounds, whereunto Doctor George Cary, Dean of this church, hath been a liberal benefactor.

Richard Crossing noted: In his [the mayor's] year at least 600 houses were burned in London & Southwark, the suburbs of London, & the new channel was cut to bring up vessels nearer to Exeter.

1676

William Glyde

Bishop Sparrow having well governed this church about nine years space, was translated to the Bishopric of Norwich; in whose stead Thomas Lamplugh, Doctor of Divinity, was 3 October elected bishop of this diocese and 12 November at Lambeth by Gilbert Arch-bishop of Canterbury consecrated thereunto.

1677

George Tuthill

PART THREE

Memorials of the City of Exeter

Samuel Izacke 1678–1722

1678

William Sanford
Esquire

Nowell Pearse of this city was elected one of the stewards for this year ensuing; but refusing to execute that office, was therefore fined, and paid the same accordingly; in whose room and place Thomas Horn of the said city, grocer, was elected.

1679

John Collings
Esquire

John Starr of this city, junior, was elected one of the bailiffs for this year; but refusing to execute that office was therefore fined and paid the same accordingly. In whose room and place Andrew Jeffery of the said city, fuller, was elected, who likewise refusing to execute the same, was fined and paid the same. And in his place Joseph Pince of the said city, serge maker, was elected, who also refused to execute the same, was likewise fined and paid the same. In whose room Nicholas Savery of the said city, linen draper, was elected, who also refusing that office was likewise fined and paid in accordingly. And in his room and place Thomas Gould of the said city, silk weaver, was elected and he likewise refusing to execute that office was also fined and paid the same.

1680

Henry Smith Esquire

In this year William Glyde and Malachy Pyne, Esquires, were elected Members of Parliament for this city.

1681

Isaac Mawditt
Esquire

In this gentleman's mayoralty, on the death of George Cary, Doctor of Divinity and Dean of this Cathedral, who, in his lifetime, had twice said *Nolo Episcopari* in earnest (being offered that See twice) was born at Clovelly in Devon. Richard Annestey, Doctor of Divinity, was elected Dean thereof.

Three of those gentlemen (bailiffs John Carwithen, Charles Alden, William Southmead, Nathaniel Gist) – sons in law to the Mayor.

1682

Endymion Walker Esquire

1683

Christopher
Brodridge Esquire

In this gentleman's mayoralty King Charles the II, calling for a surrender of the charter, the same was accordingly done and on the New Charter granted the following gentlemen were therein nominated and appointed, to wit,

1684

James Walker Esquire

James Walker, Esquire, Mayor
   Thomas Gibbon, Esquire, Recorder
   Henry Smith, Endymion Walker, Robert Dabynott, George Saffin, John Snell, John Cholwell, Christopher Bale, Aldermen
   Edward Cross, Esquire, Sheriff
   John Carwithen, Malachy Pyne, Humphry Leigh, Christopher Coke, John Gandy, Richard Pidgsley, John Mathew, Charles Alden, Thomas Hill, Edward Dally, William Jope, Tristram Bowdage, Thomas Potter, Common Councilmen.

James II

1685

Robert Dabynott
Esquire

In this gentleman's mayoralty the Honourable John Earl of Bath, Lord Lieutenant of this County of Devon, and City and County of Exon, was admitted to the Freedom of the said City.

1686

George Saffin
Esquire

In this gentleman's mayoralty the Honourable George Earl of Dartmouth was admitted to the freedom of this city.

1687

John Snell Esquire

The 28th day of November following, an order of the Privy Council was sent hither in these words (to wit)
   James Rex
   Trusty and well-beloved, we greet you well. Whereas we have, by our order in Council, thought fit to remove John Snell Esquire from being Mayor, and one of the Aldermen of that our City of Exeter; George Saffin, John Cholwill, James Walker, and Henry Smith, from being Aldermen; Christopher Coke, from being one of the Sheriffs, and of the Common Council; Humphrey Leigh, Charles Alden, Thomas Potter, Nathaniel Gist, Malachy Pyne, Edward Dally, John Carwithen and William Jope from being of the Common Council; and Richard Rous from being Sword Bearer of Our City. We have thought fit hereby to Will and Require you forthwith to elect and admit Our Truly and Well-beloved Thomas Jefford, Esquire, to be Mayor, and one of the Aldermen; George Tuthill, Merchant, William Glyde, Gentleman, Edmund Starr, Merchant, and Thomas Atherton, Merchant, to be Aldermen; Richard Cunningham, Gentleman, to be one of the Sheriffs and of the Common Council; John Curson, Receiver, and of the Common Council; John Starr, Merchant, John Pym, Merchant, John Boyland, Merchant, Robert Buckland, Vintner, Jeremiah King, Grocer, Robert Tristram, Merchant, Tobias Allen, Merchant, and Hugh Bidwell, Fuller, to be of the Common Council; and Joseph Bradshaw to be Sword Bearer of Our said City, in the room of the person above mentioned. And Humphrey Bawden, Fuller, to be one of the Aldermen, in the room of Endymion Walker, deceased, without administering to them any other

oaths, but the usual oath for the executing of their respective places, with which we are pleased to dispense, in this behalf. And for so doing, this shall be your Warrant, and so we bid you farewell. Given at our Court at Whitehall, this 28th day of November 1687, in the third year of our reign.

By His Majesty's Command, Sunderland

To our Trusty and Well-beloved the Deputy, Recorder, Aldermen, Common Councilmen and Freemen of the Corporation of the City of Exeter

Thomas Jefford Esquire

The first Court held before the Mayor and the preceding bailiffs (John Gandy, John Burell, Richard Peryam, Thomas Salter) was the fifth of December.

The second day of January following John Curson, Anthony Vicary, and William Atkins took the oaths for executing the office of bailiffs.

In the same manner the 30th day of January William Reynell took the oath for executing the office of a bailiff.

The 24th day of January 1687 Mr Jefford the mayor was desired by the then Chamber to surrender into His Majesty's Hand the former Charter, which was done accordingly.

The 27th day of March, 1688, the new Charter was first executed.

The 27th day of September 1688 the King's Mandate was sent hither, to elect and continue Sir Thomas Jefford (who had lately had the Honour of being knighted) to be Mayor of the said city and Richard Cuningham, Esquire, to be Sheriff of the said city for the year ensuing, in the words following, (viz.)

James *Rex*
27 *die Septembris*, 1688

Trusty and Well-beloved, We greet you well. Whereas We are well satisfied of the Loyalty and Ability of Our Trusty and Well-beloved Sir Thomas Jefford, knight, the present Mayor and Richard Cuningham, Esquire, the present Sheriff of that Our City of Exeter, we have thought fit hereby to Require you to elect and continue him the said Sir Thomas Jefford to be Mayor and the said Richard Cuningham, Esquire, to be Sheriff of our said City for the year next ensuing, with all the rights, profits, and advantages thereunto belonging, without administering to them any Oath or Oaths, but the usual Oath for the execution of their respective places with which we are graciously pleased to dispense in this behalf; and for so doing this shall be your warrant, and so we bid you farewell. Given at our Court at Windsor, the 27th day of August, in the 4th year of our reign.

By his Majesty's Command, Sunderland

Which day Sir Thomas Jefford was sworn accordingly.

Mr Jefford was a dyer in this city, and in that art very curious, by means whereof he got a great estate; being somewhat ambitious, and aspiring after honour, he procured to himself the government of this city, but his continuance was of a short date.

The 4th of November, 1688, the Prince of Orange landed at Torbay, sent a detachment to take possession of this city, and himself a few days after made his entrance, and during his stay here he lodged at the deanery, when he marched towards London, he left Sir Edward Seymour Governor thereof.

1688

Sir Thomas Jefford

In November 1688 a order of Privy Council, pursuant to a proclamation for restoring corporations to their ancient charters, was sent hither, in the words following (to wit)

At the Court at Whitehall, the first of November 1688
Present, The King's Most Excellent Majesty
Whereas in his Majesty's late Proclamation, issued, for restoring corporations to their ancient charters, liberties, rights, and franchises, the ancient corporation and body corporate of the city of Exeter is one of those therein excepted, upon a supposition, that the deed of surrender by them made to his late Majesty was recorded, but upon further examination, and producing the said deed of surrender, it appearing that the same never was recorded; his Majesty in Council (designing the same benefit to the said city, and the ancient corporation thereof, as to other cities in the said proclamation not excepted) in pursuance to the power reserved to his Majesty in the Charter of Incorporation lately granted to the said city, is pleased to order, and it is hereby ordered, that the mayor, sheriff, recorder, town clerk, aldermen, common council men and all and every other magistrate, officer and minister of or in the said city, be, and they are hereby removed, displaced, and discharged of and from the said offices, magistracies, and places; saving always, and reserving to them, and every of them, such right, privilege, place or office as they have or lawfully may claim by the ancient charter or franchises of the said city; and it is further ordered, that the mayor, sheriff, aldermen, recorder, town clerk, and common council men, and all, and every other minister and officer of the said city, that were such at the time of the sealing of the said deed of surrender, do take upon them the execution of their respective offices and magistracies, and proceed to make due elections, and to act and do as they lawfully might, if no such deed had ever been had or made.

Phil. Musgrave

In this year, on the Prince of Orange's landing at Torbay, Dr Lamplugh, the bishop of this diocese, quitted his palace here and went to King James. The Arch-bishopric of York being then translated the king immediately translated him to the same. Shortly after, Sir Jonathan Trelawny baronet, then Bishop of Bristol, was translated hither, being descended to an honourable family in the county of Cornwall, he was of a generous mind, and pious disposition, and one of those seven bishops that were, in the reign of King James the second committed to the tower, for being steadfast and immoveable in the principles of the Church of England, as established by law.

Pursuant to the above order Mr Bodridge was reinstated, and the 8th day of December following, Christopher Bale, Esquire, was elected Mayor.

In this year Sir Edward Seymour, baronet, and Henry Pollexfen Esquire were elected members of the convention for this city.

William III

1689

John Snell, Esquire

Mr Edward Cross executed the office of Receiver for some part of the year in order to qualify him to be on the election for a new mayor for the succeeding year.

In this year Christopher Bale Esquire was elected a citizen in the room of Henry Pollexfen Esquire who was made Lord Chief Justice of the Common Pleas.

1690

Edward Cross, Esquire

In this Gentleman's Mayoralty, John Bidgood, Doctor of Physic, and a native of this place, very eminent in his profession, by his last will and testament, gave to St John's Hospital within this city the sum of six hundred pounds, towards the maintenance and education of three poor children, to be admitted into the hospital; which, with some addition freely given by the chamber, an annuity or rent-charge of thirty pounds per annum, issuable from Duryard Mills within the parish of St David's in the county of the said city, was purchased and settled according to the donation.

1691

Edward Seaward, Esquire

1692

Christopher Coke, Esquire

In this gentleman's mayoralty the Right Honorable the Earl of Danby was admitted to the Freedom of the City.

1693

John Gandy, Esquire

1694

Roger Dabynott, Esquire

In this gentleman's mayoralty, the Chamber taking into consideration the benefit and advantage that might accrue to the city in general, contracted and agreed with certain persons for the erecting and building of an engine or water-work from and out of a certain water course called the New Mill Leat, issuable from and out of the River Exe, and from thence to place and lay pipes, whereby to convey and furnish the inhabitants thereof, at reasonable terms, with sufficient quantity of water for their domestic and other uses, for and during certain number of years.

1695

Gilbert Yard, Esquire

About this time, the Right Honourable Thomas Earl of Stamford, Baron of Grooby, and one of his Majesty's most Honourable Privy Council, was appointed Lord Lieutenant and *Custos Rotulorum* for the county of Devon and City and County of Exeter.

John Tucker, Merchant and native of this city, by his last will and testament, gave the sum of one hundred pounds, towards the education and maintenance of the poor children of St John's Hospital here.

In this year, Edward Seaward and Joseph Tiley, Esquires, were elected Members of Parliament for this city.

1696

Christopher Bale

In this Gentleman's Mayoralty the privilege of a mint was granted, and erected within this city; several officers appointed, and silver money coined here, and distinguished by having the letter E impressed under the King's bust, &c.

1697

John Curson, Esquire

In this Gentleman's Mayoralty, it was consulted and agreed on by the Chamber, for the greater conveniency and advantage of the merchants and other traders of this place, to make the river navigable home to the quay of this city. According to which projection this affair was begun and carried on with great success, at the expense of several thousand pounds, by the said Chamber, exclusive of the great assistance from the city in general and of all the neighbouring clergy, gentlemen and others who contributed their kind assistance therein; by which means ships of a hundred ton came up to this city;

whereas, before this great undertaking, goods and merchandise were unloaded from the shipping at Topsham, and conveyed hither by lighters, or large boats. Anciently there was a sea port here but by a misunderstanding between Hugh Courtenay the Earl of Devon and the then Chamber, the Channel was stopped up, by which the navigation was obstructed; and the Earl being possessed of the manor of Topsham, took his opportunity to advance the trade there, he being a person at that time of great power and interest. But the Chamber having obtained an Act of Parliament in the reign of Charles II, made such works through the dams, tho at great expence, that lighters of the greatest burden did after that come up to the city quay.

Likewise, in this mayoralty a patent, under the common seal, was granted to the Right Honourable James Duke of Ormond, Lieutenant General of all his Majesty's Forces in his kingdoms of England, Scotland and Ireland, Knight of the most Noble Order of the Garter, and one of his Majesty's most honourable Privy Council, to be Lord High Steward of this city, and admitted to the freedom thereof.

In this year an Act of Parliament was obtained, for the erecting and building of a workhouse within this city and county of Exon, for the relief and maintenance of the poor and indigent. Since which, there have been several benefactions towards the better support and continuance of that great work.

In this year Sir Edward Seymour, baronet, and Sir Bartholomew Shower, were elected Members of Parliament for this city.

1698

John Burrell

1699

Joshua Hickman

1700

John Snell, Esquire

Queen Anne

1701

John Cholwell, Esquire

On the death of the Right Honourable the Lord Altham, who had been dean of this church for the space of twenty years, William Wake, Doctor of Divinity, was elected dean thereof, whose father was a gentleman of the county of Dorset, a great sufferer for his loyalty to King Charles the First, and on that account a long time imprisoned in the High Gaol for the county of Dorset.

In this year Sir Edward Seymour and Sir Bartholomew Shower were elected Members of Parliament for this city.

1702

John Gandy, Esquire

In this gentleman's mayoralty, on Friday the 13th day of March, on the death of King William, Anne Princess of Denmark was here proclaimed Queen of England, Scotland, France and Ireland, at six several places (to wit) at the Guildhall, in St Peter's Churchyard, in the serge market, at the Conduit, at Saint John's Bow, and before the New Inn, with great solemnity; the mayor, aldermen, and common council men in their scarlet gowns and robes, the officers and several incorporations in their liveries.

In this gentleman's mayoralty, the Right Honourable the Earl of Rochester coming to this city, continued here for some days, and was entertained by the mayor; he was pleased to honour the city, in being made a free and franchised man thereof.

John Lethbridge of this city, merchant, by his last will and testament (int' al') gave the following charities (to wit) Item, 'I give to the mayor, bailiffs, and commonalty of the city of Exon, the sum of two hundred and sixteen pounds, upon this special trust and confidence, and to and for the only uses, intents, and purposes herein after mentioned, (that is to say) that the said mayor, bailiffs, commonality, or such person or persons to whom the same shall be lent, (as I will the same shall be lent) shall pay for the same after the rate of five pounds per cent per annum, and that the interest thereof shall be distributed by the said mayor, bailiffs, and commonality, in manner following forever, (that is to say) ten shillings, part thereof, amongst the prisoners for debt, lodging in the room called the Shoe, in the prison of the South Gate of the said city, on the fifth day of November in every year, for ever; and fifty shillings, other part thereof, to the Hospital of St John in the said city, yearly, for ever, towards the maintenance of the poor boys therein. And seven pounds, sixteen shillings, yearly for ever, to the almshouses near the South Gate, founded by the late Alderman Lethbridge, so that every one of the six poor persons that now do, or hereafter shall live in the said almshouses, may have and receive six pence weekly, for ever. Item, I likewise give to the said mayor, bailiffs, and commonalty, the further sum of fifty pounds, the interest thereof to be employed for and towards the better maintenance of the poor children in Hele's Hospital within the said city.'

1703

John Newcombe, Esquire

In this gentleman's mayoralty, on the 26th day of November, about eleven at night, there arose a terrible tempest of wind, which continued till past four in the morning, and most of the houses in this city felt the effects thereof, several stacks of chimneys thrown down, beating the very roofs before 'em; but, by the good Providence of God, not any person hurt. A beautiful range of tall elms, which were of a long standing in St Peter's Church-Yard, and very ornamental to the walks there, were, by the violence of this storm, rooted up, some few only remaining, which not being uniform, were taken down; and shortly thereupon, by the direction, and at the costs and charges of the dean and chapter of this church, a parcel of lime trees were planted in their room, with a considerable addition, which adorns that place, and admits a pleasant prospect.

Sir Edward Seaward, knight, who had been mayor of this city, and sometime served the same in Parliament, gave towards the education of the poor children in St John's Hospital, the sum of six hundred pounds, which, together with the sum of one hundred and nineteen pounds and four shillings, freely given, and advanced by the governors of the said hospital, an estate was purchased and settled accordingly.

1704

Gilbert Wood, Esquire

1705

Thomas Barons, Esquire

Thomas Jeffery, Benjamin Brown and John Southcombe, having executed their office, as bailiffs for the year, refused to keep their respective feasts according to ancient usage and custom of this city, and pursuant to a bye-law for that purpose; whereupon they were fined, and prosecuted; and on that prosecution, petitioned the chamber, submitted, and paid their several fines accordingly.

William Wake, Doctor of Divinity, and dean of this cathedral, was made bishop of the diocese of

Lincoln. On whose removal, Lancelot Blackborne (sometime sub-dean of this church) was elected dean thereof.

1706

Nicholas Wood, Esquire

1707

Edward Dally, Esquire

In this gentleman's mayoralty, the Right Honourable – Earl of Abingdon coming to this city, was entertained by the mayor.

In the same year, Sir Edward Seymour baronet, who had executed the office of recorder for this city for several years, being in his declining age, voluntarily resigned that place, in whose room Sir Nicholas Hooper, her then Majesty's Serjeant at Law, was elected.

In the same year, Bishop Trelawny was translated from this see to the diocese of Winchester; in whose room Offspring Blackhall, Doctor of Divinity, was elected Bishop of this place, and soon after consecrated and installed here by proxy.

1708

Edward Spicer, Esquire

Thomas Townshend, Edward Edmonds and Philip Bishop, having executed the office of bailiffs for this year, refusing to keep the respective feasts, according to ancient usage and custom, and pursuant to a bye-law for that purpose, were every of them fined, and prosecuted. But they persisting in their obstinacy, a trial was brought against one of them, at the next assizes held for the said city and county and tried before the Lord Chief Justice Parker; when the Customs was proved, and maintained, and the bye-law corroborated; and thereon a verdict was obtained and the fine and costs of suit paid. Upon which, the two other bailiffs humbly petitioned, and submitted to their fines, and paid the same, together with their proportionable costs.

In this gentleman's mayoralty the good bishop of this diocese, observing with concern the great number of poor, illiterate children, whose parents were not of ability to educate them, preached a sermon concerning the rules and measures of alms-giving, and the manifold advantages of charity schools for the instruction and education of the poor of this city, and other places of his diocese; and out of zeal for his design, his lordship annexed to his excellent sermon a pious letter to his clergy, thereby exciting them to a greater zeal for this work of piety and charity. And the very next day after the sermon, a great number of the inhabitants of this city voluntarily subscribed for the erecting charity schools within this place, and there are now four (to wit) two for boys and two for girls. There are likewise appointed two masters for instructing the boys and each master is allowed for his yearly salary thirty pounds; two mistresses for the girls and each of them allowed yearly twenty five pounds. All the poor children entirely clothed, the boys are taught to read, write and cast accounts; the girls to sew and knit. They have all bibles, common prayer books and spelling books given them and are examined every Sunday evening in their catechism. The subscriptions and collections for the maintenance of these schools amount to two hundred and fifty pounds yearly and since the erection of these schools, several benefactions have been given.

1709

Edward Collings, Esquire

About this time the Right Honourable the Lord Poulet, Baron of Hinton St George, and one of Her Majesty's Most Honourable Privy Council, was appointed Lord Lieutenant and *Custos Rotulorum* for the County of Devon and City and County of Exeter, and was admitted to the Freedom of this City.

1710

Thomas Salter, Esquire

In this year Sir Copleston-Warwick Bampfield, and John Snell, Esquires, were elected Members of Parliament for this city.

1711

Joshua Hickman, Esquire

Edmond Cock of this city, fuller, having executed the office of bailiff for some part of the year, and being under an indisposition, petitioned the chamber for his quietus the remaining part; which, on account of his past service, and otherwise, was accordingly granted him; and in his room John Hellier of this city, grocer, was elected and executed the office accordingly.

1712

Jacob Rowe, Esquire

In this gentleman's mayoralty, Mr William Eakins of this city, goldsmith, an eminent, pious and charitable person, by his last will and testament gave £50 per annum to the Charity Schools within this city, for ever, for the instruction of boys to be here elected in the mathematics and especially in navigation.

1713

John Newcombe, Esquire

In this gentleman's mayoralty, on the death of Queen Anne, George Lewis, Elector of Hanover, was here proclaimed King of Great Britain, France and Ireland, in six several places, (to wit) at the Guildhall, St Peter's Churchyard, in the serge market, at the Conduit, at St John's Bow, and before the New Inn, with great solemnity. The Mayor, aldermen, and common council men in their scarlet gowns and robes, and other gowns, with other officers and the several incorporations in their robes of livery, respectively, with many thousand inhabitants on foot, with the greatest demonstrations of joy, the bells ringing, and the night concluded with bonfires and illuminations, and a general meeting of the chamber, and other gentlemen, at the Guildhall in drinking His Majesty's Health; Prince George, etc.

In this year Mr Nathaniel Rowland, a merchant of this city, by his last will and testament gave the sum of £200 for the benefit of the poor children educated in the charity schools here.

In this year John Harris, and Nicholas Wood, Esquires, were elected Members of Parliament for this city.

King George

1714

John Gandy, Esquire

About this time the Honourable Sir William Courtenay of Powderham Castle was constituted Lord Lieutenant and *Custos Rotulorum* for the County of Devon and the City and County of Exeter.

1715

William Sanford, Esquire

The late Duke of Ormond absenting himself from his kingdom, was dismissed from the office of Lord High Steward of this city. And his Royal Highness George Prince of Wales being pleased to honour this city with the acceptance thereof, a patent under the Common Seal was granted to him to be Lord High Steward of the same; which was presented to His Royal Highness by Sir Peter King (a native of this city) Lord Chief Justice of the Court of Common Pleas, who, by his mighty genius, and hard study in the laws of this kingdom, hath rendered himself eminent in that great capacity, a gentleman of an affable and courteous temper, beloved by all who have the honour to know him.

1716

Nathaniel Dewdney, Esquire

In this Gentleman's Mayoralty, Edward Trelawny, sub dean of this church was made dean thereof, and arch deacon of Exeter, a gentleman of great hospitality, which the poor inhabitants of this place daily experience by the gifts which flow from his bountiful hand, especially the miserable objects confined for debt in the city-compter, who, during the whole time of his residence here, are weekly supplied with his benevolence. The prays of such must pierce through the clouds &c. Tis much to be wished that so good and great an example had many followers.

In this Gentleman's Mayoralty, Offspring Blackhall, bishop of this church, having well governed the same for the space of nine years, departed this life, whose death was much lamented by those that knew him; he lies buried in an aisle on the south side of his own church, and, according to his particular direction, not any monument or tomb to be erected to certify his interment; but his good works, now made public, are sufficient for that purpose, much more durable than inscriptions, which time may soon deface. He was a very learned and pious prelate, the great ornament of his age, and made this see happy under his government, and was the author of many excellent treatises now extant. In whose room Lancelot Blackburn, Doctor of Divinity, who had been dean of this church for some years past, was elected bishop thereof and soon after consecrated and installed.

The Right Honourable the Lord Carteret was constituted Lord Lieutenant and *Custos Rotulorum* for the County of Devon, and City and County of Exon.

In this year Francis Drew and John Bampfield, Esquires, were elected Members of Parliament for this city.

1717

Philip Pear, Esquire

In this gentleman's mayoralty, in the month of -, about the middle of the day, a sudden fire happened without the East Gate of the said city, in a street there called Paris Street, which burnt several houses to the ground, but through God's Mercy and Blessing on the means used, a stop was put to its further progress.

1718

John Burell, Esquire

1719

Thomas Copleston, Esquire

In this gentleman's mayoralty, a suit was commenced and carried on by the Chamber against Captain Bond of Topsham, for non-payment of the petty customs, or town duty; this cause was tried before my Lord Chief Justice King; the custom maintained was proved, and a verdict given in favour of the chamber.

1720

William Gandy, Esquire

In this Gentleman's Mayoralty the Front of the Guildhall of this city was beautified.

About this time the Right Honourable – Fortescue, Lord Clinton, a title of honour, resumed and which had been nigh one hundred years since in this family, was made Lord Lieutenant and *Custos Rotulorum* for the County of Devon, and City and County of Exeter.

1721

John Phillips, Esquire

In this gentleman's Mayoralty, the voluntary feasts, that had been usually kept for the entertainment of the judges who come into this Western Circuit, were discontinued, and in lieu thereof, the Governors of this City, out of a tender regard and deference to their Lordships, show their respects in another manner.

In this years, Richard Sanford, gentleman, a native of this city, by his last will and testament gave the sum of three hundred pounds, and ordered that the same be laid out in the purchase of an estate, the produce whereof to be appropriated for the benefit of the poor children educated in the charity schools here.

1722

Thomas Salter, Esquire

In this year, John Rolle and Francis Drew, Esquires, were elected members of Parliament for this city.

INDEX